A miniature painting by Sehr Sayeed from the private collection of Sugata Bose and Ayesha Jalal

The couplets from Muhammad Iqbal's 'Khizar-i-Rah', used in the painting

دیکھتا کیا ہوں کہ وہ پیکِ جہاں پیما خضر
جس کی پیری میں ہے مانندِ سحر رنگِ شباب

Dekhta Kya Hun Ke Woh Paik-E-Jahan Peyma Khizar
Jis Ki Peeri Mein Hai Manind-E-Sahar Rang-E-Shabab

There that world-measuring courier I had sight of—Khizr,
That ancient in whom youth's colours fresh as the daybreak dwell.

کہہ رہا ہے مجھ سے، اے جویائے اسرارِ ازل!
چشمِ دل وا ہو تو ہے تقدیرِ عالم بے حجاب

Keh Raha Mujh Se, Ae Joya'ay Asrar-E-Azal !
Chashm-E-Dil Wa Ho To Hai Taqdeer-E-Alam Behijab

'Seeker,' said he, 'of eternal secrets!
When the heart sees clear vision, the fates that rule earth wear no veil.'

Oceanic Islam

Oceanic Islam

Muslim Universalism and European Imperialism

Edited by

Sugata Bose and Ayesha Jalal

B L O O M S B U R Y
NEW DELHI • LONDON • OXFORD • NEW YORK • SYDNEY

BLOOMSBURY INDIA
Bloomsbury Publishing India Pvt. Ltd
Second Floor, LSC Building No. 4, DDA Complex, Pocket C – 6 & 7,
Vasant Kunj New Delhi 110070

First published in India 2020
This edition published 2020

Bloomsbury Academic
An imprint of Bloomsbury Publishing Plc

ISBN: HB: 978-93-89714-27-2; eBook: 978-93-89812-49-7

2 4 6 8 10 9 7 5 3 1

Typeset in Minion Pro by Manipal Technologies Limited
Printed and bound in India

Contents

Preface

The Indian Ocean interregional arena is a space of vital economic and strategic importance characterized by specialized flows of capital and labor, skills and services, and ideas and culture. Islam, in particular, and religiously informed universalism, in general, once signified cosmopolitanism across this wide realm. This historical reality is at variance with contemporary conceptions of Islam as an illiberal religion that breeds intolerance and terrorism. The future balance of global power will be determined in large measure by policies of key actors in the Indian Ocean and the lands that abut it, rather than in the Atlantic or the Pacific. The interplay of multiple and competing universalisms in the Indian Ocean interregional arena is in urgent need of better understanding. This volume bridges the divide between sophisticated scholarly research and superficial public knowledge regarding this key web of human interactions. The essays compiled bring together the best academic scholarship on Islam in South Asia and across the Indian Ocean in the age of European empire to a wide reading public.

The essays have emerged out of a series of intensive lectures, workshops, and conversations at the Center of South Asian and Indian Ocean Studies at Tufts University. The Tufts Center has been especially well placed to take on this ambitious project. It is the only center in North America devoted to South Asian studies with an Indian Ocean scope. This has enabled it to creatively trespass the arbitrary area studies on boundaries that separated the subcontinent from its neighboring regions of the Middle East and Southeast Asia. Research and programmatic activities under its aegis have always imaginatively crossed the nation-state's frontiers between India, Pakistan, Bangladesh, Afghanistan, and Sri Lanka. Its location within the Fletcher School of Law and Diplomacy has made it a natural meeting place of academics and practitioners. These advantages have been deployed to good effect in the execution of this book project.

All the contributors have presented their work at Tufts and have revised their essays in light of comments by the editors and other participants. As a result, this book of essays has a degree of intellectual coherence that is rare in collected volumes. Each essay is based on original archival research and, at the same time, offers an interpretation that is of general relevance to an understanding of Islam across the Indian Ocean.

This volume is a fresh contribution to Islamic and Indian Ocean studies alike, placing the history of modern South Asia in broader interregional and global contexts. It also refines theories of universalism and cosmopolitanism while at the same time drawing on new empirical research.

Sugata Bose and **Ayesha Jalal**

Introduction

Islam Is the Ocean

Sugata Bose and Ayesha Jalal

The influence of oceans has never been limited to the lands that abut them. "Mediterranean civilization," Fernand Braudel observed, "spreads far beyond its shores in great waves that are balanced by continual returns...We should imagine a hundred frontiers, not one, some political, some economic, and some cultural." Tracing the connections between Europe and the Mediterranean, he pointed to "a series of north-south routes, natural isthmuses that are still decisive influences on exchanges today: the Russian isthmus, the Polish isthmus, the German isthmus and the French isthmus." These represented "four skeins of history, each tied more or less securely to the warm sea, the source of prosperity, but also linked to each other."[1]

Historians exploring the ties between the South Asian subcontinent and the Indian Ocean in the early modern and modern periods have paid a great deal of attention to the ports and emporia that have dotted its coasts and littoral zones. There is an impressive body of scholarship on trade and culture in cosmopolitan port cities, such as Cambay, Surat, and Bombay, in different eras.[2] Yet, to unveil a hundred horizons of the Indian Ocean in all its hues, it is necessary to navigate the great rivers that link the mountains to the seas.[3] The river routes of South Asia supplied the warp and woof that tied the continent to the ocean much in the same way as the land isthmuses of Europe.

The ports that have been the focal point of scholarly attention were doubtless venues for the expression of various forms of cosmopolitanism in which Islam was a key constituent element. However, these were urban settings where Muslims were in a numerical minority. The delta of the Ganga and the valley of the Indus emerged as the Muslim-majority regions of the subcontinent. Their articulation to the Indian Ocean interregional area merits a more detailed and textured study. This opening essay sets the intellectual stage for the contributions to follow by tracing the contours of oceanic Islam in the modern age, especially the period from the 1850s onwards. The era from 1850 to 1930 has been defined in a recent work as the age of steam and print.[4] Even though these new technologies quickened the pace of global communication, technological determinism in defining an age misses the more significant shifts in the balance of global power. This was a period of a relentless European onslaught on the Islamic world and Muslim resistance against difficult odds on both the intellectual and political planes. While taking the vast seascape of the Indian Ocean as the canvas for scholarly inquiry, this introduction pays special attention to the river basins of the Indus and the Ganga that today straddle India, Pakistan, and Bangladesh and link them to the Arabian Sea and the Bay of Bengal. By choosing a large oceanic space transcending territorial nation-states as a capacious unit of analysis, and then training the spotlight on two regions in the north-west and north-east of the subcontinent on both sides of the partition lines of 1947, we seek to map new directions in comparative, connective, and border-crossing historical scholarship. A depth of understanding of the strands of Islamic universalism emanating from this complex interregional arena in the century spanning 1850 to 1950 may be of vital importance in addressing intractable contemporary problems facing the region and the world.

Rivers and Seas

The Indus and the Ganga have nurtured cultures and polities for several millennia. For our present purposes, it is sufficient to begin with the discovery of these riverine tracts by the vanguards of Britain's seaborne empire. James Rennell, a renowned late eighteenth-century imperial cartographer, found the Ganga and the Brahmaputra (or the "Ganges" and "Burrampooter" as he called them) intersecting "the country of Bengal" in such a way as to form "the most complete and easy inland navigation that can be conceived." In most parts of the country, a navigable stream could be found within a maximum range of twenty-five miles. This river navigation gave "constant employment to 30,000 boatmen" ferrying salt and food for ten million people and transporting commercial exports and imports amounting to perhaps two million pounds sterling every year in the immediate aftermath of the British conquest of Bengal. The boats could be as large as 180 tons but more commonly had a capacity of thirty to fifty tons. Rennell regarded the Ganga and the Brahmaputra as "twin sisters, from the contiguity of their springs" in the Himalayas, one moving west and the other east. They resembled each other not just in length and volume but also "the smoothness and colors of their waters," "the appearance of their borders and islands," and "the height to which their floods rise with the periodic rains." The Ganga traversed mountainous paths for 750 miles to Hardwar, where gushing "through an opening in the mountains" it flowed with "a smooth navigable stream through delightful plains" to the sea some 1,350 miles away. From a military perspective, Rennell thought it "infinitely surpass[ed] the celebrated inland navigation of North America." In its journey through the plains, it received eleven rivers, some of which were "equal to the Rhine and none smaller than the Thames." The delta bordering on the sea was "a labyrinth of rivers and creeks," the Sunderbans. It was "enveloped in woods and infested with Tygers."[5]

The river and the sea were bound in an intimate relationship. The water of the Ganga taken at its height contained a quarter portion of mud. "No wonder then," Rennell commented, "that the subsiding waters should quickly form a stratum of earth; or that the Delta should encroach upon the sea." The ocean in its turn exercised its dominion in the winter and the monsoon in two very different ways: "in the one by the ebbing and flowing of tides; and in the other by depressing the periodic flood, till the surface of it coincides as nearly with its own, as the descent of the channel of the river will admit."[6]

The Ganga was well known to European travelers for centuries. However, the Brahmaputra was unknown in Europe as late as 1765, the year the East India Company obtained the *diwani* or the right to collect the revenue of Bengal. The twin sisters, separated at birth in westerly and easterly directions, startlingly subverted the saying that the twain shall never meet. Some 200 miles from Yunnan, the

Brahmaputra hesitated. "Here it appears," Rennell wrote in 1780, "as if undetermined whether to attempt a passage to the sea by the Gulf of Siam, or by that of Bengal; but seemingly determining on the latter, it turns suddenly to the west through Assam, and enters Bengal on the north-east." Throughout its course of 400 miles through Bengal, the Brahmaputra bore an intimate resemblance to the Ganga, "except in one particular." The exception was this: for the last sixty miles before it met the Ganga, "it forms a stream which is regularly from four to five miles wide, and but for its freshness might pass for an arm of the sea." To capture "the grandeur of this magnificent object," Rennell had to take recourse to poetry:

> Scarce the muse
> Dares stretch her wing o'er the enormous mass
> Of rushing water; to whole dread expanse.
> Continuous depth, and wond'rous length of course.
> Our floods are rills –
> Thus pouring on, it proudly seeks the deep,
> Whose vanquish'd tide, recoiling from the shock
> Yields to this liquid weight. – Thomson's Seasons[7]

It was this watery landscape that was home to the predominantly Muslim peasantry of Bengal.

Contrary to the claims of Braudel and the Annales school of historians, geographic structures are not constants. The transience of the physical environment is nowhere more evident than in the deltas of great rivers.[8] "Next to earthquakes," Rennell correctly noted, "perhaps the floods of the tropical rivers produce the quickest alterations in the face of our globe."[9] What Rennell's 1780 snapshot could not capture was the steady swing of the active delta toward the east over three centuries. The Bhagirathi in the west had given way to the Padma in the east as the main channel of the Ganga as it wove its way toward the sea. Nor could Rennell anticipate catalytic events that would change the identity of rivers. The great flood of 1787 resulted in the Tista, formerly a tributary of the Ganga, to link up with the Brahmaputra, which shifted westward to meet the Ganga near Goalundo in Dhaka district via the Jamuna. The waters of the twin sisters merged to flow into the Meghna near Chandpur in Tippera district. East Bengal's agrarian identity would henceforth be inextricably linked to the strains of the boatmen's music that wafted across the Padma and Meghna.[10]

The process of Britain's colonial conquest of India that began in Bengal took nearly a century for its completion. It was only in the 1830s that the British began to take an interest in navigating the Indus as a prelude to their conquest of Sindh and Punjab. Lahore, the capital of Punjab, was located on the banks of the Ravi. "There is an uninterrupted navigation of the Indus from the sea to Lahore," Alexander Burnes wrote in his geographical memoir of 1833, "and the distance, by course of the river, amounts to about a thousand British miles." The journey by river to Lahore took exactly sixty days. Multan was reached in forty, but another twenty days were spent "in navigating the Ravee, which is a most crooked river." Lahore had an estimated population of some 80,000 citizens, even though it was smaller at that time than its sister city Amritsar. There were about 700 boats between the sea and Lahore deployed for ferrying and other purposes. Despite this evidence of a thriving inland navigation, Burnes insisted that there were political problems in using the Indus as a channel of commerce. The people and princes, in his view, were "ignorant and barbarous."[11]

The Indus bifurcated into two branches five miles below the city of Thatta and sixty miles from the sea. They flowed into the ocean seventy miles apart and this distance constituted the span of the active delta of the Indus. If one included other moribund branches, the delta had a width of about 125 miles. Rice was the staple product of the Indus delta even though wheat was preferred in certain localities. Grain was "cheap and plentiful" everywhere, and Thatta and Hyderabad, situated three miles away from the Indus, were the ancient and modern capitals respectively. Karachi (or as Burnes spelled it, Curachee) was situated fourteen miles from the western mouth of the Indus. This port handled most of the imports as well as the most valuable export, Malwa opium. The local chiefs imposed a duty of 250 rupees on each camel load of opium, and the revenue from opium had amounted to 700,000 rupees, equal to the land revenue of the Talpur Mirs of Sind. The emirate had about a hundred dinghies or sea-vessels "of a peculiar construction, sharp-built, with a very lofty poop." The smaller boats navigated the river and were used for fishing in the estuary while the larger ones sailed from Karachi to Muscat, Bombay, and the Malabar coast. They were purely trading vessels and carried no guns. Connected on the one side to the interregional arena of the Indian Ocean, the region was also linked to an overland network of trade. Hindus of Bahawalpur traveled to Balkh, Bukhara, and Astrakhan by way of Peshawar, Kabul, and Bamiyan to carry on commerce with Central Asia. The Indus was as closely related to the Arabian Sea as the Ganga was to the Bay of Bengal. It was clear to Burnes that the land in the deltaic tract of the Indus "must have greatly encroached on the ocean." "Nothing is more corroborative of this fact," he wrote, "than the shallowness of the sea out from the mouths of the Indus, and the clayey bottom and tinge of the water."[12]

Alexander Burnes had a certain obsession with Alexander the Great's adventures in the Indus valley. This is quite understandable as the British prepared for the military conquest of Sindh and Punjab. He noted that Punjab's military resources were "immense." Looking into the future, he reckoned there were "few rivers of the world where steam might be used with better effect than the Indus," dramatically reducing the duration of the voyage between Lahore and the sea.[13] Charles Napier, who led the British conquest of Sind, wrote in 1842 about the need to abolish river tolls on the Indus, turn Karachi into a free port, protect the traders of Shikarpur, make Sukkur a marketing hub, and introduce steamboats for river navigation. Calcutta, Napier complained, was trying to run down Sindh and the Indus because they threatened the trade of the Ganga and give an advantage to Bombay and Karachi. Once the conquest of both Sindh and Punjab had been accomplished by 1849, Napier exulted: "India should suck English manufactures up her great rivers, and pour down those rivers her own varied products. Kurrachee, you will yet be the glory of the East! Would that I could come alive again to see you, Kurrachee, in your grandeur."[14] Napier's dream of the imperial economic penetration of India up its river valleys came true. However, in one technological aspect, the conquest of the classic river, the Indus, proved to be something of an anti-climax. Steamships on the Indus proved to be spectacular failures in both the economic and strategic dimensions. By contrast, country boats decisively won the contest against steam flotillas in carrying crops, commodities, and soldiers across the Sindh-Punjab frontier.[15]

The term "sindhu," from which both the region of Sindh and the river Indus took their names, was synonymous with the sea. Punjab was, of course, the land of the five rivers—Jhelum, Chenab, Ravi, Beas, and Sutlej—all tributaries of the Sindhu or Indus. Together, they formed the western expanse of the Indus-Gangetic plains. The Sutlej-Beas doab, the valley encompassing the easternmost rivers of Punjab, was not so far from the Ganga-Jamuna doab in the vicinity of Delhi. The Ganga and Brahmaputra, as we have seen, had their reunion in eastern Bengal. Having proximate origins in the Himalayan mountain ranges, the Indus, Ganga, and Brahmaputra river systems watered the world's largest contiguous stretch of alluvium. The skeins of history—economic and cultural—connecting this landmass to the ocean called *al-Bahr al-Hind* deserve a closer analysis than they have received so far from historians of South Asia and the Indian Ocean.

The Contours of Oceanic Islam

"Islam is the desert," Braudel proclaimed, echoing Essad Bey.[16] This was to confuse the place of origin of the revelation with the character of the religion and its associated way of life. It would not be far wrong to make a counterclaim: "Islam is the ocean." Islam traveled well by sea on boats and ships and not just by caravans. It did not arrive fully formed in the South Asian subcontinent but rather was shaped by the river valleys and agricultural plains where it attracted the largest numbers of the Faithful. It established an urban presence too on the coasts and the interior. The entanglement of Islam with the agrarian environment of reclamation and cultivation in Bengal as well as varied urban settings of rulership, trade, and bazaars in the Gangetic plain has been well studied by historians of the late medieval and early modern periods.[17] Placing Islam in its Indian Ocean context, combined with a closer look at the Indus valley, promises to offer fresh perspectives on its modern history in the age of European empire.

The search for cosmopolitanism by historians has been often confined to the pre-modern and pre-colonial era based on a false assumption of its antithetical relationship with modern anti-colonial nationalism. Cosmopolitanism across the Indian Ocean did, of course, have pre-modern and early modern roots. Bombay and Calcutta were latecomers in the late seventeenth and eighteenth centuries to that cosmopolitan world of port cities, of which Surat had been a shining example. During the millennium stretching from the eighth through the eighteenth century, Islam or a Muslim ecumene had signified cosmopolitanism across that wide realm. From the early eighteenth century, Parsis and then Gujarati Banias contributed to what Christopher Bayly has described as "a culture of cosmopolitan commercial sociability." The Parsi diaspora throughout western India, first in Surat and later in Bombay, "adapted their form of local assemblies and created their own modernized form of the Indian panchayat." Their early modern bulletins of commercial intelligence were the harbingers of modern newspapers. From Bombay, the Parsis went to Aden by the mid-nineteenth century. Cowasjee Dinshaw played a key role in building modern Aden. Parsis engaged in trade between India, Aden, and East Africa. The Parsis were not alone in breathing new life into early Asian modernity. A wide range of Shia sects in Bombay with a history of pre-colonial links across the western Indian Ocean—Bohras, Khojas, Memons, and Ismailis—adjusted their habits of commercial cosmopolitanism to the exigencies of a colonial transition. A medieval Ismaili text, popular in nineteenth-century Bombay, described the perfect human being in the following terms: "Persian by breeding, Arabian by faith, Iraqi in culture, Hebrew in law, Christian in manner, Syrian in devotion, Greek in science, Indian in discernment, Sufi in intimations."[18]

Calcutta and Bombay rose to positions of pre-eminence, if not dominance, as colonial port cities in the world of Indian Ocean politics and commerce from the second decade of the nineteenth century. In a recent book, Nile Green has explored the Muslim experience with industrial modernity in Bombay between 1840 and 1915. Green seems to be in two minds as to whether *Bombay Islam* was cosmopolitan or not. The book opens dramatically with the collapse of a block of the Sita Ram Building in 1903, a disaster that was rumored to have been retribution for an insult offered by its Hindu owner and British customers at a bar on its ground floor to the shrine across the street of a saint named Pedro Shah, a Portuguese sailor who had converted to Islam. Green interprets "his spectacular miracle" as "symptomatic of the larger pressures of cosmopolitan modernity that helped create a marketplace for religions in the city surrounding them." Bombay is seen to have emerged as "the cosmopolis of the Indian Ocean." Muslim writings in trans-regional languages, such as Persian, Urdu, and Arabic, circulated across the western Indian Ocean as far as South Africa. These are analyzed to explore what is described as "an industrial and cosmopolitan environment." Yet, in summarizing his argument, Green takes a contradictory position. "In the most industrialized, technological and cosmopolitan city of the west Indian Ocean," he asserts, "the most successful religious productions were not 'modern', disenchanted 'Protestant' Islams, but cults that were enchanted, hierarchical and ritualistic. They were neither uniform in characteristics nor cosmopolitan in outlook, but highly differentiated and parochially communitarian. They were neither reformed, nor modernist, but customary and traditionalist." The deployment of the market model of a religious economy leads to a second contradiction. Muslims are said to have consumed the "Islamic products and services" on offer as "rational agents."[19] That seems to toss the enchanting quality of Bombay Islams into the Arabian Sea.

An eagerness to contest Christopher Bayly's thesis about the rise of the global uniformity of world religions in the course of the nineteenth century[20] has led Green to exaggerate diversity and diversification. We need a better conceptual framework to make sense of the religious experience of subaltern groups in conditions of urban-industrial modernity. Instead of drawing a sharp dichotomy between the one and the many, reformist versus customary Islam, modernity against tradition, a subtler approach would be to accept the interplay of the singular and the plural and the many accommodations between the supposedly reformist and customary strands of Islam. Muslim shrines drew large numbers of non-Muslim devotees, as in the case of the shrine of Haji Ali in Bombay and Moula Ali Shah in Calcutta. The Haji Ali shrine on Bombay's sea face was constructed in memory of a wealthy Bukhara merchant who gave up his worldly possessions to go for haj. The relevance of the Indian Ocean interregional space in modern times was underscored by the reconstruction of the Nakhoda Mosque in Calcutta under the patronage of the Cutchi Memons in 1926. Cosmopolitanism must not be confused with global uniformity. It may be possible to delineate the features of "local cosmopolitanism" emanating from Bombay into the Indian Ocean interregional arena, much in the way that Engseng Ho has narrated so astutely in his book, *The Graves of Tarim*.[21] Bombay also served as a magnet for Muslims from across the subcontinent. For all their differences, they embarked as Muslims for pilgrimages from this port city. From the late 1860s to the 1890s, the haj from India consisted of carefully controlled flows of pilgrims from the three ports of Calcutta, Bombay, and Karachi. The outbreak of plague in 1896 led to the closure of Calcutta as a pilgrim port for thirty years. Even after the port of Calcutta was reopened for pilgrim traffic in 1926, a majority of pilgrims from Bengal continued to embark from Bombay and as many as 85 percent chose to return via Bombay. The convening power of this metropolis for the subcontinent's Muslims was formidable.

Nile Green "deliberately stops" his survey of Bombay Islam in 1915 on grounds that Mohammad Ali Jinnah became the president of the All India Muslim League the previous year. "From that period," it is claimed, "the new imperatives of nationalism and the search for a unified Indian Muslim 'community' symbolized by Jinnah pulled Bombay's Muslims in other directions, whether seen in their participation in the nationalism of the Muslim League or the internationalism of the Khilafat movement."[22] Yet, the years from 1910s through the 1940s represent the most fascinating phase in the history of aspirational cosmopolitanism in South Asia, as we will presently argue in this introductory essay, a kind of cosmopolitanism that was bound in a complex relationship with Indian nationalism and Islamic universalism.[23]

The colonial port-cities were by no means the only or even chief conduits of South Asian Islam's engagements with the wider Indian Ocean interregional arena in the nineteenth and twentieth centuries. If there is a lacuna even in the densely populated and intensely cultivated intellectual terrain of Bengal in its relations with a wider interregional arena, there are vast expanses of fallow in the scholarly fields of UP and Punjab in their connections with the Indian Ocean. Ayesha Jalal fills that void through a study of a few of the significant intellectual voyages from the upper Gangetic plain and the Indus valley to the Indian Ocean in search of a Muslim world and Islamic universalism. These include the journeys of Sayyid Ahmad Khan in 1869, Shibli Numani in 1892, Mahboob Alam in 1900, Mohammad Ali in 1928, Ghulam Rasul Mehr in 1930, and Muhammad Iqbal in 1931.

In Sunil Amrith's essay, a relatively small coastal town of Nagore emerges as the nodal point of the diffusion of a cosmopolitanism of the Tamil Muslim assortment across the eastern Indian Ocean. The spiritual center is the Sufi mystic Shahul Hamid's *dargah* or shrine, replicas of which can be found in Singapore and Penang. "Shahul Hamid," Amrith tells us, "was an apt patron saint for people on the move. The sea is at the heart of his story. Stories of his life recount his journey from the plains of North India to Mecca and back across the Indian Ocean, stopping in the Maldives and at Adam's Peak in Ceylon before settling in Nagore, where he died." In his comparative and connected history of Tamil Muslims and Chinese Muslims in Southeast Asia, Amrith gives us a vivid account of "a lived and pragmatic cosmopolitanism" rooted in particular urban contexts. His survey over the *longue duree* enables him to distinguish this modern instance of cosmopolitan practice from the romanticized versions propagated by some historians of the pre-modern era. At the same time, he is able to track its long after-life through the period of anti-colonial nationalism and beyond the attempted closure of the ocean's call by the guardians of the post-colonial nation-states' borders.

Migrant capital and labor undergirded the political economy of European colonial empires. Yet, the monitoring of mobility was simultaneously a key imperial project. The movement that was brought under strict surveillance was Muslim pilgrimage across the Indian Ocean, especially the annual haj. Eric Tagliacozzo's essay shows how the imperial control of Muslim bodies evolved from ad hoc methods of regulation to a systematic and rigorous espionage that may be seen as the defining feature of the high modernist state by the early twentieth century. Tagliacozzo sees the French, British, Dutch, and Italian projects of surveillance on Muslims in the Hejaz through a comparative lens. In time, the British apparatus of colonial control became the most elaborate and formidable in the partnership inflected with rivalry that sought to parry the threat of "Pan-Islam" and other allied transnational anti-colonialisms. "Pan-Islamism" was a pejorative colonial label for a phenomenon that is better described as a quest for Islamic universalism. The haj was one avenue of that search. The pilgrims' progress was strictly monitored by colonial rules.[24]

While Tagliacozzo provides an incisive analysis of European visions of control, Seema Alavi's essay evokes expressions of a Muslim cosmopolitanism in the interstices of the Ottoman and British empires during the late nineteenth century. She does so by following the itineraries and sifting through the textual productions of two Muslim men of religion, Maulana Rahmatullah Kairanwi and Siddiq Hasan Khan, who fled India after the British crushed the 1857 rebellion. As long as the Ottoman empire supplied an alternative locus of temporal sovereignty,[25] these *émigrés* had a space where they could articulate a global Muslim sensibility. Alavi sees this form of cosmopolitanism between empires as a challenge to the emerging power of the nation and a precursor to the idea of transnationalism in the twentieth century. Maulana Shibli Numani would take the expansive spatial imagination of a transnational Muslim world to a higher intellectual plane in his voyage to Ottoman domains in 1892.

Sana Aiyar shows the relevance of the Indian Ocean interregional arena as a horizon from which to illuminate local histories in a transnational, connective context. She analyzes the early twentieth-century anti-colonial movements in Burma where Burmese were partners and rivals with Indians. Extraterritorial solidarity based on religious identity linked the Khilafat movement in India to the politics of Burmese anti-colonialism. The affinities and animosities based on race complicated faith-based relations. Moreover, there were tensions between discourses of indigeneity and diaspora in Burma that caution against any uncritical celebration of expressions of cosmopolitanism transcending the identities of race and religion.

While Amrith, Tagliacozzo, Alavi, and Aiyar pursue connections across the vast eastern and western zones of the Indian Ocean, Iftekhar

Iqbal, and Andrew Sartori focus on Bengal, or the Ganga-Brahmaputra deltaic tract, and its articulation with broader Indian Ocean and global domains. Their contributions must be placed in the larger context of a development of immense significance for the nineteenth-century world economy going on in the agrarian hinterlands of Asia. What was fashioned in the first half of the nineteenth century was a settled and sedentarized peasantry, which, during its latter half, produced primary products for a capitalist world market. Production relations based on settled peasant labor and migrant indentured or quasi-indentured labor came to be bound in a dialectical relationship. It may have been possible until the mid-nineteenth century to advance a simple demographic typology in the eastern Indian Ocean of densely populated and sparsely populated zones. The rise of plantations and mines dramatically unsettled that dichotomy. They drew their labor from the old-settled, thickly populated agrarian regions, which got an extended lease of life through this escape hatch of migration. Large contingents of Tamil labor, for instance, moved to the tea plantations of Ceylon and the rubber plantations of Malaya, just as Chinese migrant laborers were sent to work in the tin mines of the peninsula. But the new concentrations of population also needed new sources of food, which the old rice bowls of Bengal, Tamil Nadu, Java, and northern Vietnam were in no position to supply. This spurred the opening of the rice frontiers of the Irrawaddy delta in Lower Burma, the Chao Phraya delta in Thailand, and the Mekong delta in southern Vietnam, largely financed by overseas Chinese and Indian capitalists. The triad of old agrarian zones, new plantations and mines, and newer rice frontiers, linked by specialized flows of labor and capital, remained in place from the mid-nineteenth century, until the crisis of the depression decade arrested or reversed most of these flows.[26] If Tamil peasant labor moved across the sea to Ceylon and Malaya, Bengali peasant labor in the densely populated east Bengal districts adopted two strategies of survival. First, Bengal's smallholding peasantry turned to cultivating a more labor-intensive and higher value cash crop, jute, in a process that could be termed agricultural involution. Second, a certain sizeable fraction among them migrated to the Brahmaputra valley in the neighboring province of Assam. Nearly a million Bengali Muslim peasants went in search of jute lands from eastern Bengal to Assam in the first three decades of the twentieth century.[27]

Iftekhar Iqbal views Bengal as a frontier of both the Indian Ocean and the South Asian landmass. Paralleling Amrith's tracking of Tamil Muslim migration, Iqbal examines the mobility of Bengali Muslims along the rim of the Bay of Bengal. Adapting and modifying Nile Green's analysis of "space making," Iqbal demonstrates how Bengali agrarian society was deeply influenced by the promises and predicaments of the Indian Ocean. Conversely, he also views the Indian Ocean from the vantage point of the river, or rather the Ganga-Brahmaputra delta of Bengal, as well as the Irrawaddy delta in Burma. If Rennell was interested merely in the geographical and commercial confluence of the river and the ocean, Iqbal studies trade and religion, culture and politics, at the cusp of the delta and the bay. The history of Bengalis, subalterns and elites alike, was not contained within the borders of Bengal in the age of British colonialism. The Bengali language, far from being confined to the level of a vernacular, rose as the vehicle of a universalist aspiration, not just in contestation with Urdu but through a partnership marked by rivalry with Arabic.

Andrew Sartori unravels the meaning of Muslim emancipation in Bengal, the South Asian region with the largest Muslim population. He does so by seizing upon the aspect of Lockean thought that emphasizes the property-constituting powers of labor and then exploring its articulation by the colonizer and colonized in the Bengal countryside. The quarter of a century between the passage of the Rent Act of 1859 and the Tenancy Act of 1885 saw a significant trend toward the legal recognition of moderation of rent and security of tenure for occupancy *raiyats* in Bengal, where the revenue had been permanently settled with zamindars in 1793. Sartori shows how *proja*—or tenant—claims on environmental resources came to be affiliated with a sense of Muslimness. While there were two earlier phases of a connection between rights over land and expressions of Muslim identity, he interprets a popular pamphlet from the early twentieth century as demonstrating a stronger link between peasant property and Muslim piety. By the 1940s, the demand for Pakistan tied the agrarian aspirations of smallholding peasants to Muslim self-determination.

In the early twentieth century, many peasants from densely populated Mymensingh migrated to the Brahmaputra valley in Assam. Both Iqbal and Sartori offer fresh insights into the political discourse of Maulana Bhashani, who led the Bengali peasant colonists in Assam. There remains room for more reflection on how Bhashani's "liberal" commitment to peasant property meshed with his declaration of jihad in the name of Allah and his call to peasants to become *shaheeds* in the path of Allah.

Muslim cosmopolitanism and Islamic universalism in their varied forms did not collide with a monolithic Europe. The British empire's claims of a liberal universalism were unsettled by the discourses embodying a universalist aspiration of both Germanic Europe and South Asian Islam. Kris Manjapra analyzes the deep entanglement of South Asian Muslim intellectuals with Germanic modes of scholarship that denied British universalism the hegemony it craved. He interprets the century spanning the mid-nineteenth century to the mid-twentieth as one featuring resistance to Anglo-Saxonism by European rivals and colonized subjects in Asia. This was not an anti-modern or anti-liberal protest against "progress." Scholars and activists in Central Europe and South Asia came together in intellectual and political efforts to craft Islam as a cosmopolitan thought zone seeking to shape a global future that challenged the false universalist claims of Britain's worldwide empire. "German scholars of South Asian Islam emphasized the universal," Manjapra writes, "not the particular." Among the South Asian Muslim intellectual explorers who engaged with this strand of Germanic scholarship were Muhammad Shahidullah of Bengal, Ali Akhtar Ansari of the United Provinces, and, last but certainly not the least, Muhammad Iqbal of Punjab.

The partition of Punjab and Bengal in 1947 split up the river basins of the Indus and the Ganga. Ram Manohar Lohia recalls a private conversation in Noakhali with Jawaharlal Nehru at the instance of Mahatma Gandhi in November 1946. "Mr. Nehru spoke of the water, slime, bush and tree," Lohia writes, "that he found everywhere in East Bengal. He said that was not the India he or I knew and wanted with some vehemence to cut East Bengal away from the mainland of India." Lohia found this to be an extraordinary observation. "These reasons of geography might under other circumstances," Lohia commented, "prove how necessary it is for the Ganga and Jamuna plains to stay joined with their luxuriant terminus. But once the idea of partition came to be accepted as a condition precedent to India's freedom, no matter that the acceptance was still very private and not even communicated to Mahatma Gandhi, the geography of East Bengal could well become abominable."[28] The division of land and water destroyed the organic river isthmuses that connected Punjab and Bengal to the Indian Ocean. It was a crime against nature and humanity for which the subcontinent is still paying a hefty price.

Notes and References

1. Fernand Braudel, *The Mediterranean and the Mediterranean World in the Age of Philip II* (Berkeley: University of California Press, 1995), pp. 170, 188–189, 191.
2. See, for example, K. N. Chaudhuri, *Trade and Civilization in the Indian Ocean* (Cambridge: Cambridge University Press, 1983); Ashin Dasgupta, *Indian Merchants and the Decline of Surat: c. 1700-1750* (Delhi: Manohar, 1994); Nile Green, *Bombay Islam: Religious Economy of the West Indian Ocean, 1840-1915* (Cambridge: Cambridge University Press, 2011).
3. For a discussion of the space and time in the Indian Ocean interregional arena, see Sugata Bose, *A Hundred Horizons: The Indian Ocean in the Age of Global Empire* (Cambridge, MA: Harvard University Press, 2006), pp. 1–35.
4. James L. Gelvin and Nile Green (eds.), *Global Muslims in the Age of Steam and Print* (Berkeley: University of California Press, 2014).
5. James Rennell, *An Account of the Ganges and Burrampooter Rivers*. By James Rennell, Esq. F.R.S. Read at the Royal Society. January 25, 1780. London, MDCCLXXXI. (1781). *Eighteenth Century Collections Online*. Gale. Harvard Library. November 2, 2014, pp. 3–8.
6. Ibid., pp. 18, 25.
7. Ibid., pp. 27–28.
8. See Sugata Bose, *The New Cambridge History of India: Peasant Labor and Colonial Capital* (Cambridge: Cambridge University Press, 1993), pp. 9–14.
9. Rennell, *An Account of the Ganges and Burrampooter Rivers*, p. 16.
10. Bose, *Peasant Labor and Colonial Capital*, pp. 11–12.

11. Alexander Burnes, "Navigating Indus," *Substance of a Geographical Memoir on the Indus.* By Lieut. Burnes, E.I.C.S. Communicated by the Court of Directors of the East India Company. Read 25 March, 8 and 22 April, and 13 and 27 May, 1833, pp. 113–114, 155.
12. Ibid., pp. 114–115, 121, 123, 126–127, 142–144.
13. Ibid., pp. 113, 154.
14. W. P. Andrew, *The Indus and Its Provinces* (London: William H. Allen & Co.: 1857, reprinted Lahore: East and West Publishing Company, 1976), pp. 6–9.
15. For an engaging account of "conquering the classic river," see Alice Albina, *Empires of the Indus* (London: John Murray, 2008), pp. 26–51; on the resilence of traditional country boats in the age of steam, see Clive Dewey, *Steamboats on the Indus: The limits of Western Technological Superiority in South Asia* (Delhi: Oxford University Press, 2014).
16. Braudel, *The Mediterranean*, p. 187.
17. See, for instance, Asim Roy, *The Islamic Syncretic Tradition in Bengal* (Princeton: Princeton University Press, 1983); Richard Eaton, *The Rise of Islam and the Bengal Frontier, 1204-1760* (Berkeley: University of California Press, 1993).
18. C.A. Bayly, "Penang and Bombay: Indian Ocean Port Cities in the Nineteenth Century," in Loh Wei Leng, T.N. Harper, and Sunil S. Amrith (eds.), *Proceedings of Penang and the Indian Ocean Conference 2011* (Georgetown, Penang: Think City, 2012), pp. 176–187.
19. Nile Green, *Bombay Islam: The Religious Economy of the West Indian Ocean, 1840-1915* (Cambridge: Cambridge University Press, 2011), pp. 1–3, 11, 16.
20. See C.A. Bayly, *The Birth of the Modern World, 1780-1914* (Oxford: Blackwell, 2004).
21. Engseng Ho, *The Graves of Tarim: Genealogy and Mobility across the Indian Ocean* (Berkeley: University of California Press, 2006); Homi Bhabha, *The Location of Culture* (New York: Routledge, 2004).
22. Green, *Bombay Islam*, pp. 7, 237.
23. This section on Bombay draws on arguments in Sugata Bose's Vasant J. Sheth Lecture on "Colorful Cosmopolitanisms: Bombay, Calcutta and the Indian Ocean," Vasant J. Seth Foundation, Mumbai, January 2013.
24. On the haj from India, see Bose, *A Hundred Horizons*, Chapter 6.
25. For a discussion on the different realms of divine and temporal sovereignty in Muslim thought, see Ayesha Jalal, *Self and Sovereignty: Individual and Community in South Asian Islam since 1850* (London: Routledge, 2000).
26. See Bose, *A Hundred Horizons*, Chapter 3.

27. See Sugata Bose, *Agrarian Bengal: Economy, Social Structure and Politics, 1919-1947* (Cambridge: Cambridge University Press, 1986), pp. 37–58; Bose, *Peasant Labor and Colonial Capital*, pp. 24–29.
28. Ram Manohar Lohia, *Guilty Men of India's Partition* (Allahabad: Kitabistan, 1960), p. 17.

1

Muslim Universalist Aspirations

Intimacies between the Indus-Gangetic Plain and the Indian Ocean

Ayesha Jalal

Muslim imaginings were animated by a sense of belonging to a worldwide community of believers long before the age of steam and print was heralded by colonial empires. Aural, textual, and visual expressions of Islamic universalist aspirations are imaginatively interwoven in the literature, music, arts, and architecture of the Muslim world abutting the Indian Ocean. The increased volume of travel and exchange, which came with the ease of modern travel, alone cannot explain the enduring vitality of the period from the mid-nineteenth century to the first three decades of the twentieth for an understanding of Muslim conceptions of Islamic universalism. With the Western colonial powers controlling the flow of haj pilgrims, Indian Muslim feelings of disempowerment and subjugation to Western colonial domination led to greater empathy with co-religionists in other parts of the Islamic world. Muslim intellectuals and publicists of the Indus-Gangetic plain, for instance, adjusted to the loss of formal sovereignty in 1858 by taking a heightened interest in the affairs of Ottoman Turkey. Affinities with the *ummah* did more than fulfill a religious ideal and were increasingly seen by Muslim intellectuals, newspaper editors, and politicians as a political necessity. Dubbed "Pan-Islamists" by the British colonial state and held in disdain by their Hindu counterparts for harboring extraterritorial loyalties, these Muslims had a far more expansive vision than mere sedition or disloyalty to their homeland. Aware of their minority status in the subcontinent, they looked for succor and inspiration in *Balad-i-Islam*—as they often referred to the Muslim world in preference to the more legalist

Dar-ul-Islam—for emotive and political reasons. These invocations of Islamic unity and brotherhood in an age of Western colonialism and Muslim political disunity need closer historical investigation. Was the *ummah* a mere figment of Indian Muslim imaginings and a salve for the pain of subjugation? Or could it be that Islamic universalism, encapsulated in the notion of *tawhid*, or the unity of creation, was a lived and more intimate experience. By connecting individuals across the spatial settings of the Indian Ocean and the Indus-Gangetic plain, the idea of *tawhid* generated exchanges that had a greater impact on the ideas and politics of Muslims in late nineteenth- and early twentieth-century colonial India than historians have acknowledged.

Even the preeminent Indian Muslim modernist of the late nineteenth century, Sayyid Ahmad Khan, who advocated loyalty to the British Raj and rejected any binding authority of the Ottoman caliphate over Indian Muslims, acknowledged the sovereignty of God over the entire universe. He was as attached to the sacred lands of his faith as those labeled "Pan-Islamists." On April 16, 1869, six days after boarding the Peninsular and Oriental Steam Navigation Company's ship *Baroda* from Bombay, on his way to London, Sayyid Ahmad Khan was enthralled by his first glimpse of the Hejaz. He marveled at God's grace, which had turned a barren land into the birthplace of the final prophet. Sayyid Ahmad was still in reverie when his fellow English traveler and friend, Major Dodd, the Director of Public Instruction at Nagpur, asked, "Did you see the Prophet's land?" "Yes," Sayyid Ahmad replied, "this is Arabia the blessed." When Dodd commented on a well-traveled Pathan Muslim maid, who was traveling on the ship, as belonging to Sayyid Ahmad's *qaum*, he retorted: "Yes, no doubt, our *qaum*, our *qaum*, without doubt all human beings are our brothers because they are born of the same father and all Muslims are our religious brothers who believe in one God."

He had a religious sensibility that meshed comfortably with the curiosity of a traveler who had a sense of history and interest in the everyday life of the places he visited. Revealing the contours of the Islamic universalist aspiration, as opposed to the more limited political connotations of "Pan-Islamism," this was a conception that was rooted in the local but was global in scope. Sayyid Ahmad was delighted to see the "sovereignty of Urdu" established across the Arabian Sea from India all the way to Aden. He was able to get around the bazaars of Aden speaking Urdu. The cosmopolitan ambience of Suez with its Egyptian, Turkish, German, and Greek shops captivated him. Sayyid Ahmad spoke in Arabic to the shopkeepers before being drawn to the turbaned figure of Sheikh Ismail, who, it turned out, could speak some Urdu. A middle-aged Syrian, Ismail had journeyed innumerable times to Java over the past fifty years, during which he also visited China, Australia, Hindustan, and the Deccan. Since the Suez Canal was not opened until November of 1869, Sayyid Ahmad took a train to Alexandria. Upon embarking the ship *Poona* for Marseilles, Major Dodd offended Sayyid Ahmad by casually remarking: "We have arrived in Europe … having left the land of the Prophet behind, this is the land of infidels." Miffed by Dodd's incorrigible tendency to highlight faith-based differences, Sayyid Ahmad coolly retorted that it would be more appropriate to say they had entered the land of the *ahl-i-kitab* or the people of the book. Being Muslim for Sayyid Ahmad did not mean rejecting or resenting European achievements and values. He was committed to learning from Europe. Among the high points of his trip aboard the *Poona* was meeting Ferdinand de Lesseps, from whom he learned that the canal under construction at Suez would become operational in six months. At a ceremony on the ship to honor him, Lesseps dismissed suggestions that his engineering feat be named after him and instead proposed naming it the "French Canal." Dismayed by the self-aggrandizement and lack of national feeling among Indians, Sayyid Ahmad found it uplifting to meet such a courageous and capable man, who placed the glory of his country above his own.[1]

Self-education through travel, quite as much as the religious duty of pilgrimage to the holy sites of Islam, was highly prized by the Muslim *ashraf*—literally the respectable classes—who also considered it their duty to communicate their observations and personal experiences to a broader readership. Apart from those devoted to issues of religious theology and ritual practice, the overarching thrust of the *safarnamah*s, or travelogues, written in the late nineteenth and early twentieth centuries by Muslims who sailed from Bombay and Karachi to the Red Sea ports is informational, reformist, and, ultimately, political in intent. Sayyid Ahmad Khan's undisputed lead in this regard cannot go unobserved. On returning from Europe in September 1870, he launched the periodical *Tehzib-ul-Akhlaq* to promote rational and critical discussion among Muslims. In 1877, Sayyid Ahmad laid the foundations of the Muhammadan Anglo-Oriental (MAO) College at Aligarh modeled after the University of Cambridge, which he had visited to study the British higher education system. The networks forged by Sayyid Ahmad's educational initiatives spawned a rich and vibrant intellectual tradition that continues to resonate across the subcontinent.

Before his Islamic universalist vision led him to take an alternative path, Shibli Numani (1857–1914) was closely associated with the Aligarh Movement inspired by Sayyid Ahmad Khan's leadership in the field of Muslim education. An erudite scholar and poet, Shibli was well versed in Arabic, Persian, and Urdu. He had contemplated a trip to the Ottoman Empire ever since he began writing on the heroes of Islam. Despite the voluminous historical material present in India, he needed access to Islamic works in Egypt and Syria to write a comprehensive series. The opportunity eluded him and he had lost hope. He was teaching Arabic at the MAO College when, on the spur of the moment, he decided to join Professor Thomas W. Arnold, who was going to Europe. Arnold was teaching philosophy at the MAO College and giving French lessons in private to Shibli, who, in turn, was helping the professor with his Arabic. Shibli's voyage was a personal journey for knowledge and experience. He was reluctant to write about his travels, deeming his impressions to be too cursory to merit publication. But his friends and admirers prevailed upon him. Indian Muslims knew nothing about the contemporary conditions in the Ottoman domains since travel to the Islamic countries had been in abeyance for some time.[2] Shibli was alluding to the decline in the number of haj pilgrims from India after the cholera epidemic of 1865 was traced to the Gangetic valley, leading to the imposition of the dreaded surveillance regime discussed in Tagliacozzo's chapter.

European anxieties about the influx of destitute and diseased Indian pilgrims and British fears of "Pan-Islamism" in the aftermath of the 1857 rebellion created the "twin infection" of Muslim surveillance and security.[3] Colonial concerns in India about Muslim sedition were magnified after 1880 when Sultan Abdul Hamid II reasserted Ottoman claims to the caliphate. For an ardent admirer of the Ottoman sovereign, Shibli had no difficulty boarding the ship with Professor Arnold at Bombay on May 1, 1892 without a passport. Shibli was interested to see the social effects of Abdul Hamid's modernization reforms, especially the newly set up educational institutions. European prejudices against Muslims, particularly the Turks, were so deeply ingrained that even those who were not bigoted had nothing positive to say about the Ottomans. Shibli wanted to come to his own conclusions. On May 14, upon disembarking the ship at Port Said, he was seized by the realization of being in a Muslim-ruled country for the first time. He had already performed the haj. But the Ka'aba was the House of God, and he was thinking of worldly sovereignty. Everything in the city interested him. Shibli was pleased to see Port Said's tall and beautiful buildings as signs of Muslim prosperity and progress. He was disappointed to learn that they belonged to European traders. There was not a single decent house or tall building owned by a Muslim. The only sign of Muslim architectural glory was a royal mosque at the end of the posh European settlement.[4]

At Port Said, Shibli parted company with Arnold after preferring to go to Istanbul via Syria instead of traveling for a week from the Italian port of Brindisi through places where he was unfamiliar with the language, as he had initially planned. Arnold told Shibli that the Christian pilgrimage to Jerusalem was underway and he might encounter religious bigotry. After boarding the ship to Istanbul, Shibli found that while the pilgrims were avidly religious, they were mainly French and Italian and did not have the hubris of a conquering nation. This distinction between the arrogance of the British as rulers of India toward their subjects and other Europeans is an early confirmation of Manjapra's discussion of the entanglements of South Asian and German intellectuals who rejected the hegemonic claims of the British. There had been no other Muslim on the ship from Bombay to Port Said. From Beirut, the ship was filled with Syrian Arabs. Longing for the familiarity of interaction with co-religionists, Shibli tried conversing with the Syrian Muslims, who, like him, were traveling in third class.

His efforts at socializing met with cold aloofness. Shibli tried showing off his knowledge as a religious scholar but to no avail. He felt certain something was amiss. By chance, someone asked him what his religion was. When he said "Islam," the questioner said, "Absolutely not, do Muslims wear a cap like this?" The sherwani-clad Shibli had an Irani cap on his head, and the Syrians had mistaken him for a Magian. Once the misunderstanding was removed, they warmed up to Shibli, and a few became inseparable and gave him several important tips about Istanbul. The longer lasting impression Shibli took from his trip from Port Said to Istanbul, which he calls "Constantina," was the difference between living under Muslim and Western sovereignties. Passengers traveling in third class from Bombay to Suez were treated like coolies, but the situation was completely different in the Ottoman domains. Though the officers and staff on the ship were mostly European, they treated the passengers considerately. Often issues arose in which a Muslim passenger was at fault, but the ship's officers handled the matter judiciously.[5]

Shibli's account of his travels to Suez, Cyprus, Rhodes, and arrival in Istanbul, where he did not know a soul, is interlaced with knowledge of Islamic history. Being in a Muslim-ruled country made it possible for him to experience Islamic universalism in its cosmopolitan dimensions in everyday life. Like Sayyid Ahmad, Shibli was surprised by the internationalism of Urdu when he met an Egyptian vendor at Suez who spoke the language, though he had never visited Hindustan. The experience Shibli valued the most were his scholarly exchanges with other Muslims. At Rhodes, he engaged in a religious debate in Persian with the imam of the Hisar mosque and other luminaries in the library of the mosque. The rules of discussion were extremely civilized. When matters seemed headed for contention, the conversation moved on to another subject. Shibli maintains that these educational gatherings were a major reason for his successful trip, and the contacts he made through them helped him avoid the usual difficulties faced by tourists. The friendships he made during his travels as well as a wider circle of acquaintances were other contributing factors in Shibli's ability to navigate Istanbul, and later also Cairo, where he met the Egyptian reformer Muhammad

Abduh and discussed the sorry state of traditional Muslim education, including at Al-Azhar.

On May 23, when he reached Istanbul, Shibli had nowhere to stay. He could not afford a hotel and stayed at a caravanserai with a fellow traveler, Sheikh Abdul Zattah, a Syrian whom he had befriended on the ship. Zattah was the nephew of Khalid Naqshbandi, who was highly respected by Syrian residents of the city and who called him "Hazrat." Khalid Naqshbandi was a disciple of the eighteenth-century Indian Muslim scholar Mirza Mazhar Jan-e-Janaan Dehalvi. The Syrians helped Zattah gain access to people in Istanbul. Shibli benefitted enormously from these contacts. So would other Indian Muslims who followed in his wake in the twentieth century. Istanbul captivated Shibli, and he confirmed his favorable view of Sultan Abdul Hamid's patronage of modern education. Shibli liked the emphasis on a common routine for the students, the strict discipline and uniformity of dress, food, and large residential halls rather than separate rooms, which was the case at MAO College. After returning to India, he introduced similar halls of residence at MAO College, such as the Zahoor Hussain ward. But his insights were not clouded by an uncritical celebration of the Ottomans. Shibli thought the traditional madrassa education was in as deplorable a state as in India. The Sultan had more than doubled expenditure on education, resulting in a mushrooming of primary and secondary schools. However, all the colleges were in the Ottoman capital and none in Beirut, Damascus, or Jerusalem. Overall, Shibli did not think Muslims were doing well under the Ottomans, who seemed utterly helpless against the European powers. He was shocked to discover that each of the European powers had separate post offices in Istanbul, and even Turks thought it safer to mail their letters here than in the government post office. The condition of Ottoman Muslims was strikingly similar to that of Indian Muslims. Like their Indian counterparts, they did not take to industry and had only a small percentage of the share of trade and commerce. Even the shopkeepers in Istanbul were Jewish or Christian. As in India, there was an unresolved and bitter tussle between traditional and modern education. The votaries of tradition refused to keep pace with changing times, while those with a modern sensibility promised much more than they actually delivered. An air of melancholy, or *huzun*, enveloped the Turks, who seemed hopelessly resigned to their fates.[6]

Sayyid Ahmad Khan and Shibli came from the Muslim minority areas of North India. Even though Bengal and Punjab supplied the largest number of hajis from India, more attention has been paid so far to the first-hand accounts of the pilgrimage of Muslims from the North Indian Gangetic heartland.[7] Shifting the gaze to the Indus valley reveals a regionally distinct but shared interest in engagement with Muslims across the western and eastern Indian Ocean. In 1900, Munshi Mahboob Alam, the editor of the Lahore-based daily *Paisa Akhbar* (the penny newspaper), traveled through the Ottoman territories on his way back from Europe, where he had gone to see the Paris Exhibition. His travel narratives were printed in the *Paisa Akhbar*, which sold for two rupees and had a circulation of 10,000, not an inconsiderable amount at the time. In 1908, Alam combined these articles with his diary entries to publish the voluminous *Safarnama Europe, Bilad-e-Rome, Shaam-o-Misr*, which is a treasure trove of insights into his conception of Islamic universalism. His friends and admirers gave him a tearful send-off at a function held on the premises of the Islamia College. After the opening speeches and recitations, a twenty-three-year-old Muhammad Iqbal, who was already famous for his poetic talents, read a warm and witty poem contrasting the enticement of an oceanic journey with the sense of loss felt by Alam's friends and associates in Lahore. The poem included the second line of the popular Indo-Persian verse—*ba salamat ravi wa baaz aiye*—go and come back safely—which begins with *ba safar raftand mubarak bad*, congratulations on your journey. The couplet had been repeatedly used by other speakers at the gathering and also in letters written to Alam bidding him Godspeed. In a humorous play on Alam's name, Iqbal added:

> You are the pride of Punjab, but hurry
> For there is no power of patience
> Let no one be separated from Mahboob (beloved)
> Whose heart strings for Alam's (the world's) adornment.[8]

"Progress is impossible without travel," the maverick journalist and editor of the *Paisa Akhbar* wrote. Muslims used to travel for haj even before the modern discoveries but had stopped doing so. If Muslims had continued going on haj, their condition would not have been so bad. Alam believed Hindustanis had much to learn from Europe. However, his initial impulse was to take a ship from Bombay or Calcutta to China or Japan; visit Australia and sail the Pacific to North America; cross the Atlantic to England; and then go to Paris, Berlin, Istanbul, and Egypt before returning to India. The prospect of going on his first-ever journey by ship proved to be daunting, and so he decided to go to Europe first. On the afternoon of May 27, 1900, Mahboob Alam took the train to Bombay from Lahore's railway station, where a large number of his Muslim and Hindu friends came to say goodbye. At every railway station in Punjab, where the train stopped, friends came laden with food and refreshments. Touched by the show of affection and respect, Alam realized the virtues of the *watan*, homeland. However, he was determined to see Europe. In Bombay, he obtained bank drafts that could be easily cashed but failed to get the passport needed to visit the Ottoman territories. Alam was advised to show the passport issued to him for travel to England at the Foreign Office in London, where, for a fee, he could get the passport required for travel to the Ottoman Empire.[9]

On June 1, Alam embarked the Austrian Lloyd Company's ship *Imperatrix*. "The rebelliousness of the sea was delightful," he wrote, "All day under the rays of the sun the small waves look like sparkling diamonds." Unlike the Peninsular and Oriental Company's mail ships, the *Imperatrix* stopped in Aden for a whole day to unload wheat from India and load merchandise for Port Said and elsewhere. Leather was loaded for New York and tobacco for Istanbul or "Constantina." He mentions the Parsi trader Dinshaw Cowasjee, who had migrated to Aden from Bombay around 1855 and played a leading role in the city's development. He was now the biggest contractor in Aden and owned innumerable properties and several steamers. Because of him, several Parsis had settled in Aden. At the time, there were 500 Parsis in the port city. They controlled most of the trade between the Somali coast and Aden. Alam regretted not being able to get off at Aden or Port Said because of the quarantine regulations that his fellow passengers likened to hell. Dodging the quarantine regime at Suez, he opted to go straight to Austria. In Vienna, Trieste, and Berlin, he ate only at Jewish restaurants. Alam was disappointed to see that there were only a handful of Muslims at the Paris Exhibition; they had brought no wares with them to show and were mainly employees. "This is the condition of Muslims," Alam lamented. Fortunately, some Hindu lawyers from Lucknow and Allahabad, led by Pandit Motilal Nehru, had created a performance company, ensuring the cultural presence of the Indus-Gangetic region at the Paris Exhibition. The famous wrestler Ghulam Mohammad Amritsari was there with his brother Kullu and four other wrestlers from Lahore and Amritsar. There was a dancing girl from Awadh; a few *bhands* from Punjab's folk tradition, who use mimicry, satire, and farce to entertain; a Delhi-based artist, Nazir Hussain; a Bengali master spinner of tops; a snake charmer; an eater of cloth; food and sweetmeat vendors; and several musicians.[10]

Alam was disappointed to learn that the Indian troupe started performing three months after the opening of the Paris Exhibition. He returned to London to get a passport from the Foreign Office to visit the Ottoman empire. When he came back to Paris a month later on his way to Istanbul, he was sorry to hear that all the Hindustani wrestlers and performers had left. After getting his Turkish visa, Alam dropped the idea of going to Greece and Italy because of time and cost constraints, and lack of familiarity with the languages spoken there. He boarded the Orient Express from Paris to Istanbul via Munich, Serbia, and Bulgaria, during which for thirty-two hours an enforced silence between him and four Russian passengers oppressed him. One of Alam's abiding regrets was that the imperial passport regime had prevented him from visiting the Ottoman territories on the way to Europe. If he could have done that, it would have cost the same amount of money to go to the United States and visit Japan and China before returning to India.[11]

Alam arrived in Istanbul in the first week of September 1900, just a few days after extravagant celebrations to mark the twenty-fifth year of Sultan Abdul Hamid's reign. The city's cosmopolitan population, its Asian and European parts, as well as the blending of Eastern and Western cultures charmed him. Newspapers in several languages were published here with shops carrying signs in as many as five to seven languages. People of different religions and thinking were resident here, which was one of the problems facing the Ottoman government. There were more than seventy thousand libraries in Istanbul and so many mosques that it was said that one could visit a new mosque every day for a whole year. Alam thought he could pray at a new mosque in the city for two whole years. His travelogue, like the contemporaneous one by another Punjabi Muslim, Abdur Rahman Amritsari, provides one of the most detailed accounts in Urdu of the social, intellectual, and political milieu of Ottoman Turkey at the turn of the century.

A sympathizer of Abdul Hamid, Alam thoroughly disapproved of the Young Turks' enchantment with Europe. This did not mean ignoring defects in the Ottoman system or overlooking clear evidence of authoritarianism. It took him four hours to get his luggage released from Ottoman customs. There was a book censorship desk at the customs office. A strict censorship system was in place. Any book critical of the Ottomans, derogatory toward Islam, or containing a photograph of the Sultan was banned. Only Qurans published at the Ottoman printing press were permitted. The provision was less than a decade old and had been enforced to counter rumors that the Russians had printed Qurans with the passages on jihad left out. Turkish authorities repeatedly checked his passport. For travel to Syria and Egypt, he had to get a passport in Turkish because the Turks would not accept a passport in a language other than their own. The streets of Istanbul were filled with Turkish army officers in their uniforms, medals, and swords because, as he explained to himself, "The government here is a real military government."[12]

During his stay in the Ottoman domains, Alam was warmly received by the journalistic community. An Afghan acquaintance with contacts in newspaper offices leaked the news of his presence in Istanbul. Sayyid Abdul Ghaffar, a Kashmiri who had been living in the city for twenty-five years, came to Alam's hotel and insisted that he stay with him. For the next two weeks, Alam was Ghaffar's guest and met several luminaries of the city, including the Syrian Sheikh Abul Huda of Aleppo, who belonged to the Rafai Sufi order and was a trusted aide of Sultan Abdul Hamid. A dignified white-haired man, Huda was the author of almost 175 books on Islamic knowledge in Arabic and lived in a majestic house near the sea. At the time, Huda was embroiled in a controversy with Mohammad Zafir, a Shadhili Madani sheikh to whom Abdul Hameed had given his oath of allegiance. One of Zafir's followers had published an insulting piece about Huda, who mistook Alam for a journalist and began talking about the incident, regretting that *jahalat* (ignorance) and *fitna* (sedition) was rampant among Muslims. Describing his opponent as an uneducated and ill-mannered man who was envious of him, Huda claimed that Zafir's paternal grandfather was a Jew. He presented Alam with several of his Arabic works on mysticism and the Shadhilia order, remonstrating that one Hindustani newspaper had criticized him without any evidentiary backing. Huda thought "the condition of Muslims" was "pitiful because they had ceased to be Muslims" and had lost their sense of honor and manliness. Alam and Huda discussed this and other matters in Arabic for an hour and a half.[13]

The opportunity of communicating in person with Muslims in the Ottoman empire on historical and contemporary issues was the lived experience of Islamic universalism that Alam thoroughly relished. These conversations gave him a better idea of the political dynamics underlying the Ottoman relationship with the European powers. A Turkish officer told him that his mind had been fashioned by the British colonial state in India and he would not be able to understand the Ottoman way of doing things. The observation proved to be correct to an extent. Alam was surprised to find that a government official in Ottoman Turkey was not debarred from also being a journalist. Ahmad Mihdat Effendi, not to be confused with Ottoman statesman Mihdat Pasha for whom he worked, was a government servant who owned and edited the older and more conservative paper *Tarjuman-i-Haqqiqat* (interpreter of truth). One of Alam's acquaintances described Ahmad Mihdat as the Victor Hugo of the Turks. Finding echoes of Sayyid Ahmad Khan in Mihdat's approach to miracles, Alam thought he was the Ottoman *necheri*, literally one who reduces religion to worldly matters. Mihdat praised Jalaluddin Rumi's magnum opus *Masnawi* as an excellent interpretation of the Quran but had never heard of Sayyid Ahmad. He wanted to read the Indian Muslim reformer's writings but regretted not knowing Urdu, though he was proficient in Arabic, French, and Persian.

Ahmad Mihdat's house was located in the Asian part of Istanbul in a beautiful spot on the eastern bank of the Bosphorus. Alam took a steamer to meet him three or four times and learned much about Ottoman history and contemporary politics. According to Mihdat, the Ottomans ruled effectively for 200 years. The rot started with the European intervention in the Crimean War and their pledge in the Paris Treaty of 1856 to maintain the integrity of the Ottoman Empire. European priests had misled many Turks, and like them, Mihdat was initially disgruntled with the Quran. During this dark and uncertain period, Indian ulema came to the rescue of Turks. He was especially grateful to Moulvi Rahmatullah Kairanwi, one of the "little men between great empires" discussed by Seema Alavi. Mihdat found Kairanwi's book on Christianity very useful and translated it into Turkish. Later, he wrote several books on Christianity himself and concluded that Christianity and Judaism were unworthy of being considered religions. A chip off the old block, he also did not take kindly to the Ottoman ulema. He recalled a scholar from Damascus telling him that Turkish and Arab ulema studied religion for the sake of official appointments while Indian ulema studied religion solely to gain knowledge of religion.[14]

With this overture to religious and intellectual connectivities among Muslims of Ottoman Turkey and British India, Mihdat gave Alam a spirited lecture on Turkish intelligence in numismatics and their natural resources. The collection of coins in Turkish museums was more complete than anything on display in the museums of London. Geography formed part of the Turkish classification scheme that the Europeans had now adopted. Numismatics was the name of the ancient school, he claimed, that included Asia Minor, Hindustan, Iran, and Afghanistan. There were 220 million Turks in the Ottoman empire, half of them women, most of whom did not wear the burqa, unlike their Hindustani counterparts. Another eleven million were Arab, with an additional two million consisting of other nations, or *millets*, that did not wear the Turkish fez. Turkey had an enormous advantage over Japan in terms of agricultural productivity but had labor scarcity and was financially indebted to Europe. Seven Turks occupied one square mile compared with 125 in Japan. The land was so fertile that there was no need for fertilizers. The Punjabi in Alam was amazed to see fertilizers being dumped into the Bosporus. Mihdat maintained that Abdul Hamid had repaid most of the "£150,000,000 loan incurred during the reign of Sultan Abdul Aziz" and acquired no new debts.[15]

This only affirmed Alam's own positive estimation of Abdul Hamid. He was impressed by the strides made by Ottoman Turkey in the field of education after visiting various institutions established in Istanbul over the past quarter of a century. The Sultan wanted to raise Ottoman Turkey to the level of Europe and, contrary to the charge of the Young Turks, would not have been spreading modern education if he had wanted to keep his people in darkness. However, Ottoman curbs on the press disappointed Alam. He realized that Abdul Hamid's authoritarianism and the wall of security around him were due to the threat posed by the Young Turks and Armenian nationalists, some of whom were based in Europe and engaged in subversive activities. By the time Alam wrote the preface to his travelogue on September 13, 1908, Abdul Hamid had survived a European anarchist's assassination attempt in July 1905 and exactly three years later had been forced by the Young Turks to restore the 1876 constitution and abolish espionage and press censorship.

Political freedoms did not mean a more effective exercise of sovereignty. Much of the Ottoman debt dated back to the time of the Crimean War of 1853–1856. Financial insolvency and the capitulations imposed by European powers had gravely undermined state authority. Foreign residents of these countries were subject to the laws of their respective countries. Trading privileges granted by successive Ottoman Sultans had been used to extend European control over the empire. European traders were protected from all kinds of taxes and could not be tried in the local courts. The ubiquitous presence of European power and capital in Ottoman Turkey irked Alam. He was dismayed to see shops in Istanbul filled with European manufactured goods. Carpets were Turkey's only export to Europe. Clothes were imported from Europe, while boots—a Turkish invention—came from Russia. Conversations with Ahmad Jidat, the owner and editor of the newspaper *Iqdaam* (measures) and also a high-ranking police official, provided him with historical insights into the reasons for Ottoman dependence on cheap European goods. Handmade Turkish products were more beautiful but also costly and had lost out to cheaper machine-produced goods. Alam saw tremendous potential in commodity trade between Ottoman Turkey and Hindustan and regretted that Turkey's beautiful prayer rugs were not exported to India. Although he acknowledged that handmade Turkish goods were not plentiful enough to export, he attributed the absence of trade to the same lack of commercial enterprise as shown by Hindustani Muslims.[16]

The contacts Alam forged in Istanbul, often with Indians or individuals somehow linked with India, helped him immensely in the Ottoman provinces that he visited. He boarded a ship from Istanbul to Beirut that stopped at Rhodes, where his Turkish passport was checked but not his luggage because of his Kashmiri friend Sayyid Abdul Ghaffar's extensive connections. Sheikh Huda's two letters opened doors for Alam in Beirut and Damascus. In Beirut, he visited newspaper offices and publishing houses, adding to the burgeoning collection of books he had acquired on the trip. While in Damascus, he encountered Ata Effendi Jilani, a wealthy descendant of Abdul Qadir Jilani, who was extremely fond of Indian Muslims. A man of exceptional hospitality, he invited Alam to stay with him even though the two had never met before. Alam valued the common practice of hospitality among Arabs and Indians, which did not exist in Europe. But his intellectual exchanges in Damascus disappointed him. Though he met several scholars and influential people, he was sorry that not many had opened their eyes to the needs of the time. Those that had were of little use in the prevailing political climate. Damascus was a city of exiles. There were newspaper editors who had been exiled from Istanbul as well as two Afghan sardars,[17] both of whom were living on stipends from the Ottoman Sultan.

More memorable for Alam was his visit to the tomb of Muhiyuddin Ibn Arabi, the great twelfth-century Sufi master from Andalusia. Ata Effendi narrated a charming story about Arabi's father, who did not have children. When he mentioned this to Abdul Qadir Gilani, the eleventh-century Persian Sufi sheikh poked him in the back and said, "You will have a son whom you should name Muhiyuddin."

According to Arabi, while his name was Muhiyuddin Arabi, he was actually a Gilani. Alam also visited the grave of the Algerian Abdul Qadir Al-Jaziri, who had fought the French in the mid-nineteenth century. He prayed at the Ummayad Mosque and felt great pride going to the spot where Mohammad al-Ghazali, the influential Islamic philosopher and author of the *Ihya Ulum al-Din*, had spread knowledge standing under a minaret even though it had long burnt down. Alam admired the exquisite stonework of Syrian masons and the beauty of the call to prayer given in unison by as many as twenty muezzins. Salahuddin Ayubi, Saladin in European consciousness, was buried in front of the Umayyad Mosque. Europe, more than Asia, considered Saladin a brave man.

Alam's pride in belonging to a wider Muslim world drew on a sense of Islamic history that was more nostalgic than analytical. He tended to exaggerate the merits of Sultan Abdul Hamid's rule because he saw conditions in the Ottoman territories through the prism of his own political subjugation to British rule. This changed on his arrival in Egypt where the British had established their foothold after defeating Urabi Pasha's revolt in 1882 and banishing him to Ceylon. Critical of the broken promises that had enabled the British to occupy Egypt, the critical observer in Alam was not averse to acknowledging their achievements. Britain needed Egypt to control the Suez Canal, which was the gateway to India. So, in 1903, under an agreement, the French were allowed to intervene in Morocco in exchange for Egypt. Alam held out little hope for Egyptian nationalists succeeding in regaining power of their country so long as India remained in British hands. Unlike in 1884, France no longer had a say in Egypt. The Turks were too mired in problems of their own to pressure the British in Egypt even though the Ottoman Sultan was still formally sovereign. Alam thought press freedom and the development of a modern educational system were among the most significant benefits of British rule in Egypt. But there was also much that he disapproved of. He was dismayed that the colloquial, and to his mind incorrect, Arabic spoken here was also used by the prominent ulema, who otherwise wrote the language correctly. Overall, he did not form a high opinion of the collective intellect of ordinary Egyptians, whom he thought were less refined than Turks and Syrians.

When Alam visited Al Azhar University, the sight enraptured him. Thousands of students and teachers between the ages of seven and seventy were listening to lectures, debating, or studying inside Al Azhar's imposing premises. While drawn from all over the world, the vast majority of over 10,000 students at the time were Egyptian. There were a few hundred Syrians, Turks, and also Europeans but, significantly, only three Indians. When the Maghrib call to prayer was given, Alam was taken aback by the relaxed attitude of the students, some of whom did not rush to form prayer lines but continued talking and coming in and out of the university's premises. There were other aspects of the social and cultural ambience of Egypt that Alam could not easily square with his Hanafi-orientated Islam. For instance, Egyptians ate all kinds of sea life, including tortoises, because they belonged to the Shafi and Maliki schools. There were only a very few Egyptians, he thought, who did not drink alcohol. Alam had no ear for music and did not take to the Arab way of participatory listening. He quipped that he had heard enough Arabic songs to last him a lifetime. The only Arabic foods he liked were hummus and lentil-based dishes, a diminution in the quality of life for a carnivorous Punjabi.

Where Alam was culturally too steeped in his Punjabi regional identity to feel entirely at home in Cairo, the tropes of Islamic universalism came to his rescue. One of the people he met in the city was Sheikh Ali Yusuf, the editor of *Al-Muayyad*, which was considered to be the largest circulating Muslim paper in the world. A shrewd journalist, Yusuf was a disciple of Jamaluddin al-Afghani. A small, thin man, he wore the national dress and spoke only in Arabic but was very knowledgeable. He received Alam cordially and they met again on two or three occasions. *Al-Muayyad* supported the Ottoman government and refrained from displaying its opposition to the British occupation of Egypt. When Alam came to bid farewell, Yusuf complained of his early departure and gave him a photograph of himself and a copy of *Al-Muayyad* in which there was a story about his visit to Cairo. Alam was pleased to see the growing interest in newspapers among Egyptians, who were avid café goers, where they read and discussed the news over innumerable cups of Arabic coffee. Alam also met Mustapha Kamil, the editor of another popular Arabic newspaper, *Al Liwa* (the standard).

A handsome and well-built man who dressed in European clothes, Kamil was a staunch nationalist who later founded the National Party. He maintained that he was not opposed to the British, several of whom were his friends, but to their imperialism. Proficient in French, Kamil had traveled to France and Germany, where his stirring lectures against the British occupation of Egypt were well received by newspaper editors. When Kamil enquired about the situation in India, Alam said that Muslims were trying to acquire education because under British rule they had the freedom to bring about reforms.[18]

Among other mentionable vignettes of Alam's visit to Cairo was his meeting with the renowned Syrian scholar Rashid Rida, editor of *Al Minar*, and through him with Muhammad Abduh, who was the chief judge of Egypt. Alam describes Rida as a highly intelligent and accomplished young man whose articles advocating a return to the values of the Prophet's companions had been translated and published in Indian newspapers.[19] Eight years earlier, Shibli had regretted that a man like Abduh was appointed a judge when he ought to have been spearheading educational reform, most notably at Al Azhar.

Abduh had ruefully agreed with Shibli.[20] Displaying his continued interest in education, Abduh queried Alam about the educational situation in India and, on hearing the response, said: "Won't Muslims forget religion with this kind of worldly education?" Alam asked Abduh whether salvation could be gained by good people who were not Muslim. Abduh said yes, if they believed in God; the only requirement for a place in heaven was belief in *tawhid*—the oneness of the Creator. He thought those who did not believe in the oneness of God were not of the right mind. Abduh, who spoke French, wanted to spend six months in England learning English. He presented Alam with several Egyptian publications, including his own works, *Rasala-al-Tawhid* and *Taqrir-i-Mufti*. Alam also attended Abduh's lecture at Al-Azhar. Abduh's death four years later made the encounter all the more unforgettable.

An Indian Muslim, Muhammad Shukri, whom Alam had met on his first visit to the *Al-Muayyad* office, helped him contact several people in Cairo. Alam met the elderly Latif Pasha Salim Hijazi, who had played a significant role in Egyptian politics during the time of Ismail and Tawfiq Pasha. Latif Pasha had supported Yusuf in launching *Al-Muayyad.* Age and experience had denuded his former energy. He told Alam that Muslims, whether of India, Turkey, Egypt, or China, were all useless and lowly; the *ummah* was dead and unless God sent another prophet, their reform was impossible. There was no use in learning French and English or setting up factories. Alam protested that this kind of hopelessness was against the faith. Upon which Latif Pasha said that an Indian Muslim ought to translate the Quran correctly into English so that the people of Europe could understand that Islam teaches Muslims to love Christians and establish brotherly relations with them. Mirza Abdul Fazal also came to see Latif Pasha, and so Alam met him as well. Abdul Fazal was a respected scholar and knowledgeable man. He said that although he had not invented electricity, he could convert the inventors of electricity to Islam. At the time Alam did not like this bravado, but he later discovered that Abdul Fazal was a Bahá'í and had converted thousands of Christians in the United States to the Bahá'í religion. Latif Pasha gave Alam his publications on Islam.

Loaded with books and personal knowledge of places he had once only imagined visiting, Mahboob Alam took the Austrian Lloyd ship *Imperatrix* from Suez to Bombay. He stopped at Aden, where many Indians boarded the ship in third class. Alam heard that there was a lively traffic of Indians between Aden and Bombay. On November 12, the ship left Aden and reached Bombay at midnight on November 1900. Returning to India after five months once again reminded him of the importance of worldly sovereignty. British customs officials gave him a particularly difficult time. While Europeans were allowed to take trunks, the smallest items in an Indian's luggage were checked. Alam spent several days getting his things released and also had to pay a nominal duty. His friends and admirers in Bombay, including Badruddin Tyabji, received him warmly. The welcome ceremonies would have continued unabated from Delhi to Lahore if Alam had not been delayed in Bombay. A large crowd nevertheless came to greet him at the Lahore railway station and he barely escaped the ordeal of giving a public oration immediately on arrival. He soon had to make amends and on December 23 with Professor Thomas W. Arnold presiding, Alam delivered a lecture on his travels at Islamia College.

Thirty years later, another eminent Punjabi Muslim journalist, Ghulam Rasul Mehr, who had studied at Islamia College and was the co-editor of the newspaper *Inqilab* (revolution), took a train from Lahore to the port city of Karachi en route to perform haj. An Islamic universalist of a more explicit political bent than Alam, Mehr played an active role in the Khilafat movement while also strongly advocating the regionally based political interests of Punjabi Muslims. The intertwining of regional concerns with universal aspirations in the thought and politics of Muslims from the Indus-Gangetic plain was forcefully revealed in the politically decisive decades of the 1920s and 1930s. A disciple of the pro-Congress Muslim scholar Maulana Abul Kalam Azad, Mehr took his mentor's lead in supporting Ibn Saud's claims to the defunct Ottoman caliphate and control over the Hejaz against the British backed Sharif of Mecca. Other leading Khilafatists, such as Maulana Mohammad Ali and his elder brother, Maulana Shaukat Ali, as well as the ulema of Farangi Mahal and Barelvi, were opposed to Ibn Saud, whom they blamed for the desecration of Muslim shrines in Mecca and Medina. Mehr and some other Punjabi members of the Khilafat Committee were instrumental in blocking a resolution inspired by the Ali brothers against Saud's regime. With the collapse of the Khilafat movement and the end of the Ottoman empire, the political connections between Muslims in India and West Asia were tested and reinforced rather than disrupted. If Shibli and Alam thrived in the Ottoman lands through contacts they forged there, an ineffable intimacy marked the early twentieth century encounters of individuals from Hindustan who navigated Muslim lands across rival empires. Mehr's 1930 haj narrative stands in good company with the 1931 travel accounts of the Punjabi Muslim poet and philosopher Muhammad Iqbal and the pro-Ottoman anti-colonial Islamic universalist Mohammad Ali. Using his journalistic talent through the Urdu language weekly *Hamdard* and its English counterpart *The Comrade*, Mohammad Ali orchestrated the Khilafat cause in India as well as in Europe and West Asia. Mehr, Iqbal, and Mohammad Ali differed in their conception of Islamic universalism but were united in their unease about the implications of an international system based on the territorial nation-state. The pull of Islamic universalism made sure that they were not just distant observers but active participants in the politics of post-Ottoman West Asia, which, to their abiding regret, had fallen under European subjugation just like their own homeland.

Mohammad Ali, who adopted the nom de plume "Jauhar," literally, feat, and in time acquired the title of "maulana," first went to Europe in 1898, when he was only nineteen-and-a-half-years old. In 1902, he went to study at Oxford and returned to England in 1913 with the Muslim League leader, Wazir Hasan. In 1920, when he led a delegation to Europe to advocate the Khilafat cause, Iqbal wrote a critical poem questioning Ali's understanding of history that had misled him into becoming beholden to the cause of the Ottoman caliphate. Rejecting Iqbal's insinuation that he was going to plead with the British, Mohammad Ali asserted that far from stretching out his hands and begging the Europeans, he would extend them a clenched fist. Such defiance was matched by an ongoing commitment to promoting unity in the Muslim world after the collapse of the Ottoman empire. In 1913, along with his elder brother, Mohammad Ali had played a leading role in organizing the Indian Medical Mission to the Ottoman empire led by Dr Mukhtar Ansari. With Muslims politically divided in the aftermath of the First World War and unable to agree on a caliph, it was more imperative than ever to work to bridge the divisions within the ummah. Mohammad Ali was disdainful of Ibn Saud, who apart from destroying Muslim tombs had stopped the pilgrim traffic and was a British collaborator. He noted scathingly that the Syrians, who were the first to rise against the Ottomans, had chosen Saud as king. Political to the core of his being, Mohammad Ali was distressed to see Aden, a part of the Jizarat-ul-Arab, under infidel rule. "Like India, Aden too is subjugated," he rued. "India's subjugation begins from Gibraltar, which is the last link in the chain. May God break this chain soon."[21]

In December 1926, Mohammad Ali had attended the first Motamar Al-Alam Al-Islami, or the World Islamic Conference, at Mecca as part of the Khilafat Committee delegation. Portrayed as the first such assembly of believers, the conference was representative of Muslim communities across the world, with the exception of Iran, China, Libya, and the rest of the Maghrib. Called by Ibn Saud to legitimize Saudi control over the Hejaz, this attempt at forging Islamic unity on understandings between Muslim nation-states rather than the institution of the caliphate disintegrated in the face of political and ideological divisions. An influential section of the Khilafat Committee in India, led by the Ali brothers, wanted to prevent a Saudi takeover of the Hejaz, since the management of the holy places was a matter of direct concern for the entire Muslim *ummah* and not just the Arabs. They justified their stand on the grounds that rule by a family was unacceptable. The Hejaz had already suffered enough under the rule of the family of Sharif of Mecca and the result was the complete neglect of the haj pilgrims.

In its resolution accepting Ibn Saud's invitation to attend the Motamar Al-Alam Al-Islami in Mecca, the Central Khilafat Committee demanded immediate improvements in the conditions for the haj pilgrims. The Indian Muslim sense of entitlement flowed from the knowledge that a considerable portion of the annual expenditure on the pilgrimage was funded by Indian princely states, such as Hyderabad, Rampur, and Bhopal. Interpreting Saud's implicit endorsement of the nation-state form as an effective separation of religion and politics—an unwarranted innovation in Islam—the Indian Khilafat delegates left the conference with "bitter feelings."[22] The discovery of oil in the late 1930s would eliminate any leverage Indian Muslims thought they possessed in matters to do with the Hejaz, but even at the time there were those in the Khilafat Committee, such as Mehr and Maulana Zafar Ali Khan, who thought supporting the Saudis, who were already in physical control of the Hejaz, made better sense than insisting on more "democratic" arrangements for the holy land.

By the time Mohammad Ali took a fifth trip to Europe in 1928 for health reasons, he was a known figure among the local population in Aden. The moment he got off the shore, Arab moneychangers, policemen, coolies, and taxi drivers recognized him and cried "this is Mohammad Ali, Shaukat Ali", and some even kissed his hands with affection. Mohammad Ali headed to Cowasjee Dinshaw's shop to exchange Indian rupees. Dinshaw was not there but his son met him cordially and invited him to a meal.[23] Ali declined as he wanted to meet Muhammad Yasin Khan, a Bombay lawyer who had been a magistrate in Aden for some time.[24] Mohammad Ali had met Yasin

Khan, the brother of a fellow Aligarhian Yameen Khan, on previous visits to Aden. When Ali arrived at his bungalow, Yasin Khan had just finished his meal and was enjoying an Alphonso mango. Ali had been eating mangoes on the ship from Bombay. While politely declining Yasin Khan's invitation to dinner, he could not resist the Alphonso mangos. For the next couple of hours, they discussed the politics of West Asia and North Africa centered around the families of Imam Yahya and Imam Idrisi, Sheikh Sanusi, Sultan Ibn Saud and the dispute between Najd and Yemen where some Yemeni tribes were supporting the British.[25]

Wary of Ibn Saud's Najdi followers and displeased with Mustafa Kamal Ataturk's religious policies, Mohammad Ali was drawn to the radical strand of Egyptian nationalists represented by the Hizbul Watani party, which, he noted approvingly, did not worship at the altar of nationalism. Over the years, he had forged a special bond with prominent members of the Hizbul Watani, such as Dr Ahmad Fawad, who had suffered a great deal in the national cause by siding with the Turks, and Dr Abdul Hameed Saeed, who was the vice president of the party. As he had already seen the historic sites in Cairo, Mohammad Ali's main interest in visiting the city on this occasion was to catch up with his Egyptian friends and update them with the politics of Muslims in India. He had sent a telegram from Bombay to his friends in the Hizbul Watani party saying that while he wanted to stay for a week, the air in Egypt was too dusty for his ailing diabetes-ridden body. Another reason for not overstaying for too long was that the high commissioner in Cairo was Lloyd George, the former governor of Bombay, who had been Mohammad Ali's jailor. Not wanting to create trouble for his friends, he asked them to meet him at Suez in their personal cars so that they could spend the three-and-a-half-hour drive to Cairo exchanging thoughts on their respective political woes. On failing to get a response, Ali feared that the imperial networks had foiled his plans and Lloyd George had intercepted the telegram. But imperial authority had its limits. Hours before disembarking the ship, he received a wireless message from his friends, who were there to receive him at Suez and drove him to Cairo.

Mohammad Ali successfully dodged the system of imperial controls and arrived unnoticed in Cairo. He enjoyed the dumbfounded expression of the British Police Commissioner, who was taken aback to see him in Dr Saeed's company at the Continental Hotel wearing his handspun clothes and *hilal-o-ahmar* (crescent) cap. This fleeting triumph was cast into the shadow by the all-pervasive signs of Britain's military occupation of Egypt. A British air fleet was stationed in Heliopolis, the ancient heart of Cairo, even though the Egyptians had not received a single plane of their own. Mohammad Ali was appalled to learn that a British regiment was juxtaposed against the barracks of each Egyptian army regiment. "I think the condition of Egypt is like India's ... there is a great deal of talk but little by way of implementation," he bemoaned. "Even people who were not selfish wanted the easy life." When they had last met in Rome, Dr Saeed was carrying a walking stick that had a golden handle with an engraving of the pyramids and the words "Egypt for Egyptians." Mohammad Ali objected to this narrow territorial nationalism and proposed that it should be replaced with a picture of the world and the words "the creation of the creator" or "the world of Islam." These exhortations to Islamic universalism had some effect. When Dr Saeed established the Jamiat-ul-Shaban-ul-Muslimeen as the Muslim counterpart of the Young Men's Christian Association (YMCA), he made sure to combine lessons in nationalism with those on Islamic universalism. Welcoming his Indian guest to the Jamiat-ul-Shaban-ul-Muslimeen, Dr Saeed in a soaring speech said that Indian Muslim leaders ought to visit Muslim countries instead of just going to Europe. Mohammad Ali countered by saying that while India was poor compared to Egypt, Indian Muslims visited Islamic countries and were familiar with circumstances there. But Egyptian leaders rarely ever visited India and were oblivious of the condition of Indian Muslims to whom they offered no help. In a lighter vein, he added that Indian Muslims not only came to Egypt but also sent experienced colonial officers like Lloyd George, his former tormentor in Bombay jail. Mohammad Ali regretted that some Muslim countries were in deep sleep. Far from practicing Islam, they did not even understand the religion. Indians were the first to lose sovereignty, but they had also awakened before the Egyptians, Turks, Iranians, and Syrians.[26]

Elaborating on his idea of Islamic universalism, Mohammad Ali told the Jamiat-ul-Shaban-ul-Muslimeen that no two people in this congregation or the world at large looked alike. People had distinctive faces in different parts of the world, but whether someone was a Moroccan or Chinese, an inhabitant of the North Pole or the South Pole, whatever their faces, no one regarded them as outside the human race. The same was the case with thoughts and ideas, but sameness was also apparent in them. Despite all the differences, there was oneness. There was no one better than the creator of this world to guide his creation on the right path in social organization. This guidance was called Islam, and the Quran was the system for all ideas and the entire world, and the Prophet was the best example for all. Mohammad Ali's speech stirred the young men of the Jamiat-ul-Shaban-ul-Muslimeen, who gave him a long round of applause.[27]

Direct exchanges of this kind were less usual than the continuous circulation of information between India and Egypt through the exchange of newspapers. During Mohammad Ali's brief sojourn in Cairo, he heard that a telegram from a Mohammad Khan in Karachi had been published in the local newspaper *Al-Siyasa* in which Shaukat Ali was accused of plotting with Imam Yahya of Yemen to assassinate Ibn Saud. Both the *Hamdard* and *The Comrade* demolished the notion of this supposed conspiracy. On reading a copy of the *Hamdard* in London, Mohammad Ali learned that Ibn Saud's representative in Damascus had debunked the conspiracy. Heaving a sigh of relief, he wondered, "If in the monsoon season the rivers of Punjab had enough water in which Mehr Sahib could drown." A clear reference to Mehr's intrigues against him through the medium of the press, an embittered Mohammad Ali complained that he too had been accused of conspiring to kill Ibn Saud with the help of the Egyptian general Urabi Pasha.[28] The point was well taken. Urabi had been living in the splendor of isolation in Ceylon's Kandy district since 1882. The "disclosure" of the conspiracy, however, gave Mohammad Ali the opportunity to publicize his opposition to Ibn Saud's use of force in an interview with the Egyptian newspaper *Al Akhbar*, copies of which were sent to India.[29]

During the remainder of his stay in Egypt, Mohammad Ali was feted like a celebrity. He met with several scholars, journalists, and government functionaries and visited Al Azhar, where students from all over the Islamic world were present, nearly all of them poor and destitute. Mohammad Ali prayed to God to protect them from the worldly ulema so that they could understand Islam and emulate the early companions of the Prophet. Only then could Muslims once again become Muslims and spread Islam in its true light to all corners of the world. With these fervent thoughts in his mind, he headed for Port Said to board the ship to Europe. In an otherwise uneventful trip, Mohammad Ali encountered an Englishman who out of the blue asked him about Egyptian politics, adding that he had kept his eyes on him all the while and knew exactly what he had been up to. Irritated by the impertinence, Mohammad Ali replied that he did not know about Egyptian politics, but his job was to make the political situation in India as difficult as possible for the British. By the grace of God, there were many Egyptians working to make the going tough for the British. The Englishman superciliously said: "You only think of your own country, we keep an eye on all the countries." Not one to miss a beat, Mohammad Ali retorted: "You belong to a nation about whom Lord Salisbury had said that it always insisted on immediately conquering the moon because otherwise the inhabitants of Mars would take it over." This silenced the Englishman and they never spoke again.[30]

Firmly grounded in the rhythms of the Punjab's regional culture, and more conservative in his ideological orientation, Mehr lacked Mohammad Ali's fiery temperament and transnational appeal but shared his keen antipathy to Western imperialism. He describes his voyage in letters written to his brother that were published in the *Inqilab* between April 29, 1930 and July 23, 1930. Unlike a standard haj account, Mehr's travel narrative is marked by attention to worldly matters and a relative lack of emphasis on the purely religious. Not being able to smoke his hookah on the train from Lahore to Karachi upset him no end, until the clouds of dust from the Indus plain drove him to distraction. Even with the windows of the train firmly shut, it took less than fifteen minutes for an inch of Indus soil to cover everything from the baggage to the seats. Though a great supporter of Sindh's separation from Bombay, Mehr was dead opposed to the idea of making Karachi the permanent port city of northern India until the land around the railway tracks was either cultivated or the railway authorities found a way to prevent the dust from inundating the train.

One could want to see lively Mashad, but which "miserable creature from Lahore would want to come to dust filled Karachi?"[31]

On April 23, 1930, Mehr boarded the ship *Khusro* for Jeddah along with 739 others, all of whom had got the required smallpox and cholera injections to avoid the "horrors of Kamaran." But they had to pay for the sins of the fifty-seven pilgrims who took the ship from Bombay without getting inoculated. Mehr thought Indian Muslims needed "*por zoor jid-o-jihad*" (intensive struggle) to escape the "hell of Kamaran." Otherwise, there was no avoiding the first trial of the haj being a colonial imposition. By the time the ship docked at Kamaran to get the Bombay passengers inoculated and their clothing fumigated, Mehr was at his wit's end with the tasteless English and Indian cuisine on the ship. The Central Khilafat Committee was involved in the arrangements for Indian food. But "from the point of view of the Punjabis, the food was not good" as the cooks in the kitchen had "no ability to prepare food according to the temperaments of people from different provinces." There was no dining room to eat Indian food, which could only be eaten sitting on the floor. The bread served was inedible. Made out of white flour and cooked in butter on English stoves, the sight of the bread made Punjabis anxious since they fell sick after eating it for a few days. A fellow passenger, Hafiz Mohammad Sadiq, had brought his domestic servant and rescued Mehr from his misery. For the rest of the journey, he not only enjoyed smoking his hookah but also devoured delicious curries and sweets.[32]

When the monotony of the sea was finally broken on the fifth day by the sight of the "dry and sagging mountains" of Arabia, Mehr was gripped by angst at the subjugation of one Muslim country after the other. He could only see the flags of foreign powers. The distant lights on the shore thrilled his fellow travelers. But for him, these lights were like "tears of fire." The only comfort in this grim scenario was the warm welcome he received on arrival at Jeddah, courtesy of a fellow Punjabi named Ehsanuddin, who was a clerk at the Turner Morrison shipping company. Although he had become completely Arabized, Mehr was relieved to see that Ehsanuddin had not forgotten his homeland and the memory of Punjabi climes remained deeply embedded in his heart.

At his home, Ehsanuddin served Mehr lassi, the traditional Punjabi yogurt-based drink with salt, which was known locally as *chaach* and was a perfect antidote to the scorching heat of the Hejaz. Mehr marveled at the cooling effect of the drink and made a mental note to tell the Khilafat Committee members responsible for arranging food on the ships to serve lassi to the pilgrims. The intimacy of his welcome to the Hejaz took an even more charming turn when Ehsanuddin, who knew his passion for the hookah, produced a local version with the coal tray in the base that looked like a beautiful decorative bowl once the pipe was removed. Upon enquiring about the backdrop of this curious looking hookah, Mehr learned that when the Sauds came to the Hejaz from Najd, they declared war on smoking and drinking and closed down all the taverns. Hejazi smoking enthusiasts responded by inventing this camouflaged hookah. Realizing that it was a safer option while performing haj under a Najdi government, Mehr borrowed the hookah. Later, one of his traveling companions liked the hookah so much that they both decided to get it replicated in Muradabad on their return to Hindustan.[33]

Hindustan's many presences in the Hejaz—whether in the form of material objects or Indians dressed like Arabs—made for an intimacy that was both electrifying and endearing. One of the high points for Mehr was meeting Ubaidullah Sindhi, a Deobandi scholar and anti-colonial nationalist, who had been living in Mecca for the past few years. Sindhi had gone on self-exile to Afghanistan during the First World War in order to seek help from the Central Powers to end British colonial rule in India. With the two men sharing a common mentor in Abul Kalam Azad, Sindhi met Mehr with great respect and affection. He had read Mehr's writings in newspapers and wanted to meet him for some time. Mehr was a college student when Sindhi left India in 1915 and had vague memories of his face. He had first seen Sindhi in Lahore with Abul Kalam Azad. Mehr and Sindhi met regularly and had discussions on subjects ranging from the religious to the political. Contacts with men like Sindhi and Ehsanullah facilitated Mehr's access to the ruling circles in the Hejaz, who had their own reasons for wanting to cultivate support among Indian pilgrims. Mehr was able to rub shoulders with Ibn Saud and high-ranking Najdi officials with remarkable ease, an opportunity he used to the fullest to convey the innumerable issues that faced Indian pilgrims during the haj. However, even with his reach to the higher echelons of power, Mehr was unable to get permission to visit Medina after performing haj. Indicative of Najdi aversion to Muslims thronging the Prophet's grave and showing undue reverence, it signposted unprecedented new restrictions on the believers' movements in the Hejaz. For a Khilafatist, Mehr might have raised his voice in protest but thought better to console himself with the thought that he was due to make another trip to West Asia the following year.

In late November 1931, Mehr returned to the Hejaz in the company of Muhammad Iqbal to attend the second Motamar Al-Alam Al-Islami at Jerusalem. Iqbal was on his way back from England where he had attended the Second Round Table Conference in London to discuss the future constitutional setup in India. Never a supporter of the Khilafat issue, Iqbal's reasons for participating in the Motamar called by the Grand Mufti of Jerusalem Haj Amin al-Husseni were two-fold: promoting international Islamic solidarity and safeguarding Palestinian interests in the face of aggressive Jewish Zionism backed by Western imperialist powers. Iqbal was a vocal critic of territorial nationalism, which he regarded as the source of all modern conflicts. After boarding the ship from Bombay to England in September 1931, Iqbal gave an extended interview to the *Bombay Chronicle* in which he regretted that the spirit of Islamic universalism had been misconstrued in Europe as something akin to the "Yellow Peril." Denying any prejudice toward another community, religion, or nation, he maintained that the Muslim desire for unity was being wrongly viewed as "Pan-Islamism," a term that was the product of the fertile imagination of a lone French journalist. Considered to be a purely political movement against European powers, "Pan-Islamism" gave quite the wrong meaning to Muslim sentiments for worldwide unity in the face of European aggression against their countries. Iqbal's proposed dropping "Pan" from the phrase as "Pan-Islamism" sufficed to convey the Muslim desire for a faith-based solidarity that was more of a social experiment than the political project Europeans imagined it to be. He explained that his opposition to the European model of nationalism stemmed from the fact that it clashed with Islam's more elevated point of view. "Nationalism was against rising above differences of race while Islam was the purveyor of a spiritual unity of all mankind."[34]

Iqbal experienced this spiritual unity in intimate encounters with fellow Muslims he met during his voyage in 1931. With his fame preceding him, admirers thronged Iqbal even before he had disembarked the ship. He had not intended to get off at Aden but was left with no choice by the insistent exhortations of a young lawyer Sheikh Abdullah, who took him home for a lavish meal. Over several cups Yemeni coffee, Iqbal chatted with his host and an Iranian trader who gifted him with a Yemeni *aqiq* (cornelian), which is considered blessed by Muslims because of its association with the Prophet of Islam. Iqbal had last visited Aden twenty-two years ago when there was virtually nothing there but dry parched earth. Now it was a busy city that was rapidly advancing. Arab traders from Hadramat were there in strength as were many Punjabis, with Sindhi shopkeepers occupying an especially prominent place. Touched by the affection with which he was greeted, Iqbal regretted that his limited finances prevented him from making a more extensive tour of Muslim countries to fulfill his ambition of writing a book entitled *Modern World of Islam* on contemporary developments in the Muslim world.

At Port Said, a young Egyptian doctor woke Iqbal up at 3 am, and soon a group of young men from the local branch of the Shaban-ul-Muslimeen joined them. Iqbal discovered that Congress propaganda had led most Egyptians to see Indian Muslims as obstructing the cause of India's independence. Moreover, Iqbal's call for a Muslim state in northwestern India at the All-India Muslim League's December 1930 session also appeared to contradict his clear stance against territorial nationalism. But the proposal aimed at consolidating Muslim power in the northwest and, far from being the separatist demand for an Islamic state or confederation, as some of his detractors claimed, was strictly placed within the context of India.[35] So, during his brief stopover at Port Said, Iqbal took the opportunity to clarify matters for the Egyptians:

> The Hindus are always worried that Muslims with the help of Muslim Afghans and Baluch will take control of Hindustan. But is it possible

> that Egypt once it becomes independent will hand over their country to the Turks simply because they are Muslim? In sum, Congress' non-violence is simply a response to English oppression, otherwise the situation in Mirpur, Kanpur and Srinagar makes it plain that in relation to the Muslims it is violence.

Elaborating on Iqbal's points, the poet and scholar Mushir Hussain Kidwai, who was also traveling on the ship, told the young Egyptians that Indian Muslims were afraid that Mohandas Karamchand Gandhi and the Hindus did not really want independence and merely wanted to seize the government in India and the British Indian army to use them against the Muslims. In fact, Indian Muslims were restless for independence because on their freedom rested the freedom of Muslim countries. However, in getting independence from the British, the Indian Muslims did not want to become subjugated to Hindu majoritarian rule. In a subsequent statement, Iqbal blamed Egyptians for failing to understand Indian politics. It was imperative for Egyptian journalists and opinion makers to visit India to see things for themselves. In India too there was mischievous propaganda against Egyptian Muslims, who were said to have departed from the Quran, Allah, and Islam.[36]

Iqbal spent a little more time in Egypt on his return trip from England. Accompanied by Mehr, who had covered the Second Round Table Conference as a journalist, he met with several of the same individuals and organizations as Mohammad Ali, who had passed away in January 1931 and was buried in Jerusalem according to his wishes. It was at Ali's funeral that his elder brother Shaukat Ali and the Grand Mufti of Jerusalem Haj Mohammad Amin al-Husseini decided to hold the second Motamar Al-Alam Al-Islami as a way of promoting the Palestinian cause to counter mounting pressure from the forces of Jewish Zionism backed by Western imperial powers. When Iqbal and Mehr arrived in Alexandria on December 1, 1931, members of the British Indian Association and the Jamiat-ul-Shaban-ul-Muslimeen greeted them with flags and welcoming slogans along with a large contingent of newspaper correspondents. The train from Alexandria to Cairo took three and a half hours. The lush green fields, style of cultivation, and small villages on both sides of the railway tracks reminded Iqbal of Punjab. At Cairo railway station, they were met by a large contingent of people, including the leader of the Shaban-ul-Muslimeen, Dr Abdul Hameed Saeed; the editor of *Al Manar*, Rashid Rida; several Indian Muslim residents of the city as well as Indian students studying at Al Azhar. In Cairo, Iqbal also met with the Rector of Al-Azhar; Mohammad Ali Pasha, the former minister of Auqaf; Mirza Mehdi Bey, president of the Council of Trade and innumerable journalists and scholars.[37]

The main topic of discussion invariably was the upcoming meeting of the Motamar Al-Alam Al-Islami in Jerusalem. With the idea of reviving the caliphate now virtually dead, among the suggestions the Egyptians made to Iqbal was to persuade the Motamar to raise funds to buy land from debt-ridden Palestinians, who were being forced by the effects of the worldwide depression to sell their properties to European Jews. The question of the Indian Muslim role in the anti-colonial movement also came up for discussion. Iqbal and Mehr were astonished to find that in Egypt there was no recognition of the political issues that concerned Indian Muslims, who were seen as little more than British pawn. Gandhi was considered to be the real leader and Congress the representative nationalist organization. So, they took the opportunity to educate the Egyptians by meeting with a number of journalists and newspaper editors. Among those whose minds Iqbal succeeded in changing was the Syrian nationalist doctor, Abdur Rahman Shahbandar, who had fled to Egypt after the failure of his revolt against the French in 1927. Iqbal also lectured Ali Abdel Razziq for arguing in his book *Al-Islam Wa Usul Al-Hukm: Bahth Fi-l Khilafa Wa-l Hukuma Fi-l Islam* (translated as *Islam and the Foundations of Governance*) that there had always been a separation of the religious and political in Islam. Other prominent Egyptians Iqbal met included Muhammad Hussain Haykal, editor of the *Al-Siyasa*, which was the mouthpiece of Egypt's largest party, Hizbul Ahmar, a liberal constitutionalist organization. Iqbal explained social and political matters with reference to the Quran, leading the Egyptians to say that they had never seen the Muslim holy book in this light. Mehr had a longer meeting with Haykal lasting three hours, during which he explained the political situation facing Indian Muslims.

Haykal wrote a four-column piece on the subject and followed it up with more later.[38]

In Cairo, Iqbal and Mehr were treated to elaborate meals by their Egyptian and Indian Muslim hosts. Many complained at the brevity of Iqbal's visit, with some offering him money to stay on for a longer period of time. It was with some difficulty that he extricated himself from his Egyptian admirers to take the train to Palestine in time for the opening of the Motamar Al-Alam Al-Islami. At some of the stations on the way from Cairo to Jerusalem, groups of Punjabi Muslims greeted them with slogans of "zindabad" (long live). It was raining when the train reached the Jerusalem railway station at 9 am on December 6. Amin al-Husseini, Shaukat Ali, and a few others were at the station to receive them. With the exception of Turkey and Afghanistan, Muslims from all over the world were represented. The delegates included influential personalities, some of them world-famous on account of their scholarship, such as Rashid Rida, and others better known within the confines of their own countries. Several unsuccessful efforts had been made to sabotage the conference. Iqbal blames the British, other imperialist powers, and the forces of Zionism, noting that the local Christian and Jewish population was not hostile. In fact, relations between Muslims and Christians in the city were extremely cordial. George Habib Antonius, the famous historian who was in Jerusalem at the time, met Iqbal and gave a dinner in honor of the delegates attending the conference. It was mainly Jews imported from outside who tried to stop the proceedings of the Motamar from taking place, while international newspapers gave distorted reports of its proceedings. Two local Palestinian groups were rabidly against Amin al-Husseini. Until the eve of the conference, Shaukat Ali exerted much effort to reconcile them but could only manage to persuade the Mufti's opponents to agree that, while boycotting the conference, they would desist from criticisms and support resolutions that were for the betterment of the country.[39]

On December 6, 1931, at the conclusion of the opening session, the delegates left for the Masjid-i-Aqsa accompanied by volunteers who sang Palestinian national songs. On the way, they prayed at the grave of Mohammad Ali Jauhar and said their Maghrib prayers at the Masjid-i-Aqsa.

After dinner, Amin al-Husseini in his address stressed the need to bridge Muslim differences to put up a collective front against Zionist and imperialist machinations, and also emphasized the need to promote Islamic teachings in their correct light and save the religion from discord and division. Iqbal and various others spoke briefly in response. Dr Abdul Hameed Saeed of the Hizbul Watani party asked the delegates to vow to give up their lives to defend the sanctity of the Muslim holy places, which they all solemnly did.[40]

When the conference formally started on December 7, 1931, Husseini was elected president and Iqbal honored with one of the positions of vice presidents. Shaukat Ali made his impact felt on the proceedings by suggesting that the delegates be allowed to choose which of the seven committees they wanted to serve on. The conference's deliberations revealed an underlying tension between the vision of a worldwide community of Muslims and the practical realities of an international system based on nation-states. Symbolism and emotional rhetoric found bigger play than concrete evidence of political unity and realistic action. Reacting to the French control of the Damascus railway station a few days earlier, the committee on the Hejaz Railway proposed placing control of the railways in Muslim hands in the form of a *waqf* or charity, which was easier said than done. Another rallying cry of the conference was the establishment of a new Islamic university in Jerusalem. Iqbal was not opposed to the idea in principle, but favored an educational institution that taught both modern and traditional knowledge according to contemporary needs. His main objection to the scheme was that Jerusalem, apart from lacking stature as a center of Muslim learning like Cairo, Tehran, Damascus, or Mecca, was by then a Jewish majority city. However, Iqbal did not press the point and went along with the decision favored by a majority of the delegates. Later, when Amin al-Husseini came to India to promote the cause of the university, Iqbal went out of his way to help him in raising funds.[41]

The Palestinian focus of the conference was evident in the main resolutions adopted. These included a call to boycott Jewish businesses; establish an agricultural bank to assist Palestinian Muslims in extricating themselves from debt; and make the rest of the Muslim world aware of the threat Zionism posed in Palestine. Resolutions were also passed opposing the recommendations of the Commission on the Wailing Wall and opposing further Jewish emigration to Palestine. But with almost all the Muslim countries either under colonial subjugation or mired in problems of their own like Iran, Afghanistan, and Turkey, there were no prospects of them helping the Palestinians or any other nation. Delegates heard of the treatment of Muslims in Soviet Turkestan where mosques had been padlocked, madrassas closed, and the faithful divided into various nationalities to weaken them politically. Representatives from North Africa for their part elaborated on the oppression of the French authorities. Amid much hue and cry, the conference considered efforts to find a way of addressing these problems but to no avail.[42]

In his farewell address on the evening of December 14, Iqbal spoke in English with a simultaneous translation into Arabic. He regretted leaving the conference early and not being able to fully partake in the discussions because of his lack of proficiency in Arabic. Islam was facing two kinds of challenges, Iqbal maintained, one from materialism and the other from nationalism. Muslims had a duty to defeat both these dangers. He urged the delegates to promote the spirit of brotherhood upon returning to their respective countries. The spirit of Arab youth had impressed him. "It is my belief that the future of Islam is linked to the future of Arabia, and the future of Arabia is based on Arab unity," Iqbal asserted. "Islam will be successful when the Arabs unite. It was imperative on all of us to expend all the force to achieve that end so that God gave us success." The speech was well-received with cries of "Allah-o-Akbar" with Arab students promising to spread Iqbal's message everywhere.[43]

On December 15, with the conference still underway and the cause of international Muslim unity that had brought them to Jerusalem far from realized, Iqbal and Mehr headed to the railway station, where they were personally seen off by Amin al-Husseini and other leading Muslim delegates. The emotive bonds of Islamic universalism that they had tried converting into real political strengthen through participation in the Motamar Al-Alam Al-Islami remained a distant aspiration. On setting foot on the ship *Palna* at Port Said, they were drawn into the familiar world of politics in colonial India that their travels in

Europe, Egypt, and Palestine had at best momentarily eclipsed. By sheer coincidence, Gandhi was returning to India after the Second Round Table Conference on the same ship. There is no indication that Iqbal encountered the Mahatma. But there was plenty of time and opportunity to discuss politics under the "blue of the sky spread across the earth" with political luminaries like Sir Muhammad Saleh Akbar Hydari, who was in charge of the finance department of the Nizam of Hyderabad, and Dr Shafaat Ahmad Khan and Shafi Daudi, both of whom had also attended the Second Round Table Conference.[44]

On December 28, 1931, the ship reached Bombay. Members of the Khilafat Committee greeted Iqbal and Mehr and took them to the Dar-ul-Khilafat. Iqbal declined Attiya Faizi's invitation to attend a reception in his honor since he was eager to return to Lahore as soon as possible. At the Bombay railway station, Iqbal issued a press statement welcoming the British decision to raise the status of the North West Frontier Province to that of a governor's province and expressed disappointment with Gandhi's unhelpful attitude toward a solution of the minorities' problem. Unlike Shaukat Ali, Iqbal had avoided publicly blaming Gandhi for the failure of the Second Round Table Conference. However, fifteen weeks ago on starting the journey, he had issued a warning that would loom large on the Indian political horizon in the remaining years of the British Raj. Iqbal was convinced that if the demands of the Muslim majority in Bengal and Punjab were not accepted, whatever constitution was introduced in India would be smashed into smithereens by the Muslims. In the end it was the Congress High Command—with Mahatma Gandhi dissenting from the decision of his erstwhile lieutenants—that the Muslim-majority provinces of Punjab and Bengal were partitioned in 1947, dividing both the valley and delta of the Indus and Ganga that flowed into the Indian Ocean.

Notes and References

1. Sayyid Ahmad Khan, *Musafaran-i-London*, comp. Sheikh Muhammad Ismail Panipati, reprint (Lahore: Majlis-i-Taraqia Urdu, 1961), pp. 86, 90, 103–104, 114–115, 117–121.

2. Shibli Numani, *Safarnamah Rom-o-Misr-o-Shaym*, reprint (Lahore: Sang-e-Meel, 2012), pp. 2–5.
3. William R. Roff, "Sanitation and Security: The Imperial Powers and the Nineteenth Century Hajj" in *Arabian Studies* VI (London: Scorpion Comm. and the Middle East Centre, University of Cambridge, 1982).
4. Numani, *Safarnamah Rom-o-Misr-o-Shaym*, pp. 13–14.
5. Ibid., pp. 12, 15–16.
6. Ibid., pp. 6, 40–42.
7. Sugata Bose, *A Hundred Horizons: The Indian Ocean in the Age of Global Empire* (Cambridge, MA: Harvard University Press, 2006), Chapter 6.
8. Mahboob Alam, *Safarnama Europe, Bilad-e-Rome, Shaam-o-Misr* (Lahore: Paisa Akhbar Press, 1908), p. 18.
9. Ibid., pp. 2–16.
10. Alam, *Safarnama Europe, Bilad-e-Rome, Shaam-o-Misr*, pp. 29–31, 44, 50, 62, 113, 196.
11. Ibid., pp. 575–577.
12. Ibid., pp. 624–626, 804.
13. Ibid.
14. Ibid., pp. 756–759.
15. Ibid., p. 761.
16. Ibid., pp. 840–841.
17. The political interconnections between the Ottoman Empire and British India mapped out by Alavi's essay in this volume are extended to Afghanistan in Alam's travel narrative. There were two Afghan sardars living in the city on a stipend from the Ottoman government.
18. Ibid., pp. 958–959.
19. Ibid., p. 961.
20. Numani, *Safarnamah Rom-o-Misr-o-Shaym*, p. 148.
21. Mohammad Ali, *Mohammad Ali ka Safar-i-Europe*, comp. Mohammad Sarwar (Lahore: Kitan Khana Punjab, no date), pp. 48–49.
22. See Imran N. Hosein, *The Caliphate, The Hijaz and the Saudi Wahabi Nation State*, (eBook available online at http://imranhosein.org/n/the-caliphate-the-hijaz-and-the-saudi-wahabi-nation-state/), p. 66.
23. Ibid., p. 55.
24. See Scott S. Reese, "'A Leading Muslim of Aden': Personal Trajectories, Imperial Networks, and the Construction of Community in Colonial Aden," in James I. Gelvin and Nile Green, *Global Muslims in the Age of Steam and Print* (Berkeley: University of California Press, 2014), pp. 50–77.
25. Ali, *Mohammad Ali ka Safar-i-Europe*, p. 56.
26. Ibid, pp. 58–59, 68, 77, 80.

27. Ibid., p. 82.
28. Ibid., p. 95.
29. Ibid., p. 84.
30. Ibid., pp. 85, 91.
31. Ghulam Rasul Mehr, *Safarnama Hijaz*, comp. Abu Sulaiman Shahjahanpuri (Karachi: Maktaba-i-Asloob, 1984), p. 16.
32. Ibid., pp. 27–31.
33. Ibid., pp. 41–44.
34. Mohammad Hamza Faruqi (comp. and ed.), *Safarnama Iqbal: 1931 mein Inglistan, Italia, Misr aur Falasteen kay Safar ki Rawadad* (Karachi: Maktab-i-Mayar, 1973), pp. 19–20.
35. See Ayesha Jalal, *Self and Sovereignty*, pp. 324–334.
36. Faruqi, *Safarnama Iqbal*, pp. 28–29.
37. Ibid., pp. 123–134.
38. Ibid., pp. 136–137, 142, 145.
39. Ibid., pp. 157–159.
40. Ibid., p. 160.
41. Ibid., pp. 162–167.
42. Ibid., p. 170–171.
43. Ibid., pp. 171–173.
44. Ibid., pp. 182–187.

2

Islam's Eastern Frontiers

Tamil, Chinese, and Malay Worlds

Sunil S. Amrith

This chapter takes a comparative and connected view of Tamil- and Chinese-speaking Muslim communities in Southeast Asia. Tracing their journeys across the Bay of Bengal and the South China Sea brings new dimensions to our understanding of Islam on the Indian Ocean Rim—bringing to light the cultural encounters that took place on its eastern frontiers. Over centuries, Tamil and Chinese Muslim traders laid down roots in the Malay societies through which they traveled, and in which many of them settled. Intermarriage between Tamil or Chinese men and local Malay women was common—though it grew less common from the nineteenth century as the demographic weight of migration increased. At the same time, Muslims constituted a vital part of the Tamil and Chinese diasporas, which developed within firmer boundaries in the twentieth century along with new ideas of belonging and citizenship. Tamil Muslims—as journalists and writers, shopkeepers and providers of sustenance—were ideally placed to act as intermediaries between their fellow Muslims and their fellow Tamils. Similarly, Muslims among the overseas Chinese developed complex affiliations that enriched local cultures of Islam while also connecting with the social and political world of the Chinese diaspora.[1]

Theirs is an instance of cosmopolitan practice in the Indian Ocean world, rooted in specific urban situations: it was a lived and pragmatic cosmopolitanism that bears little resemblance to the romanticized notions that some historians of the pre-modern Indian Ocean have put forward. The history of Tamil and Chinese Muslim networks in the Indian Ocean pushes us to rethink chronology as well as geography. Writing of the Hadrami Arab diaspora, Engseng Ho has suggested that diasporas often outlast the boundaries of empires and nations: Tamil and Chinese Muslims' connections across the Indian Ocean and the China Sea long predate the rise of European dominance, and they have outlasted the closure of the sea by the borders of nation-states.[2] To reflect the longevity of these interregional connections, this chapter adopts the perspective of the *longue durée,* with a particular focus on moments of transition and encounter.

India, China, and the Frontiers of Islam

Within two centuries of the time of the Prophet, Arab traders had settled along the Coromandel Coast and brought their faith with them. Islam established a foothold in the trading towns along the southern coast—Kilakkarai, Kayalpatnam, Nagore, Nagapatnam, Porto Novo, Karaikal, and Pulicat.[3] Across the Bay of Bengal, Islam expanded its reach from the late thirteenth century of the common era, beginning with the kingdom of Pasai in northern Sumatra. Parts of the northern Malay Peninsula, eastern Java, and the southern Philippines followed in the fourteenth century. The turning point in the rooting of Islam in Southeast Asia came with the conversion of Melaka—the region's foremost trading center--at the beginning of the fifteenth century, after which Islam spread rapidly in the region.[4]

Over centuries, South Indian Muslims had forged a distinctive culture, rooted in the Tamil language and embracing a wider Muslim world. Tamil Muslims, in particular the elite Maraikkayar community, made, in Ronit Ricci's words, an "important contribution to Tamil literature by way of expanding the limits of existing genres, and of introducing novel combinations and entirely new models."[5] This cultural versatility is clear in the *Cirappuranam* of Umaru Pulavar, the preeminent Tamil Muslim poet of the seventeenth century. Produced under the patronage of Sidakaddi—a Maraikkayar merchant, close to the Hindu court of Ramnad—and under the tutelage of the renowned scholar Sheikh Sadaqatullah, Umaru Pulavar's poem brought together the Arabic genre of the Sirah with the Hindu Puranam to relate the Prophet's life using Tamil literary conventions. In its construction, it was a Kavya—lyrical verses linked together in a narrative.[6]

The blending of forms and vocabularies produced a melding of sacred landscapes. The *Cirappuranam*'s opening description of the marvels of the Hijaz substitute the wet-rice landscape of the Tamil country for the Arabian desert:

> Milling in crowds, those who labor in the fields
> gather and praise Earth.
> Their right hands shake the sprouting seeds
> and scatter them thick on the ground.
> They fall like golden rain on earth.[7]

As the Tamil Muslims of the Coromandel Coast traveled, their sacred geography expanded to encompass the eastern as well as the western Indian Ocean.

It is to the ninth or the tenth centuries that we can also date the arrival of Islam in China. Scholarship on Islam in China has focused on communities formed by the Inner Asian conquests of the northern heartlands; yet in China, as in South Asia, the earliest Muslim communities were coastal, maritime communities.[8] The Muslim communities of the southern Chinese coast were known as Hui—a term used also for Chinese-speaking Muslim communities of Yunnan and the interior. There is evidence of a Muslim community in Guangzhou (Canton) around the ninth century. As in South India, these communities were formed through the settlement and intermarriage with local women of Arab and Persian traders from the west. The Huai-Shang mosque in Guangzhou enters written records in 1206, but it quite likely dates from much earlier.[9] Muslim communities thrived in China's coastal towns—above all, in Quanzhou (known often by its Arabic name, Zaitun), a trading port that thrived in the thirteenth and fourteenth centuries.

Zaitun finds mention in the writings of both Marco Polo and Ibn Battuta. "It is the port where all ships from India come laden with much costly merchandise and a multitude of extremely valuable precious stones and big and rare pearls," Marco Polo wrote. For his part, Ibn Battuta declared that "after our sea crossing, the first Chinese city where we disembarked was that of Zaitun … it is a big, superb city, where damask velvet cloth, known as *zaitunniyah*, is made."

Zaitun, he declares, was "the biggest of all ports," and he found that "Mohammedans stay in a separate quarter." Even if some doubt has been cast on whether Ibn Battuta actually visited China, his mention of Zaitun nevertheless suggests that its fame as a cosmopolitan port had spread by the time of his chronicling.[10] Evidence of a thriving community of Muslim merchants in Quanzhou survives in material culture: the earliest known mosque in Quanzhou was the Sheng Yu mosque, built in 1009. The Aishuhabu Mosque dates from the eleventh century. and was rebuilt in 1309. It is still in existence. Arab and Persian traders inhabited a distinct quarter of the town, set aside for the *fan*, the foreign traders. Many of them settled and formed a local Muslim community. The Lingshan cemetery contains funerary epigraphs in Arabic and Persian, though many of the tombstones are adapted in a Chinese style.[11] At the same time, Quanzhou was home to a community of Hindu traders: they left traces of their journeys in a Tamil language inscription (discovered during an excavation in 1956), and in Shaivite and Vaishnavite statuary, "probably the further pennants of Hinduism in the north-east."[12] Islam was central to making Quanzhou a cosmopolitan port city, but the city was also the site of commercial and cultural interactions between Muslim and non-Muslim traders. We lack the evidence to do anything more than speculate about the codes they developed, the inter-cultural understandings they forged, and the basis on which they built relationships of trust. It is clear, though, that Islam's expansion into the eastern seas was bound up with travel, trade, and translation. With the rise of the Southeast Asian port polities of the early modern period, this relationship deepened; so too did interactions between Muslims of distant origins and between Muslims and others.

Trading diasporas from across Asia converged upon the port towns that dotted the Southeast Asian littoral. From the fifteenth century, port polities emerged in quick succession, each founded on entrepot trade; maritime relations were more significant to many of them than links with their own hinterlands. In Burma, the seat of power shifted from Bagan to the coastal settlement of Pegu. Along the western coast of the Malay Peninsula, Melaka emerged as the greatest of the region's ports. The conversion of Melaka's ruling family in 1419 cemented the relationship between Islam, trade, and the port polities of the Indian

Ocean Rim. Port cities with Muslim rulers were hospitable to Muslim and non-Muslim merchants from across Asia. Along Java's northern coast, Gresek, Tuban, Demak, and Banten, all rose to prominence in the fifteenth century; in the sixteenth and seventeenth centuries, Ternate, Hitu, Brunei, Aceh, Makassar, and Manila flourished (Manila was under the rule of a local sultanate before the Iberian conquest).[13]

The port cities of Southeast Asia evolved a new urban form, one that persisted through the European conquest. Arguably, its contours are still faintly discernible today.[14] Where the older, inland cities (including Angkor and Pagan) depended on their agrarian base, the new port polities had the encouragement of trade as their main aim. Where the old capitals' structure reflected a holistic royal cosmology, the new port polities' layout was a testament to the diversity of their residents. After the ruler, the most important political office in many of the Southeast Asian polities was the harbormaster—the *shahbandar*, who was very often a foreigner. The shahbandar's chief aim was to smooth the wheels of commerce: to show visiting and resident merchants that prices were fair and taxes were moderate, that agreements were honored and disagreements resolved honorably. The larger communities—Gujaratis, South Indians, and Fujianese—each had a nominated representative with a voice in decision-making. The residential structure of the port cities was distinctive too. Each was a mosaic of ethnic quarters, distinct but overlapping.

When Afonso de Albuquerque's Portuguese forces attacked Melaka in 1511, they conquered a port city at the heart of Asian commerce. In his travel account, the *Suma Oriental*, the apothecary Tome Pires counted no fewer than eighty-four languages spoken on Melaka's streets and in its bazaars. He lists the peoples and languages he encountered:

> Moors from Cairo, Mecca, Aden, Abyssinians, men of Kilwa, Malindi, Ormuz, Parsees, Rumes, Turks, Turkomans, Christian Armenians, Gujaratees, men of Chaul, Dabhol, Goa, of the kingdom of Deccan, Malabars and Klings, merchants from Orissa, Ceylon, Bengal, Arakan, Pegu, Siamese, men of Kedah, Malays, men of Pahang, Patani, Cambodia, Champa, Cochin China, Chinese, Lequeos, men of Brunei, Lucoes, men of Tamjompura, Laue, Banka, Linga (they have a thousand other islands), Moluccas, Banda, Bima, Timor, Madura, Java, Sunda,

> Palembang, Jambi, Tongkal, Indragiri, Kappatta, Menangkabau, Siak, Arqua, Aru, Bata, country of the Tomjano, Pase, Pedir, Maldives.[15]

Rarely has the hardened modern language of "identity" seemed more ill-fitting than in describing a pre-modern port city like Melaka. In all of these ports, Islam "attenuated ethnic differences," while "conversions, intermarriages, and the use of Arabic characters in writing the Malay language went a long way in unifying a society."[16] At the same time, other sorts of rituals, other bonds of trust underpinned the business partnerships—and indeed, the personal relations—between Muslim and non-Muslim traders.

Tamil- and Chinese-speaking Muslims found a fruitful field of opportunity in these Southeast Asian port polities. Shared faith smoothed their integration into local societies; very often, Tamil and Chinese Muslim traders married into ruling aristocracies. At the same time, their command of language meant that they could act as intermediaries between local rulers and others from their lands of origin—Tamil and Gujarati Hindus, Han Chinese.

Tamil Muslims traded with and settled in Kedah, Aceh, Java, and right across the Indonesian archipelago. Malay chronicles make frequent reference to South Indian Muslim teachers, traders, and holy men. The *Sejarah Melayu*—the "Malay Annals," a sixteenth-century genealogy of the rulers of the Malay Peninsula (based on an earlier chronicle written in Melaka)—gives an account of Pasai's conversion to Islam, in which an Indian emissary from Ma'abar, the Arabic term for the Coromandel Coast, features prominently. A story of intrigue in the Melaka court involves a Tamil Muslim called Raja Mudeliar, who, as shahbandar, was "easily the richest man of his time." Raja Mudeliar and the king's advisor, the Bendahara, are great rivals: "That's just what one would expect from a Kling who doesn't know how to behave!" the Bendahara says to Raja Mudeliar after a misunderstanding over money. Using the help of "a certain man of Kalinga named Kittul," Raja Mudelier persuades the Sultan to have the Bendahara executed. When he learned later of the plot, the Sultan orders Raja Mudelier himself to be killed.[17] This combination of myth and chronicle hints at how prominent Tamil Muslims were in Melaka's court; it is likely that they played a similarly important role in other port polities across the region.

Muslims played a central role, too, in the expansion of Chinese trade to the *nanyang* ("southern ocean"). China's coastal Muslim communities flourished under the rule of the Mongol Yuan and Ming dynasties—they played a leading role in the Chinese imperial navy. Between 1405 and 1431, Chinese maritime expeditions led by the admiral Zheng He, a Muslim eunuch in the service of the Yongle emperor, traversed Southeast Asia and crossed the Indian Ocean to eastern Africa. Even after the Chinese state turned its back to the sea, faced with a restive inner Asian frontier, Zheng He's voyages left small communities of Chinese along its route, as "precursors of China's modern emigration history." Early European settlements in Southeast Asia had significant Chinese populations, and so too did many indigenous kingdoms.[18]

Ma Huan, a Muslim of humble background—a "mountain-woodcutter," as he described himself—was on the fourth of Zheng He's expeditions in 1413. His memoir is a richly observant record of the journey.[19] In the thriving ports of East Java, Ma Huan found large settled communities of Chinese and many Muslims (Huihui) among them. By the end of the sixteenth century, Dutch visitors to Banten (West Java) distinguished between "natural Chinese" and "those who have lived here for a long time, and who have adopted the Mohammedan faith." Chinese Muslims left their trace on the mosque architecture of the Indonesian archipelago—the Japara mosque, for example, showed clear evidence of "the hand of Chinese artisans." Along the coast, harbor *keramat*—burial places of revered figures associated with Zheng He's voyages—emerged as places of spiritual power. Members of his vast crew settled at the many stops along their journey. When they died, some of their burial sites became places of pilgrimage as we see at Gedung Batu at Semarang, the tomb of one of Zheng He's pilots who converted to Islam and married a local woman.[20]

Eastern Frontiers in an Age of Empire

Writing of the Indian context, Partha Chatterjee has cautioned historians against rendering "the slide from the precolonial to the era of colonial modernity in the nineteenth century" as somehow "smooth and unproblematic."[21] The expansion of British power across the Bay of Bengal in the early-nineteenth century undoubtedly brought a sea-change in sovereignty to the port polities of Southeast Asia.[22] The Straits Settlements—Singapore, Penang, and Melaka—adopted outwardly some of the forms of the pre-colonial port cities: their ethnic quarters, their system of communal representation (initially, the British retained the position of *kapitan*), their plurality of faiths and languages. But the colonial state categorized, enumerated, and governed its subjects in unprecedented ways. Within a few years of the establishment of an English settlement in Penang, in 1786, the island's first governor, Francis Light, wrote of the "great number of Strangers constantly coming and going"; he recommended the "strict police" of the "great diversity of Inhabitants differing in religion, laws, language, and customs."[23]

British observers understood the diversity of peoples they ruled over in Southeast Asia through the emerging category of race. John Crawfurd, a Scottish administrator and amateur ethnographer, observed that the "race" of people from the Coromandel Coast were "shrewd, supple, unwarlike, mendacious and avaricious." The Chinese, on another view, were "the most successful traders and most patient toilers in the East," whose "love of combinations, of the guilds and unions in which all Chinamen delight, tempts them too far." Southeast Asia's creole communities caused Europeans particular anxiety. Of the hybrid Tamil-Malay families of Kedah and Penang, formed through intermarriage, Crawfurd wrote that "the motley race formed by these unions is a compound character of no very amiable description, partaking of the vices of both parent stocks."[24] Many British governors and administrators around the Bay of Bengal believed fervently in the immutable divisions of race; many ruled to make this a self-fulfilling prophesy in Southeast Asia. But ideas about "race" were confused and incoherent.

British economic policy, too, undermined the old trading and financial world of the Indian Ocean—though, as Rajat Kanta Ray showed in an influential essay, the imperial economy never wholly supplanted, and indeed depended on, the "bazaar economy."[25] Though Singapore and Penang were "free ports" relatively free of restrictions and duties, Tamil Muslim merchants along the Coromandel Coast suffered from shipping restrictions imposed by the Government of India—often on "humanitarian" grounds—which undermined their ability to compete with highly-capitalized European firms, particularly with the advent of steam shipping in the second half of the nineteenth century. Notwithstanding these pressures, in the nineteenth century, Tamil Muslims used the bridgeheads of imperial capitalism to deepen their already extensive contacts with Southeast Asia. As the trade of Penang and Singapore flourished, Tamil Muslims prospered. Through their patronage of shrines, Tamil Muslim merchants shaped the sacred architecture of Southeast Asia's port cities. Through their control of shipping from India, they transported working men across the Bay of Bengal. Through their command of capital, they financed a torrent of textiles and pepper and rice.

The biography of one well-known figure from within the creole Tamil Muslim community of the Straits Settlements evokes this world of multiple affiliations across the Bay of Bengal—an ancient maritime world that adapted to the new openings and constraints presented by colonial rule. "Munsyi" Abdullah abd al-Kadir worked as a scribe and translator for the East India Company. He is famous in Malay history as a social reformer, as author of the "first Malay autobiography," and as a servant of the British Empire, but he was also deeply embedded in a Tamil-speaking world. Abdullah's great-grandfather was a Hadrami Arab from Yemen, who settled in Nagore and married a local Tamil woman. The couple had four sons. The first, Abdullah's grandfather, traveled to Melaka, where he met and married a Tamil Muslim woman, "Peri Achi, the daughter of Schaikh Mira Lebai." The other three sons all traveled to "Java"—in this case, a general term for the Indonesian archipelago—and settled in Ambon, Sumatra, and Java, married, and had children. As a boy, Abdullah bridged creatively the many sides of his cultural inheritance. He wrote, "My father sent me to a teacher to learn Tamil, an Indian language, because it had been the custom from the time of our forefathers in Malacca for all the children of good and well-to-do families to learn it. It was useful for doing computations and accounts, and for purposes of conversation because at that time Malacca was crowded with Indian merchants." "Many were the men," he continued, "who had become rich by trading in Malacca, so much so that the names of Tamil traders had become famous. All of them made their children learn Tamil." There was no contradiction for "Munsyi" Abdullah in recognizing his Tamil heritage while devoting himself to the uplift of the Malay "race" (*bangsa*), with which he identified most closely.[26]

The South Asian Muslim community in Southeast Asia was far more diverse than traders alone, nor was it exclusively South Indian.[27] Many of the earlier East India Company soldiers in Southeast Asia were Muslim sepoys from the heartlands of North India. The convict workers transported to the penal settlements in Bencoolen, Penang, and Singapore included Hindus and Muslims in roughly equal numbers, many of them from Bengal and from North India. Tamil Muslims worked as dockworkers, mariners, shopkeepers, food-vendors, and rickshaw pullers. Before the mass migration of indentured workers to Malaya's plantations, which took off in the 1880s, Tamil Muslims were a clear majority among the "Indian" population of Singapore, Penang, and other Southeast Asian port cities.

Their influence was clear on the landscape of these port cities. There stand, to this day, dargahs to Shahul Hamid of Nagore on Telok Ayer Street in Singapore and on Chulia Street in Penang. The Penang shrine was built in 1801 and the structure in Singapore in the late 1820s. Both were replicas of the original dargah. They became places of devotion and healing, attracting local worshippers far beyond the Tamil Muslim community, just as the original shrine in Nagore had always attracted Hindu devotees. Shahul Hamid was an apt patron saint for people on the move. The sea is at the heart of his story. Stories of his life recount his journey from the plains of North India to Mecca and back across the Indian Ocean, stopping in the Maldives and at Adam's Peak in Ceylon before settling in Nagore, where he died. Shahul Hamid's protection of voyagers incorporated the coming of Europeans. A modern chronicler narrates one the saint's miracles:

> ... A Dutch ship was on her way to Nagapattinam port. At a little distance from the shore that ship had been caught in the midst of sudden storm, that caused a big hole on the bottom of the ship ... At the critical moment some one on board the ship suggested the name

> and help of our Quthub be invoked. The captain and crew did so. What a miracle! The inflow of the sea water suddenly ceased. The ship was saved.[28]

To this day, shops that line the passageway leading to the main Nagore shrine sell small pieces of foil imprinted with the images of boats, which devotees offer at the shrine when they pray for the safety of their voyages. To this day, these voyages often have Southeast Asia as their destination.

Shahul Hamid's story links his descent from Sayyid 'Abd al-Qadir al-Jilani—founder of the Qadiri tariqa in twelfth-century Baghdad—to the dispersal of his followers across Southeast Asia. A trustee of the dargah in Nagore told me that, as well as the surviving Nagore dargahs in Singapore and Penang, there were once shrines to the saint of Nagore dispersed in Burma, Ceylon, Indonesia, and Vietnam. These signs of the saint's presence charted his followers' circulations. Stories of the saint's life helped in "imagining Muslim space for mobile communities of Muslim traders and seamen in the Bay of Bengal." Susan Bayly has argued that the Nagore saint and his cult were always situated "in a wider world of *hajj* pilgrimage, trade, and teaching, which his devotees still visualized [in the 1980s] ... as a living and expansive arena in which the saint continued to radiate his presence."[29]

The dispersal of Shahul Hamid's followers across Southeast Asia was no coincidence: Nagore was, for centuries, an important center of the Maraikkayar shipping business across the Bay of Bengal. As the community of Indian migrants in Penang and Singapore diversified, in the second half of the nineteenth century, Shahul Hamid's followers were drawn from all walks of life—and from many communities. In Penang, one European observer claimed to have seen the saint's devotees in Penang throwing their valuables into the sea, firm in the belief that they would cross the Bay of Bengal and wash up on Nagore's shores. The boatmen of Penang harbor set aside a portion of their earnings to sponsor a day's feasting and procession in the saint's honor each year. In a poem written at the end of the nineteenth century—and published by a Chinese printer—Koca Maraikkayar describes the annual procession through Penang in honor of Shahul Hamid, naming the streets and sights and notables along its route. The poet describes, too, the diversity of peoples who witnessed or participated in the procession: "Klings" and "Hindus," Malays, Burmese, Chinese, Chettiars, Bengalis, Japanese, "Coringees," "Pariahs," and Portuguese. On another occasion, when the annual procession in Singapore led to a confrontation between marchers and the police, the legal proceedings that followed revealed a list of witnesses from virtually every ethnic and linguistic group on the island.[30]

But the circulation of Tamil Muslim cultural symbols in Singapore and Penang took place amid many other sites, symbols, and practices. Telok Ayer Street in Singapore stands as a symbolic point of intersection between the Bay of Bengal and the China Sea. Within a few steps of one another stand the Nagore dargah, the Chinese Temple of Heavenly Blessings—dedicated to Mazu, protector of seafarers—and another mosque built in the Tamil style, the Al-Abrar (also known as *kuchi palli,* or "small mosque"). From Rangoon to Saigon and even Vientiane, wherever small communities of Tamil Muslim traders settled, they took with them the sacred architecture of Islamic South India.

By the end of the 1860s, the chief secretary of the Straits Settlements observed a community becoming steadily more diverse: "Almost all the boatmen, caulkers, and laborers on boardships and in the town, syces, watermen, and a large number of hawkers, traders and domestic servants, are men from the Madras Coast," he wrote. Most of these men were Tamil Muslims from the Coromandel Coast. In the early twentieth century, and even after migration to the plantations had reached mass proportions, Tamil Muslim migration to Singapore and Penang became more diverse, now moving inland from the coasts, and involving whole communities from depressed weaving villages like Kadayanallur and Tenkasi. Even after the British squeezed out the Tamil shipping merchants, imposing the monopoly of the British India Steam Navigation Company, the Maraikkayar firms continued to operate on a smaller scale. Many of these agents took migrants out from the French port of Karaikal, long the heartland of the Maraikkayar shipping companies, evading the restrictions imposed by the British authorities.

As steam shipping gained dominance over the Bay of Bengal and the South China Sea after 1880, a fundamental demographic shift took place. Tamil-speaking Muslims, always a majority among those who crossed the Bay to the Melaka Straits, were now dwarfed in number by the mass migration of Dalit and low-caste Hindu laborers to the rubber plantations of Malaya—some of them under indenture, others indebted to recruiting agents. Though Tamil Muslims continued to form a large proportion of migrants destined for the urban economy—traders, petty shopkeepers, small-time merchants, food vendors—they were now outnumbered. The easy intermarriage open to an earlier generation of Tamil Muslim men arriving in the Straits was no longer open, not least because the Tamil Muslim migrants, too, were increasingly of working-class origins. This shift was more pronounced still in the case of Chinese migrants to Southeast Asia. If Chinese Muslims were prominent among the settled communities in the early modern port cities, they formed a tiny proportion of the Chinese communities of Southeast Asia in the nineteenth and twentieth centuries. Mass migration from China in the nineteenth century displaced Chinese Muslims from some of their earlier economic niches—for example, Chinese Muslims dominated the tin mines of Bangka from the early eighteenth century; in the nineteenth century, Dutch authorities sponsored the mass migration of (non-Muslim) Hakka labor to work the mines. Social tension and economic competition emerged between the Totok—"pure" Chinese newcomers from the mainland—and the local-born Peranakan. Non-Muslim Chinese Peranakan adapted to the new situation by incorporating ambitious newcomers from the mainland into their families. Chinese Muslim Peranakan were marginalized from this new, fused Chinese elite—and many of them opted to deepen their identification with indigenous communities with whom they shared faith, language, and culture. Demography might help to explain why Chinese Muslim communities have played such a minor role in the scholarship on the Overseas Chinese. But, as the next section will suggest, their cultural influence remained important.[31]

Public Spheres

The 1870s saw an opening of the public sphere in the Straits Settlements through the medium of print and an efflorescence of associational life.[32] Here, too, Tamil Muslims played a creative, bridging role.

The introduction of the movable-type lithograph led to a proliferation of small-scale Tamil publishing in Singapore and Penang, beginning in around 1873, with the production of newspapers—most of them short-lived—and books, which ranged from manuals of Islamic instruction to genealogies of saints, which connected the sacred landscapes of South India directly with the Straits Settlements, as well as back in time, and westwards, to the Arabian Peninsula and the time of the Prophet. The *Keerthanathirattu* (1896), for example, began with songs of God and the Prophet, followed by poems in praise of ʻAbd al-Qadir al-Jilani, followed by the saint of Nagore, and ending with three local saints buried in Singapore.[33]

The press was as polyglot as the society it served. The first Tamil-language newspaper in the Straits Settlements, *Tankainesan* ("Our Friend"), appeared in 1876; it was edited by Muhammad Saʻid and published by the *Jawi Peranakan* company. The very same publishers started the first-ever Malay-language newspaper, the eponymous Jawi Peranakan.[34] The Tamil-Malay community of the Straits descended from mixed marriages, stood quite naturally astride the Tamil and the Malay cultural worlds. In their content, the early urban newspapers mirrored their world in motion. A typical issue of *Jawi Perakanan* began with a list of market prices, government circulars, and notices from the government gazette; local news and correspondence was followed by news from the surrounding region, "and it is worthy of notice that so large a number of places contribute news from this part of Malaya. Such names are found as Semarang, Serubaya, Bogor, Pariaman, Menado, Bantan, Cherbun, Ambun, Karawang and Pulau Banda." News of the world came from other newspapers (including the *Rangoon Times* and the *London and China Express*); telegrams were "copied from the *Straits Times*," with stories from France and Russia and Ireland and the Bolivian Republic.[35] The Chinese press in the Straits was slower to develop, but it took off in the 1880s. Some newspapers were printed in the romanized Malay favored by local-born Peranakan Chinese, others were written in Chinese characters, still others in English, including the *Daily Advertiser* and the *Straits Chinese Magazine*. The newspaper *Lat Pau*—established by See Ewe Lay, a Straits Chinese who worked for the Hong Kong and Shanghai Bank—had 800 subscribers by the 1890s and correspondents from Rangoon to Saigon.[36] The early newspapers of the Straits were cosmopolitan in their production: most presses churned out newspapers and books in many languages. Many of the early Tamil Muslim publishing houses were backed by Tamil Hindu or Chinese capital.[37] Penang's first Tamil newspaper, *Vidya Vicarini* (published in 1883) was mobile in a more literal sense: the press followed its founding editor, poet Ghulam Kadir Navalar, back across the Bay of Bengal to Nagore.[38]

The first of the early Tamil newspapers to survive in a full run is *Singainesan* ("Friend of Singapore"). It was published between 1887 and 1890 by the Denodaya Press, which also printed texts in English and Malay. The very first edition declared (in English) that it was "designed to commemorate the Jubilee of Her Majesty the Queen-Empress Victoria," and dedicated to "the monarch whose sway extends to every quarter of the globe, and whose beneficent reign will mark an epoch in the history of the world;" on the same page, it also contained a small dedication, in Tamil, to Sultan Abdulhamid II—ruler of the Ottoman Empire and the symbolic leader of Muslims everywhere. Layers of loyalty were nothing strange in the fluid cultural world of the port cities. In his insightful analysis of its contents, Torsten Tschacher shows that *Singainesan* had subscribers across the Malay Peninsula, in Sumatra, Java, Siam, Indochina, and India. He shows, too, that the newspaper's authors addressed different audiences and adopted shifting terms of self-identification: "Tamils," in the newspaper's terms, referred largely to Hindus; the term "Tamil Muslim" did not often appear—however, it did refer to "we Kling Muslims," and also to "Kling Hindus."[39]

In an early message to its subscribers, *Singainesan* vowed that "from now on, we will print news of Singapore, Penang, Melaka, Europe … Nagapatnam, Nagur, Karaikal, Madurai, Chennai [and] Jaffna," suggesting the span of its subscribers' interests. The layout of this, as of every, newspaper resembled a collage—the juxtaposition of stories, from the serious to the trivial, from the local to the very distant, conveying a sense of simultaneity and of worldliness: the globe was laid out on the page, in columns and paragraphs. The order of news ranged from the local (the committee politics of local mosques and temples, cases in Singapore's high court, celebrations of the Queen's jubilee by Singapore's Chinese associations, the racing results, robberies and murders, and people running "amok"), to the regional (covering the Malay states, "Netherlands India," Siam and Indochina), and from there to news of India, China, and Europe. *Singainesan* borrowed liberally from other newspapers, often English-language papers, and reproduced Reuters telegrams from around the world, which encompassed everything from war reports to news of the king of Bulgaria. It gave its readers a history of Malaya's colonization—and a history of the Zulus.[40]

If they were less prominent in the development of newspapers than their Tamil counterparts, Chinese Muslim writers played an important role in the Malay world of the nineteenth century, particularly in Java. Ching Sa'idullah Muhammad, a Chinese Muslim, was a famous copyist who transcribed many Javanese manuscripts while working at the Secretarial Office in Batavia; Chinese Muslims played an important role in the development of Javanese and Malay literature. Print enabled new engagements with faith, and new experiments with language. In Southeast Asia, the first local translation of the Koran into Chinese was published in 1932 by Wang Wentjhing. At the same time, the development of the Malay language as a means of literary expression provided new arenas for dialogue across religious lines. The non-Muslim Peranakan Chinese of the Straits Settlements and Java adopted romanized Malay as their primary means of literary and journalistic expression in the early twentieth century through newspapers like *Bintang Timor*.[41]

In his important work on the history of ideas in the modern Malay world, Joel Kahn writes that "Islamic reformers in the Malay world from the early twentieth century imagined new forms of global community." They imagined a "trans-border" Malay world that transcended the territorial boundaries imposed by European empires.[42] The journeys of Malay (as also South Asian) pilgrims, scholars, and seekers to the Middle East and later to Cairo, brought them into contact with a wider Muslim world. This led to a heightened awareness of their interconnectedness, but also awareness, and even a sharpening, of difference and distinction. From these encounters came a vision of the Muslim world that was much less territorially specific, and at the same time a clearer vision of a Muslim world divided into nations. Associated with the teachings of Muhammad Abduh and his disciple Rashid Rida, Muslim modernists sought to reconcile Islamic teachings with industrial modernity and modern ideas about nationality; they emphasized the importance of rigorous scriptural interpretation *(ijtihad)*. These ideas had a great impact on Chinese-, Tamil- and Malay-speaking Muslims from Southeast Asia, who imbibed them through their travels and through circulating texts. Through practices of citation and republication, Muslim newspapers in many languages in Southeast Asia engaged with global debates on Islam. At the same time, Tamil and Chinese communities overseas were absorbed in debates over diaspora. For Tamil- and Chinese-speaking Muslims, these two concerns intersected.

By the turn of the twentieth century, a sharper sense of diasporic consciousness pervaded the large Indian and Chinese populations of Southeast Asia. Colonial administrations' addiction to racial categories, the influence of rising nationalism in India and China, the schools and libraries and temples built by second- and third-generation migrants in Southeast Asia—all of these strengthened a sense of diasporic identity.[43] The connection between the Tamil and Chinese diasporas in Southeast Asia and their homelands was reinforced by the constant arrival of newcomers from home in this age of mass migration. In different ways and at different moments, Tamil- and Chinese-speaking Muslims embraced or distanced themselves from their respective diasporas. In some circumstances, diasporic consciousness could sharpen the distinctions of faith. Among the Peranankan Chinese of Indonesia, for example, the early-twentieth century process of "re-sinicization"—a rediscovery of Chinese cultural roots—took the form of a Confucian religious revival that explicitly rejected the accommodations that earlier generations had made with local practices. Kwee Tek Hoay, founder of Java's Tiong Hoa Hwe Koan (THHK), or Chinese Association, lamented that "a laughable combination or mixing developed ... Not a few native customs slipped into the patterns and habits of the Chinese." Ultimately, he argued, "the customs, beliefs and religions of the Chinese of Java grew extremely chaotic and burdensome."

From their mothers, Peranakan children were "engulfed in native practices and customs ... firmly and fanatically." The THHK was "awake to the need for the Chinese herein Java to reform in order to lighten the oppressive burden of great variety" in their culture.[44]

In response—almost in mirror image—the Chinese Muslims in Java emphasized not their Chineseness, but their indigeneity to Java. Some of the community's leaders criticized the residues of Chineseness that remained within their practice of Islam. Lombard and Salmon cite the poem of a converted Chinese Peranakan in Java, excoriating his Chinese Muslim brethren for participating in the popular rituals of the Chinese Hungry Ghost Festival:

> Here they are reunited, these insane Muslims,
> Swallowing their saliva and shaking their heads ...
> They also gobble down Chinese food,
> There are lots of vegetables, and pork ...
> And if there is alcohol in a bowl,
> They waste no time in lapping it ...

The poem was published in the early 1920s after an episode of anti-Chinese violence by activists of the Sarekat Islam (the first Indonesian nationalist organization), and at a time when many Peranakan Chinese Muslims were trying to associate themselves with the Sarekat Islam.[45] The painful choices that the hardened political divisions of the time forced upon people is made clear by another poet's sadness at the violence between the Sarekat Islam and the local Chinese community:

> Many have told
> At the time of the events of Semarang,
> That the Sarikat Islam had clearly said
> That they were going to attack the Chinese,
> All these mad words,
> It is to be hoped that you do not listen to them.[46]

The mixed Tamil-Malay community of Malaya, known in the nineteenth century as the "Jawi Peranakan"—"Munsyi" Abdullah's community—faced a similar if less acute dilemma of identification. According to the colonial census, and on the request of a section of the community's elite, the category "Jawi Peranakan" ceased to exist in 1911. From that point, the creole community was declared to be "Malay"—a statistical assimilation to match a much broader process of cultural integration that had taken place throughout the nineteenth century. From 1917, Jawi Peranakan leaders mounted a concerted campaign against the celebration of Boria—the distinctive Penang variant of the Muharram celebration, which in the nineteenth century had attracted Tamil Hindu, Malay, and Chinese participants, and which had often turned into a riotous carnival.[47] Mohamed Yusoff bin Sultan Maidin published a pamphlet on "Boria and its Evils" *(Boria dan Bencananya)* in 1922, condemning it as un-Islamic, and indicative of a shameful past that needed forgetting—a practice brought by convicts from India in the nineteenth century.[48] At the same time, faced with an increasingly racialized Malay nationalism, Jawi Peranakan were not allowed to forget their "foreign" origins. They were not *betul Melayu*—"real" or true Malays—and their history of usurpation of the mantle of Malayness emerged from newspaper editorials, short stories, and pamphlets. The assault increased, particularly in Singapore, in the 1930s, as the question of community leadership on colonial councils came to a head.[49]

The 1920s and 1930s saw the flourishing of associational life in the Straits Settlements. These associations transcended any divide between the religious and the secular, with crosscutting concerns and overlapping memberships. But they also raised questions of belonging, of inclusion and exclusion. There were tensions between Tamil-speaking Muslims and Hindus over who could represent the community—and indeed, over where the boundaries of the community should be drawn. But there were tensions, too, between Malay and other Muslims. Journalists, editors, and activists of Tamil Muslim background had played a leading role in the development of Malay print culture; they fostered early Malay nationalism and ethnic consciousness. By the 1920s, however, tensions arose. The Singapore Malay Union, formed in 1926, made an explicit claim to wrest the community's leadership, the right to speak, out of the hands of Indian and Arab Muslims; branches of this organization spread to Penang and Melaka, the Penang branch in 1938 deciding that only "pure" Malays could be members. The measure of that "purity," of course, remained in question. When a rival organization, the Straits Settlements Malay Union offered membership to non-Malay Muslims, not all of them were flattered. In a sarcastic letter to Singapore's *Straits Times*, one reader wrote that "all these days I have been under the impression that as a Muslim local-born Indian I can only claim to be what I am." Now, this new Malay Union offered to embrace him. But he had no wish to become, in the Malay phrase, *umang umang*—which he translated, from Wilkinson's dictionary, as "a hermit crab, a term of derision applied to a man decked out in borrowed plumes." "I would prefer to remain," he signed off, "AN INDIAN MUSLIM."[50]

The quest for reform inspired many political projects in the 1920s and 1930s—creating cleavages within, and links across, the lines of community. Debates over religion and diaspora energized a process of secularization in the public sphere—an open-ended, reflexive inquiry into religious difference and public norms of the kind that Ayesha Jalal has distinguished from state secularism's harder separation between faith and politics.[51] When "Periyar" E.V. Ramasamy visited Malaya in 1929, he was received enthusiastically by many members of Penang's Tamil Muslim community, even as some caste Hindus vehemently opposed his visit, and protested against it. Periyar's positive reception among many Tamil Muslims in Southeast Asia built on the success of the Self Respect Movement in Madras in attracting Muslim support. The particular political configuration in South India—with the rise of an assertive, reform-minded and anti-caste movement—created political space for Tamil-speaking Muslims to braid their religious concerns and their linguistic affiliations in what Abdul Fakhri has called a "Tamil Muslim matrix."[52] Because of this distinctive caste of Tamil politics, which encompassed the diaspora in Southeast Asia, Tamil Muslims perhaps found it easier than their Chinese counterparts to continue to bridge the worlds of diaspora, faith, and local community.

Tamil Muslims were essential to constituting the "Tamil diaspora" in Southeast Asia, which emerged with much firmer boundaries in the 1930s. They were also central to the debates, the practices, and the conflicts of local Muslim society within the "Malay world." Their particular history can just as easily be situated in the context of the development of Tamil society overseas as it can in the history of Southeast Asian Islam; to reduce it to either frame would be to impoverish the complexity and creativity of the culture that emerged from this history of circulation across the Bay of Bengal. Chinese Muslims, too, continued to play a role in fostering different kinds of community. The cosmopolitan practice of both communities merits more attention than it has received. As Kris Manjapra has written in another context, it is important "to see social and cultural distinctions in more detailed ways, but also to bring to light the mediated and bridged communities of affiliation that connected individuals and groups across lines of difference."[53]

Post-Colonial Echoes

The geopolitical shifts of the 1940s transformed both the Bay of Bengal and the Malay world: and in some ways, it narrowed both. One consequence of the Indonesian revolution was, paradoxically, the final hardening of the border that had first been drawn in 1824 between the British and Dutch empires in Southeast Asia—from the 1940s, it marked the border between the Republic of Indonesia and Malaya, which remained under British rule until 1957. Many radical dreams of a "Greater Indonesia"—a political entity that would encompass the expansive "Malay world"—died after the Second World War, even if they remained as a glimmer in the political imagination. At the same time, the world of the Bay of Bengal became a region of contested territorial sovereignty, governed by complex restrictions on mobility across borders. These new conditions of mobility were governed by the passport, which came into widespread use almost everywhere in the 1940s and 1950s.[54]

This period saw the end of mass migration, and many instances of families divided and "stuck" on either side of the sea. Many had to make a choice about their citizenship on terms not of their choosing. The political logic of "minority" status impinged on the lives, and the political rights, of many communities of Indian and Chinese descent across Southeast Asia. Muslims of Indian or Chinese descent were often confronted by the equally unpalatable alternatives of complete assimilation as "natives," or the double bind of being "minorities within minorities"—to put it another way, they had to choose between melding into an ethnoreligious majority, or to continue as religious minorities within ethnic minorities. Yet even in this changed context, Tamil Muslims in Singapore, Malaysia, and further afield, managed better than many of their Hindu counterparts to maintain links with South India. As traders, shopkeepers, food vendors, moneychangers, many families retained vital connections between the Muslim towns on the Tamil Nadu coast and the other side of the Bay of Bengal. While circular migration in the old pattern was no longer possible, a significant degree of both migratory and cultural circulation continued to bind the Coromandel Coast to the Straits of Malacca. In part because of this continued circulation, the Tamil Muslim community remained predominantly male for much longer than many other migrant groups in Southeast Asia.

The history of Chinese Muslim communities in independent Indonesia presents some contrasts. Partly because of the Communist revolution in China and the Maoist state's strict controls over religious institutions and expression, and partly because of the brutal anti-Chinese pogroms that erupted during and after the Indonesian revolution, the Chinese Muslims oriented their political and cultural horizons oriented primarily toward the Indonesian nation-state. The 1940s and 1950s saw a significant wave of conversions to Islam by Indonesian Chinese—this had no parallels among non-Muslim populations of Indian origin anywhere in Southeast Asia. Many prominent Chinese Muslims involved themselves in the *dakwah* movements of the 1950s, and the Chinese Muslim Union (The Persatuan Islam Tiongoa Indonesia) emerged as a powerful voice to represent the community's interests. In keeping with the need to downplay Chinese ethnic origins in post-colonial Indonesia, the organization was re-named the Pembina Imam Tauhid Islam ("Action for the Faith and the Unity of Islam") in 1972. Though the new generation of Chinese converts to Islam had very little tangible connection with China; many of them located themselves firmly within a maritime imaginary—as true heirs to Zheng He. "The conversion of Chinese to Islam today is simply to bring back history," on one view.[55]

The world of Indonesian Islam in the 1950s and 1960s was a crowded field of debate and contestation—from the armed separatism of the Darul Islam movement to the cautious constitutionalism of the Masjumi. Indeed, Indonesia merits a far more central place than it is usually afforded in the intellectual history of Islam in the second half of the twentieth century.[56] In post-colonial Indonesia, debates over Islam's constitutional and political role link back in unexpected ways to a longer intellectual history of interregional connections. Consider the example of Ahmad Hassan, who became one of the leading Muslim intellectuals in post-colonial Indonesia.[57] Hassan was born in 1887 in Singapore. His father was a locally born Tamil scholar; his mother came from a Tamil family settled in Surabaya, East Java. By the time he was a teenager, he was fluent in Malay, English, Tamil, and Arabic. His father was an eminent writer and scholar, and editor of the Tamil-language publication *Nurul-Islam*. Ahmad Hassan was attracted by the modernist ideas that spread throughout the Malay world in the early twentieth century—through print and through the teachings of local students recently returned from Al-Azhar. He wrote for *Utusan Melayu*, the leading Malay modernist newspaper. He worked as a teacher in religious schools, as a perfume vendor, and as a cloth merchant. In the 1920s, he visited Surabaya in connection with his family's batik business and delved into the raging debate between the "new" and "old" factions of Islam: the Kaum Tua and the Kaum Muda. He settled in Bandung a few years later and became a leading figure in the Persatuan Islam (Persis): he was its intellectual guiding light. In 1934, he conducted a private correspondence with Sukarno while Sukarno was exiled in Flores: though they were often on opposite sides of the political debate, Sukarno respected Hassan as a teacher and a scholar. Though his worldview and his ideas were clearly forged by the facility with which his family had straddled the Tamil and Malay worlds of Islam in the late-nineteenth century, he chose to develop his insights and wage his struggles rooted in Java, and then in Indonesia. Hasan's is an intellectual life that has been confined by national history: he is seen as an "Islamic intellectual" in modern Indonesia—yet his intellectual genealogy is much more complex than that, and his origins lie very much in the circulating world of Tamil-speaking Muslims in the Bay of Bengal. For his part, Haji Abdul Karim (also known as Oey Tjen Hien), one of the preeminent Chinese Muslim leaders, developed his political thinking in his native Sumatra, forging links between currents of Chinese diasporic thought, Islamic reform, and Indonesian nationalism.[58]

Conclusion

The second decade of the twenty-first century provides a curious vantage point from which to view the long sweep of connections between Chinese and South Asian Islam and their global points of intersection: many of these are connections that are undergoing a revival after a period of relative decline during the heyday of the post-colonial nation-state. Many of the regional migrants in the age of globalization come from places, or even from families, that had been mobile in the past. The town of Nagore, for centuries tied to Southeast Asia by its merchants and seafarers, now sends many of its young men to the Middle East and to Southeast Asia as contract workers. In other port towns, including Parangipettai, deep histories of mobility across the sea are being revived—contemporary paths of migration are located in these traditions that, for part of the twentieth century, were forgotten. The annual festival in celebration of Shahul Hamid of Nagore attracts pilgrims from across Southeast Asia. And today even Quanzhou—the legendary Zaitun—seeks to re-establish its connections with the wider world of Indian Ocean Islam. The mid-sized town is at the heart of China's rise as the world's factory. Known as "shoe city," its factories manufacture over 500 million pairs of shoes for export each year. Many of its younger residents, descended (however distantly) from the Arab traders who settled there in the thirteenth century, have a renewed curiosity about the town's maritime past, and about their own connections with the Middle East. An increasing number of young people from Quanzhou have gone to study in the Middle East over the past decade, a few of them returning to teach Arabic.[59]

Over centuries, Tamil and Chinese Muslims have developed the capacity to translate between cultures and worldviews, and they have done so in ways far more creative than a bloodless term like "intermediaries" could ever convey. The history of the Indian Ocean's cosmopolitan cultures would benefit from greater attention to these two communities. And in our discussions of Islam in the Indian Ocean world, a vital new dimension might be added by considering the "other side"—the South China Sea—as well.

Notes and References

1. For helpful comments on earlier versions of this work, I would like to thank the participants at the two Tufts workshops on Islam and the Indian Ocean Rim in 2010 and 2012—I am particularly indebted to the editors of this volume, Sugata Bose and Ayesha Jalal, and also Kris Manjapra. The material in this essay on Tamil Muslim society draws on research that is presented more fully in my book, *Crossing the Bay of Bengal: The Furies of Nature and the Fortunes of Migrants* (Cambridge, Mass.: Harvard University Press, 2013); the comparative material on Chinese Muslims relies on the work of others. I have drawn, in particular, on the deeply illuminating works of Denys Lombard and Claudine Salmon, and especially their article, "Islam and Chineseness," *Indonesia*, 57 (1993): 115–131.
2. Engseng Ho, "Empire Through Diasporic Eyes: The View from the Other Boat," *Comparative Studies in Society and History*, 46, 2(2004): 210–246, 214.
3. Susan Bayly, *Saints, Goddesses and Kings: Muslims and Christians in South Indian Society, 1700-1900* (Cambridge: Cambridge University Press, 1989).
4. Anthony Reid, *Southeast Asia in the Age of Commerce, 1450-1680, Volume 2: Expansion and Crisis* (New Haven: Yale University Press, 1993); Torsten Tschacher, "Circulating Islam: Understanding Convergence and Divergence in the Islamic Traditions of Ma'bar and Nusantara," in R. Michael Feener and Terenjit Sevea (eds), *Islamic Connections: Muslim Societies in South and Southeast Asia* (Singapore: ISEAS, 2009), 48–67.
5. Ronit Ricci, *Islam Translated: Literature, Conversion, and the Arabic Cosmopolis of South and Southeast Asia* (Chicago: University of Chicago Press).
6. David Shulman, "Muslim Popular Literature in Tamil: The Tamimancari Malai," in Yohanan Friedmann (ed.), *Islam in Asia, Volume 1: South Asia* (Jerusalem: Magnes Press, The Hebrew University, 1984), 175; Vashudha Narayanan, "Religious Vocabulary and Regional Identity: A Study of the

Tamil *Cirappuranam*," in David Gilmartin and Bruce B. Lawrence (eds), *Beyond Turk and Hindu: Rethinking Religious Identities in Islamicate South Asia* (Gainesville: University Press of Florida, 2000), 74–97; Ki. Nayinar Mukammatu, "Cirappuranattil kappiya panpukal," *Proceedings of the Second International Conference Seminar of Tamil Studies* (Madras, 1968), v. 3, 95–103.

7. M. Ceyyitu Muhammatu "Hasan" (ed.), *Cirappuranam* (Chennai: Ulatak Tamilaraycci niruvanam, 1984), Vilatattuk Kantam, Nattu Patalam, 26: translation from Narayan, "Religious Vocabulary and Regional Identity," 86.
8. On Chinese Muslim communities, see Dru C. Gladney, *Dislocating China: Muslims, Minorities and Other Subaltern Subjects* (Chicago: University of Chicago Press, 2004); Dru C. Gladney, *Muslim Chinese: Ethnic Nationalism in the People's Republic* (2nd ed., Cambridge, Mass.: Harvard University Press, 1996).
9. "China," in *Dictionary of Islamic Architecture*, available online at http://www.archnet.org/publications/8803, accessed November 26, 2019.
10. Stewart Gordon, *When Asia Was the World* (New Haven: Yale University Press, 2010), 113; Hugh R. Clark, "Muslims and Hindus in the Culture and Morphology of Quanzhou from the Tenth to the Thirteenth Centuries," *Journal of World History*, 6, 1(1995): 49–74.
11. Lombard and Salmon, "Islam and Chineseness"; Chen Dasheng, *Islamic Inscriptions in Quanzhou* (Fuzhou: Ningxia & Fujian People's Publishing House, 1984).
12. Lombard and Salmon, "Islam and Chineseness"; Clark, "Muslims and Hindus"; John Guy, "Tamil Merchant Guilds and the Quanzhou Trade," in Angela Schottenhammer (ed.), *The Emporium of the World: Maritime Quanzhou, 1000-1400* (Leiden: Brill, 2001), 283–308.
13. Denys Lombard, "Pour une histoire des villes du Sud-Est asiatique," *Annales:* Économies, Sociétés, Civilisations, 25, 4(1970): 842–856; Denys Lombard, "The Malay Sultanate as a Socio-economic Model," in Denys Lombard and Jean Aubin (eds), *Asian Merchants and Businessmen in the Indian Ocean and the China Sea* (New Delhi: Oxford University Press, 2000), 113–120; Engseng Ho, "The Language of Malay Sovereignty in Malay Texts and in Episodes from History" (forthcoming in a special issue of *Indonesia and the Malay World* edited by Sumit K. Mandal).
14. Eric Tagliacozzo, "An Urban Ocean: Notes on the Historical Evolution of Coastal Cities in Greater Southeast Asia," *Journal of Urban History*, 33, 6(2007), 911–932.
15. Tomé Pires, *The Suma Oriental of Tomé Pires*, trans. Armando Coresao (London: Hakluyt Society, 1944), v. 2, 268.

16. Lombard, "The Malay Sultanate as a Socio-economic Model."
17. *Sejarah Melayu, "Malay Annals,"* trans. C. C. Brown (Kuala Lumpur: Oxford University Press, 1970), 70–71, 184–185. "Kalinga," an ancient kingdom in Odisha, was used a general term to refer to people from South India in the Malay world: later, the term transmuted to "kling" and acquired pejorative connotations by the end of the nineteenth century.
18. Philip A. Kuhn, *Chinese among Others: Emigration in Modern Times* (Singapore: NUS Press, 2008), 8; Leonard Blussé, "Batavia, 1619-1740: The Rise and Fall of a Chinese Colonial Town," *Journal of Southeast Asian Studies,* 12, 1(1981), 159–178; G. William Skinner, "Creolized Chinese Societies in Southeast Asia," in Anthony Reid (ed.), *Sojourners and Settlers: Histories of Southeast Asia and the Chinese* (Sydney: Allen and Unwin, 1996), 50–93.
19. Ma Huan, *Ying-Yai Sheng-Lan: The Overall Survey of the Ocean's Shores,* trans. J.V.G. Mills (Cambridge: Cambridge University Press, 1970).
20. Lombard and Salmon, "Islam and Chineseness"; Claudine Salmon and Denys Lombard, *Les Chinois de Jakarta, temples et vie collective/The Chinese of Jakarta Temples and Communal Life* (Paris: Editions de la Maison des Sciences de l'Homme, 1980).
21. Partha Chatterjee, *Black Hole of Empire: History of a Global Practice of Power* (Princeton: Princeton University Press, 2012), 75.
22. On sovereignty, see Sugata Bose, *A Hundred Horizons: The Indian Ocean in an Age of Global Empire* (Cambridge, Mass.: Harvard University Press, 2006).
23. Francis Light (George Town) to Sir John Shore (Fort William), 1 August 1794: British Library, Asian and African Studies Collection, Straits Settlements Factory Records, G/34/6, 111–112.
24. John Crawfurd, *History of the Indian Archipelago: Containing an Account of the Manners, Arts, Languages, Religions, Institutions and Commerce of Its Inhabitants,* vol. 1 (Edinburgh: Archibald Constable and Co., 1820), 133–134.
25. Rajat Kanta Ray, "Asian Capital in the Age of European Domination: The Rise of the Bazaar, 1800-1914," *Modern Asian Studies,* 29, 3(1995): 449–554.
26. *The Hikayat Abdullah: The Autobiography of Abdullah bin Kadir (1797-1854),* trans. A.H. Hill (Singapore: Oxford University Press, 1969); Anthony Milner, *The Invention of Politics in Colonial Malaya: Contesting Nationalism and the Expansion of the Public Sphere* (Cambridge: Cambridge University Press, 1995); Amin Sweeney (ed.), *Karya Lengkap Abdullah bin Abdul Kadir Munsyi* (Jakarta: Kepustakaan Populer Gramedia, 2005).

27. The following section is a condensed version of material in Chapters Two and Three of my *Crossing the Bay of Bengal.*
28. Janab Gulam Kadhiru Navalar, *Karunaik-katal Nakur Antavaravarkalin Punita Vazhkkai Varalaru* (Madras, 1963); S.A. Shaik Hassan Sahib Qadhiri, *The Divine Light of Nagore (The Whole History and Teachings of Nagore Great Saint)* (Nagore: Nagore Dargah, 1980).
29. Torsten Tschacher, "Witnessing Fun: Tamil-Speaking Muslims and the Imagination of Ritual in Tamil Southeast Asia," (forthcoming); Susan Bayly, "Imagining 'Greater India': French and Indian Visions of Colonialism in the Indic Mode," *Modern Asian Studies*, 38, 3(2004): 704.
30. Koca Maraikkayar, *Pinanku, urcava tiruvalankarac cintu*, (Penang: Kim Ceyk Hiyan, 1895), 4–6; see also Tschacher, "Witnessing Fun"; *Singapore Free Press*, February 26, 1857, "Coroner's Inquests."
31. Kuhn, *Chinese among Others*; Skinner, "Creolized Chinese Societies."
32. E.W. Birch, "The Vernacular Press in the Straits," *Journal of the Straits Branch of the Royal Asiatic Society*, 4 (December 1879): 51–55.
33. Muhammad Abdul Kadir Pulavar, *Kirthanathirattu* (Singapore, 1896).
34. Birch, "The Vernacular Press in the Straits."
35. Ibid.
36. Chen Mong Hock, *The Early Chinese Papers of Singapore, 1881-1912* (Singapore: University of Malaya Press, 1967); Mark Ravinder Frost, "*Emporium in Imperio*: Nanyang Networks and the Straits Chinese in Singapore, 1819-1914," *Journal of Southeast Asian Studies*, 36, 1(2005): 29–66.
37. Helen Fujitmoto, *The South Indian Muslim Community and the Evolution of the Jawi Peranakan in Penang up to 1948* (Tokyo: Tokyo Gaikokugo Daigaku, 1988).
38. S.M.A.K. Fakhri, "Print Culture amongst Tamils and Tamil Muslims in Southeast Asia, c. 1860-1960," Madras Institute of Development Studies Working Paper, no. 167 (Madras: MIDS, February 2002).
39. Torsten Tschacher, "Kling, Tamil, Indian: Being a Tamil-Speaking Muslim in Singapore" (forthcoming).
40. See, *inter alia*, "Ippattirikaiyin Nokkam" ("This Paper's Goal"), *Singainesan*, June 27, 1887; "Kaiyoppakkararkalukku" ("For Our Subscribers"), *Singainesan*, July 4, 1887; "Accai" ("War in Aceh"), *Singainesan*, March 4, 1888; "Ittalikkum, Abshiniyavukkum Candai" ("Italy and Abyssinia Go to War"), *Singainesan*, April 16, 1888; "Malay Decam" ("A History of Colonization in Malaya"), *Singainesan*, April 22, 1889. Newspapers consulted at the Lee Kong Chian Reference Library, National Library of Singapore.

41. Claudine Salmon, *Literature in Malay by the Chinese of Indonesia, A Provisional Annotated Bibliography* (Paris: Editions de la Maison des Sciences de l'Homme, 1981); Lombard and Salmon, "Islam and Chineseness."
42. Joel S. Kahn, *Other Malays: Nationalism and Cosmopolitanism in the Modern Malay World* (Singapore: Singapore University Press, 2006).
43. I make this argument at greater length in my article "Tamil Diasporas Across the Bay of Bengal," *American Historical Review*, 114, 3(2009); more broadly, see Sunil S. Amrith, *Migration and Diaspora in Modern Asia* (Cambridge: Cambridge University Press, 2011), Chapter 2.
44. Kwee Tek Hoay, *The Origins of the Modern Chinese Movement in Indonesia*, ed. and trans. Lea E. Williams (Ithaca, NY: Modern Indonesia Project, Southeast Asia Program, Cornell University, 1969), 8–10.
45. Takashi Shiraishi, *An Age in Motion: Popular Radicalism in Java* (Ithaca: Cornell University Press, 1990).
46. The poem is reproduced in part and translated in Lombard and Salmon, "Islam and Chineseness." The original verse reads:

    Koempoel semoea Slam jang gila
    Manelen loeda gojang kepala …
    Mangikoet gagares makanan Tjina,
    Sajoer babi banjak disana …
    Kaloe ketemoe arak di mangkok,
    Tidak oeroeng dia mandekok.

47. Helen Fujimoto, *The South Indian Muslim Community and the Evolution of the Jawi Peranakan in Penang up to 1948*, (Tokyo: ILCAA Tokyo Gaikokugo Daigaku, 1989), 176–177.
48. Muhammad Yusuf bin Sultan Maidin, *Boria dan Bencananya* (Penang: Mercantile Press, 1922).
49. Fujimoto, *South Indian Muslim Community*; Joel S. Kahn, *Other Malays: Nationalism and Cosmopolitanism in the Modern Malay World* (Singapore: NUS Press, 2006).
50. *Straits Times*, August 2, 1939.
51. Ayesha Jalal, *Partisans of Allah: Jihad in South Asia* (Cambridge, Mass.: Harvard University Press, 2008), 13–14; see also Talal Asad, *Formations of the Secular: Christianity, Islam, Modernity* (Stanford: Stanford University Press, 2003).
52. S.M.A.K. Fakhri, "Tamil Muslims and the Self-Respect Movement," in Mushirul Hasan (ed.), *Living with Secularism: The Destiny of India's Muslims* (New Delhi: Manohar, 2007).

53. Kris Manjapra, "Introduction," in Kris Manjapra and Sugata Bose (eds.), *Cosmopolitan Thought Zones: South Asia and the Global Circulation of Ideas* (New York: Palgrave, 2010).
54. Amrith, *Crossing the Bay of Bengal*, Chapter 7.
55. Muhamad Ali, "Chinese Muslims in Colonial and Postcolonial Indonesia," *Explorations: A Graduate Student Journal of Southeast Asian Studies*, 7, 2(2007): 1–22.
56. On the longer history of Indonesian Islam, see Michael Laffan, *The Makings of Indonesian Islam: Orientalism and the Narration of a Sufi Past* (Princeton: Princeton University Press, 2012).
57. This account of Hasan's career is drawn from Howard Federspiel, *Indonesian Muslim Intellectuals of the Twentieth Century* (Singapore: ISEAS, 2006); however, Federspiel treats Hasan entirely in an Indonesian national context.
58. See Haji Abdul Karim's memoir, *Mengabdi Agama, Nusa dan Bangsa, sahabat karib Bung Karno* (Jakarta: Gunung Agung, 1982).
59. Xiao Jia Gu, "Muslims of Quanzhou," *New Statesman*, December 18, 2006.

3

Spies in the Hejaz

Colonial Espionage in Jeddah

Eric Tagliacozzo*

Modern, state-sponsored surveillance requires two principal activities, it has been argued: the accumulation of coded caches of information, and the implementation of direct supervision over subject populations.[1] One of the most important aspects of the colonial pilgrimage to Mecca was the attempt—and ultimate success—of a range of European colonial powers to surveil and control the passage of Muslim bodies to the holiest sites of global Islam. At first, this was done on a piecemeal, ad-hoc basis. Yet by the middle decades of the twentieth century, structures were in place to make this process as scientific and as rigorous as colonial states could possibly make it. If the connection between power and the sovereign was crucial to ruling in early modern times, then by the turn of the twentieth century the ties between efforts at domination and various forms of "high modernist" government were the driving force of colonial governments.[2] Indeed, the art of state-sponsored surveillance, it might be argued, is one of the best ways to see the evolution of the modern state in all of its terrifying power. In the surveillance and criminalization of parts of the Hajj European regimes found a vast transnational vehicle to test their advancing abilities of control. This essay examines this dialectic through three discrete windows, each of which sheds light on these processes.

The Red Sea region was a "test-arena" of sorts for various colonial projects and their surveillance systems from the mid-nineteenth century to the middle decades of the twentieth. The first part of the essay examines the outlines of the three projects situated on the northern/eastern rim of the Red Sea (French, British, and Dutch), before touching on the most important colonial apparatus of knowledge/control on the southern and western side of the waterway—the emerging project of colonial Italy in the horn of Africa. Southeast Asian Hajj ships had to pass the gauntlet of all four of these powers en route to Jeddah and were watched by each in turn. The second third of the essay then concentrates more fully on the Dutch architecture of vision and control in the latter decades of the nineteenth century, and the connections between the Red Sea region and the Netherlands' most important global colony, the Dutch East Indies. The final third of the essay then proceeds onto the British surveillance project, as London's optic vis-à-vis the pilgrimage became the most important of all of these systems, particularly after the turn of the century. By the middle decades of the twentieth century, a huge and ever-expanding apparatus of colonial control was put into place, and all of these colonial partners (and sometimes, rivals) depended on the information that this project was able to acquire. With the advent of international socialism and nascent "third world" nationalisms after 1900, the stakes at hand comprised not solely those of international Pan-Islam and the specters associated with this term. I argue that control over the Hajj became seen as fundamental to ensuring the bedrock of European rule, a state of affairs that lasted until after the middle decades of the twentieth century.

Spying across the Red Sea: The Width of European Projects

As has been noted elsewhere, French scholarship was vital in decoding and codifying the "threat" of cholera and other diseases on pilgrim ships in the late nineteenth and early twentieth centuries. Not only were the French one of the principal European presences in the Hejaz in both diplomacy and trade, but also the Gallic vision of the political aspect of the Hajj was important and was commented upon regularly in French-language publications. Nineteenth-century French tracts on this topic tended to focus mainly on the connections between the Hajj and Paris's interests in the Arab world, which included parts of the Middle East and stretches of the North African Maghreb.[3] Other French publications of this period were written by Francophone Muslims, who saw an opportunity to explicate—and in some cases demystify—the Hajj for larger French-speaking audiences, including in Paris.[4] As the nineteenth century bled into the twentieth, more and more Francophone authors weighed in on these topics.[5] The pilgrimage went from being a relative cipher to increasingly passing through fields of French vision on the Middle East, mostly via ever-larger numbers of pilgrims from French-dominated lands.[6] Paris kept a close eye on all of this emerging literature—and carefully archived it—for their own geopolitical interests.

Credit: Map drawn by Lee Li-kheng, Geography Department, National University of Singapore

The British in the Red Sea region also constructed an intelligence edifice in the area, which was ultimately bent at least partially toward carefully monitoring and tabulating the Hajj, including its Southeast Asian varieties. Their intelligence narrative began with the occupation of Egypt and then continued on through the Saudi restoration, Faisal's first reign, the renewed occupation of the region, and Faisal's second reign, as well as through the rise of ʻAbd Allah and the house of Saud.[7] The British capture of Aden in 1839 was crucial in this story, as were the geostrategic dealings with Abyssinia on the other side of the Red Sea waterway in the 1840s and 1850s, and finally, intrigues with the Ottoman court for many decades after this. England slowly realized—concomitant with the growth of its own power in the world—that London would be embroiled in politics in this maritime chokepoint for many years to come.[8] The bedrock of London's covert empire in the region, however, despite these precedents, was really laid during the late nineteenth and early twentieth centuries. At that time, the worlds of Edwardian agents and Great Power politics collided with the discovery of oil in the region, alongside the perceived emergence of the Hajj as a feared transmission vehicle of "militancy and subversion" for colonial powers generally.[9] This British story will be picked up in earnest later in this chapter to show how the trends identified in thumbnail fashion here relate to the passage of Southeast Asian Muslims on Hajj in particular.

The Dutch were also vital players in the Red Sea espionage game of the international Hajj. Perhaps no one exemplified this complicated history more than Daniel van der Meulen, who was Dutch consul in Jeddah for two stints both before and after the Second World War. Van der Meulen's diaries kept a close eye on the Southeast Asian pilgrimage to Mecca. The consul's scribbles take in the travels, customs, and predilections of the "Jawa community," much as Snouck Hurgronje had done before him in Snouck's own capacity as a scholar/official resident in the Hejaz for six months. The difference is that van der Meulen was in Arabia far longer, and his travel diaries show his cognizance and watchfulness of Southeast Asians as he moved around the vast desert peninsula between the mid-1920s and the early 1950s, a period of nearly thirty years. Van der Meulen wrote on Muslim brotherhoods, murders of Southeast Asian pilgrims, and proto-nationalist "conspiracies," and his observations were eagerly sought by the Dutch political apparatus in Jeddah and in The Hague.[10] Yet he also published a number of his reflections, in missionary journals, newspapers (such as *De Telegraaf*, the *Deli Courant*, and the *Palembanger*, all with large circulations) as well as in other periodicals such as *The Moslem World*, the latter for an English-speaking audience. His topics of interest, in addition to the diary notations mentioned above, included what happened upon the return of pilgrims to the Indies, as well as the contours of Muslim revival movements.[11] His reflections were only the "tip of the spear," though, when it came to Dutch reportage on this huge phenomenon, as materials later in this chapter will soon show.

Finally, on the southern/western side of the Red Sea waterway, the Italian project of colonialism was also increasingly coming into contact with pilgrim ships. Surveillance was also important here as Rome attempted to grow its empire in the Horn of Africa over a period of several decades on either side of the *fin de siecle* period. Geography was in many ways at the heart of this endeavor: Italian militarists and civil servants of the burgeoning colonial bureaucracy tried to map out the terrain of the envisioned Italian sphere in increasingly broad sweeps. Much of this, at least in the cartographic realm, had to do with drawing accurate hydrographic charts of the Red Sea, which Italian ships had to traverse on their way to Rome's colonial settlements in Eritrea and Somalia.[12] This brought Italian scientists into contact with the pilgrim traffic up and down this waterway on a regular basis. Italian knowledge and expertise on the African coasts of the Red Sea was well-known to be accurate and was eventually utilized by the other great powers in their own map-making and charting of the arena as a whole. Italian expertise also was reflected in an active geographical publishing industry that circulated information about the parameters of the Red Sea coasts of Africa in increasingly minute detail after the turn of the twentieth century.[13] The letters of Italian explorers and missionaries back to the fascist fatherland also contained important information in this regard, which was kept on file in Rome as Mussolini's Italy grew into a regional power of note.[14]

Yet the Italian knowledge-project went beyond this one branch of science. Because the coastal parts of the Horn where Italy began its colonies were largely Muslim, Rome's planners became interested in the study of Islamic societies in the 1920s and 1930s. By the early 1900s, Italian authors had already been writing serious journal articles about Muslim interaction in places like Yemen and Eritrea.[15] The pace of publication of these contributions picked up in subsequent decades.[16] The birth and development of anthropology as a field of study throughout Europe also aided the production of knowledge; eventually, Rome had ethnographers in the arid landscapes of the Horn talking to a vast range of people, trying to understand their life-ways.[17] Produced under the Fascist regime, the studies were rarely critical of Italian colonialism and usually presented the "light of Rome" coming to the "dark continent" as only a good thing. The private letters written from the field by Italian ethnographers to their home institutes and by Italian missionaries to their own superiors echo these conclusions.[18] Yet their contributions supported larger European opinions on Islam in general, and the pilgrimage in particular, as a trans-local phenomenon with long roots and deep importance in the region. Alongside similar kinds of French, British, and Dutch reportage, Italian surveillance encircled the Red Sea as a geographic entity. The sea flowed in and out of this waterway, both through Suez and at the Bab-al-Mandab, and pilgrims flowed with the currents in both directions. On both sides of this international waterway, Muslims brought into this space were in fact constantly being studied and entered into the ledgers of an expanding colonial machinery.

Dutch Surveillance: The Early Years of an Imperial Project

Despite the fact that the Dutch East Indies were technically the Muslim-majority location furthest away from Mecca on the planet, from a relatively early date, these islands were supplying large numbers of pilgrims to the holy cities. By the eve of the First World War, these numbers were 24,025 in 1911, 26,321 in 1912, and 28,427 in 1913, but the more telling statistic is that these were roughly one-quarter of the global totals of pilgrims for these years.[19] In the eyes of the Dutch, this paradoxical fact necessitated the beginnings of a surveillance network on these subjects. From the mid-nineteenth century in Java, especially, voluminous documents were produced to keep track of the Hajj, with much of the information centering on a community-level basis. From Besoeki in the 1850s exist notations on whether the pilgrimage was deemed a threat by local administrators at this time, for example.[20] Semarang around the same time produced reams of sea-passes that noted the date, the pilgrim's name, the ship's name, as well as the vessel's.[21] From Tegal come records of the routes that some of these ships took, often jumping from the Java coasts to places such as Pontianak, Riau, and Singapore, human collection-depots along the maritime routes within the archipelago.[22] The Tegal pilgrims were away for two years at a time in the 1850s according to these statistics, while others were gone for three and occasionally for six years or more.[23] One document bundle from this residency in the early 1860s, "*Rapporten Dari Perkara Hadji Hadja njang Minta Pas dan njang Baru Datang dari Mekka, 1860-64,*" chronicles in Rumi (romanized Malay) and Dutch the comings and goings to Mecca from this single regency in over 500 pages. It gives little away about the feelings or details of individuals, but as a source for data-compilation, it is an astonishing record of movement from a very small place.[24]

Documents of a more personal nature from this period also exist. Writing primarily in Rumi, local indigenous officials supplied information about individual pilgrims who were leaving the Java coasts for Mecca in large numbers. Other documents in Dutch, record the names of those leaving in short, patterned detail:

> "Wordt bij deze verlof aan den Javaan Peto, behoorende tot de desa Wanatawang district Lebaksioe Regentschap Bribes Residentie Tagal, om verkeer naar Mekka ter vertrekken." Tagal, 22 Augusuts 1855, De Resident
>
> "By this document is permission granted to the Javanese Peto, who is from the village Wanatawang, district Lebaksioe, Bribes Regency, in the residency of Tegal, to go to Mecca." Tagal, 22 August 1855, signed, The Resident[25]

A number of pilgrims decided to change their names after coming back from their Hajj, a personal act that was sometimes committed at the conclusion of a successful trip to Mecca. Fasilan, the Dutch censors in Semarang in the 1850s noted, became Abdullah; Fasidjan wanted to be known as Abdulmajid; and Arseah turned into Abdusjamad.[26] This kind of very personal, individual attention to Hajjis and surveil even in small villages started early in the Indonesian records but eventually became more detailed as surveillance and record-gathering became more important to the Dutch later in the 1800s. By the early twentieth century, Batavia was using this Hajj-reportage apparatus to look for connections between the pilgrimage and Sarekat Islam membership on a local level, using the information for political ends, and eventually for repression.[27]

If the Jakarta archives provide a view into local surveillance, in nineteenth-century Java other repositories demonstrate how Dutch oversight over the Hajj was becoming more and more transoceanic in nature. The archives of the *Ministrie van Buitenlandse Zaken*, or Foreign Affairs Ministry in The Hague, is one such place: here surveillance material was gathered from the other side of the Indian Ocean when dealing with the Dutch-administered Hajj. As such, a certain amount of the information reflects Middle Eastern reporting. The Dutch consulate in Jeddah stockpiled boiled water, oil, spirits, and petroleum in 1878 to throw down at potential Bedouin attackers, for example. The building was designated as the city's pan-European gathering point because of its large size and its defensibility; this status shows how much the Dutch valued their toehold in the Hejaz as a means of surveilling their transoceanic subjects.[28] At other moments, an active Dutch spy-network was operationalized, as in 1881, when The Hague was informed that a man purporting to be the "second coming of Muhummad" had stepped forward ("his name is Imam Imhabil, 38 years of age, born in Mecca"). The Dutch Minister for Foreign Affairs was warned that the Ottoman Sultan had already sent out letters to Muslim lands to prepare for a jihad in two years as a result of Imhabil's birth, and the Dutch consul in Singapore performed a similar version of this preparation by writing to Batavia as the rumors were "quite enough to justify precautions" locally.[29] That same year, diplomatic correspondence warned of the arrival of three Meccan shaykhs—Syed Hussein Alkoods, Shaykh Abdul Hamid Murdad, and Shaykh

Ahmed Salawi—in Singapore, which put the Dutch Hajj-surveillance network on high alert. All three men "occupy so important a role in the Mahomedan world that their movements seldom fail to have a political object," the Governor-General of the Indies was told.[30] They needed to be watched, particularly if they were planning on moving into the Indies to preach hate against Europeans. In this, they were seen as part of a long line of "rabble-rousers and demagogues."[31]

Yet for an even more nuanced feel for how transnational Hajj surveillance had become in Dutch circles in the *fin de siecle* period, other sources from the nineteenth and early twentieth century can be examined, all of which comment upon this enormous oceanic undertaking. Some of this material was public and was put into the realm of public discourse by officials writing in their capacity as officials, but also as experts who could translate the "threat" of the Hajj for a public eager and willing to know about this phenomenon's huge global contours. The public press in journals such as the *Indische Gids* fall into this category.[32] The *Koloniaal Verslag,* a dense report of many hundreds of pages published in the Indies, also put out yearly composites of information on the Indies Hajj, showing the public the trends and directions of the pilgrimage. All of this information was important in setting a tone, and also in preserving information and a record of such carefully gleaned data.[33] Yet the majority of the material in question was private and intended only for the use of civil servants in order to keep tabs on a phenomenon that was thought to be potentially dangerous to the stability of the Dutch overseas empire. Dutch consular reports from places such as Penang and Singapore were crucial in this respect. They provided a yearly template for policy planners in The Hague to know what the Hajj looked like in ports just outside of Dutch jurisdiction but very much on the doorstep of the Indies. Religious "demagogues" were thought to use these places as bases to agitate in the Indies, for example.[34] The massive run of Colonial Office records known as *mailrapporten* (or mail reports) was also crucial in this regard, as they provide an unbroken record of many decades connecting Dutch authority in the Indies, the Hejaz, and Europe on the question of the Hajj. Dutch officials could follow the *mailrapports* (mail reports) through various colonial record offices, giving them a long-term view as they contemplated changes in policy.[35]

Chart 1: Netherlands East Indies Pilgrims

Java and Madura			Outer Islands		
Place	**1326/1909**	**1327/1910**	**Place**	**1326/1909**	**1327/1910**
Bantam	497	749	Padang Lowlands	208	379
Batavia	396	542	Padang Uplands	229	352
Preanger	1,857	2,044	Tapanoeli	44	55
Cheribon	434	494	Benkoelen	68	65
Pekalongan	396	439	Lampong	95	102
Semarang	375	380	Palembnag	310	514
Rembang	284	191	Djambi	77	93
Soerabaja	492	618	Sumatra East Coast	137	205
Madoera	380	342	Aceh and Environs	30	76
Pasoeroean	334	340	Riouw and Environs	14	78
Besoeki	344	257	Banka	121	44
Banjoemas	143	55	Billiton	22	18
Kedoe	546	256	Borneo, West	119	237
Djokjakarta	36	32	Borneo, SE	668	518
Soerakarta	54	59	Menado	51	51
Madioen	91	110	Celebes	265	536
Kediri	255	164	Amboina	83	66
			Ternate and Envir.	52	52
			Timor and Environs	10	129
			Bali and Lombok	227	232
Total	**6,814**	**6,987**	**Total**	**2,830**	**3,793**

Source: Anonymous, "De Bedevaart naar Mekka, 1909/1910" ***Indische Gids*****, 2, 1910, p. 1637.**

Ultimately, the root of Dutch uncertainty, anxiety, and fear in controlling the Hajj centered on the Indies, however, as the Dutch maintained only a tiny coterie of officials and traders in the face of a huge subject population of Muslim human beings. The Hajj might be a peaceful, unthreatening phenomenon that the Dutch were "required" to manage at the best of times, but if "extremists" did succeed in poisoning the relationship between masters and subjects in the Indies, as many Dutchmen feared in the decades leading up to the period of burgeoning nationalism in the early twentieth century, it would be the Dutch in the Indies who would pay the price. For this reason, Batavia tried to learn all it could about Islam and its permutations in every corner of the archipelago, wherever such knowledge was possible. Almost every "general report," "administrative report," and "political report" in every residency in the Indies had space for civil servants to comment on the nature of Islam in their particular area.[36] Specialized political reports were also commissioned for the so-called *Buitenbezittingen* (or residencies outside of Java and Madura, the latter comprising the "heartland" of Dutch rule) so that Islam in the "extremities" of the colony could be examined with special rigor. Some of these districts, such as Aceh, had long histories of resistance against occupation by a foreign power.[37] Finally, in the documents known as *Memories van Overgaven*, Dutch provincial officials were asked to comment about the "*geest*" or "spirit" of Islam in their particular residency when they finished their tours in a particular place and were about to hand over "their" landscape to another official. They noted at great length the details and trends in the Hajj in a vast array of Indies locales across the archipelago. All of these documents show changes over time as events unfolded in the Indies.[38]

Acting on the knowledge claimed by all of this surveillance was the province of the law. The Indies legal edifice set up to deal with the pilgrimage to Mecca required large numbers of codes, laws, and statutes to manage its sheer size and volume. From the *Staatsbladen* and *Bijbladen*, vast legal and policy compendia, it is evident that acquiring knowledge about the pilgrims themselves was deemed important by Batavia, This was so both before they set out from the Indies and once they reached the Hejaz, especially for Hajjis who wanted to stay longer in the Middle East.[39] Other laws stipulated that pilgrims were required to pay 100 guilder fines if they flaunted the Netherlands East Indies pass laws, and dictated pilgrims' responsibilities to check in with Dutch port officials in the Indies cities of their departure, then again in Jeddah with the Dutch consul, and finally back in Indies ports again upon their return to Asia.[40] Because the majority of the journey was maritime, Dutch naval authorities got involved in adjudication as well. They determined rules regarding the requisition of ships for the express purpose of the Hajj (safety matters, such as the provisioning of an adequate number of lifeboats and safety vests) and the amounts of cubic space allowed to each individual passenger to try to stave off the dangers of epidemic disease.[41] Finally, it was also legislated that the Dutch were not legally obligated to financially help pilgrims in the Middle East, which was only partially effective at preempting cost savings to protect them against shaykhs.[42] These legal protections and enforcements were eventually extended to a large number of Indies ports serving as Hajj depots, including Batavia, Surabaya, Makassar, Palembang, Jambi, Belawan/Deli, Padang, Sabang, Banjarmasin, and Pontianak by 1930.[43]

By the middle third of the twentieth century, the Dutch consular office in Jeddah had acquired a primary status as a body surveilling the Indies Hajj. Some of this oversight was actually in the interest of protecting pilgrims themselves. Reports from Jeddah on the murder of Javanese pilgrims in the Hejaz, as well as on the continuance of the slave trade alongside the Hajj, both bear this Dutch imprint of responsibility and philanthropy.[44] Shaykhs who took charge of the "Jawa" community were also listed, tabulated, and tracked—there were 241 of them in 1928 and all of their names are still known—by a wary colonial state.[45] Yet far more of the reportage is concerned with politics than protection by this time. Some of this writing concerns great power maneuvering, such as with Russian movements and oil shipments in conjunction with the Russian Hajj, and the dissemination of German propaganda (in Turkish) to local Hejazi populations, in an attempt to stir up hate against the Allies in the years leading up to the Second World War.[46] More of it has to do with ideas of Muslim linkages and potential subversion that was traveling alongside the

Chart 2: Translations of Pilgrimage Surveillance Regulations and Laws from the

Bijbladen and Staatsbladen van Nederlandsch-Indie

Bijblad #5741 (1902) p. 5740 passim:
Pilgrims' Travel Passes. We must get the most reliable information possible on the pilgrims before we give them the actual passes.

Bijblad #7130 (1909) p. 319 passim:
Pilgrims' Travel Passes. Passes must be given in to the harbor master of the departing port by pilgrims. They must also be shown to the Dutch consul in Jeddah and exchanged for a residence pass. They must be returned to the first official upon arrival back in the Indies. Pilgrims should also be classified on these passes.

Bijblad #7469 (1911) p. 444 passim:
Pilgrimage to Mecca. Pilgrims often ask for help, but they must be told firmly before they leave the Indies that they cannot expect to receive help in the Hejaz. We are indeed helpful, but we cannot be expected to be so all of the time and in every case.

Bijblad #11689 (1928) p. 381 passim:
Pilgrims' Travel Passes. There shall be a 100 guilder fine on those who flaunt the pass laws. This especially applies to those who travel though Singapore, Penang, Bombay, and Jeddah

Staatsblad #236 (1906) p. 1 passim:
Shipping and Pilgrims. The Commander of the Navy and Chief of the Department of Marine can be involved with pilgrim traffic too and lend ships for Hajjis if he feels such ships are available for use.

Staatsblad #531 (1912), p. 1 passim:
Shipping and Pilgrims. Surveillance on pilgrims during their voyages must be exercised in their own interest, too—including the insurance that there are enough lifeboats on board steamers;

that there are enough flotation devices; and that each pilgrim has a certain number of cubic meters space to stay in on deck during the voyage.

Staatsblad #15 (1923), p. 1 passim:
Shipping and Pilgrims. If an Indies pilgrim wants to stay in the Hejaz longer than his or her pilgrimage, then this must be reported to the proper Dutch authorities.

Staatsblad #44 (1931), p. 1 passim.
Travel Passes and Pilgrims. The number of Indies harbors now supporting Hajj traffic has grown; these now include Makassar, Surabaya, Tanjong Priok (Batavia), Palembang, Jambi, Belawan (Deli), Padang, Sabang (Aceh), Banjarmasin and Pontianak.

Staatsblad #554 (1932) p. 1 passim:
Shipping, Pilgrims: There must be real regulation in how the mutawwifs (shaykhs) work.

Hajj, especially vis-à-vis a number of brotherhoods and reformist sects who were shuttling between the Holy Cities and places such as the Al-Azhar in Cairo.[47] The largest single set of documents after the turn of the twentieth century focus on Dutch espionage on Indies communities themselves in the Hejaz. These provided translations of "subversive" Rumi-language letters found in Arabia and identified new organizations (such as the "Committee for the Defense of Islam in Indonesia and Malaya" or *Comite Pembela Islam Indonesia-Malaya*) that were being set up in an attempt to speed along the independence of an Indonesian nation.[48] Recruitment of the "Jawa" community was said to be high in the Hejaz during this period, and the Dutch kept careful tabs on their subjects there as a result of these suspicions.[49] Though the onset of the Second World War disrupted many of these forces, ultimately some of these people and parties did play a part in the decolonization of the Indies.

British Surveillance: The Later Designs of an Imperial Project

If the high tide of the Netherland's surveillance over the pilgrimage to Mecca began in the second half of the nineteenth century, then the British became the most important players in this transnational enterprise in the twentieth century. British reportage on the parameters of the pilgrimage was active well before then; a succession of travelers beginning in the 1800s but stretching into the 1900s saw to this with a steady stream of writing, some of which became part of the fiber of British public consciousness of the Hajj. Burton, Palgrave, Doughty, and even Philby would all come into this category.[50] Other early twentieth-century Englishmen can give us an idea of the huge range of topics that interested the British as often-allied subjects to the pilgrimage, all part and parcel of reportage on Arabia at this time. These topics ranged from meteorology, health, geology, pearl and mother of pearl-production, and date farming to missionization, telegrams, and the slave trade, to name just a few.[51] All were viewed as part of a bundle of issues that made the Arabian Peninsula "worth knowing," alongside the vast steam of Muslim bodies that made the Holy Cities centers of transnational movement. But extant accounts always stressed this proverbial stream of humanity somewhere, as if acknowledging that this was the lifeblood of the region. In his detailed descriptions of the Malay Hajj in the first third of the twentieth century, the British traveler Eldon Rutter observed dryly that "Malays die quickly if they are over-crowded," as if talking about so many hamsters put into a terrarium.[52] The origins of British surveillance of the Hajj contain much of this sort of writing, both in the Hejaz among authors and officials of Rutter's ilk, and also in Southeast Asia itself, where colonial ports such as Singapore and Penang became vast feeding-centers for Malay pilgrims.

Many British considerations on the viability of the Hajj had to do with very practical concerns, such as the effect of the pilgrimage on the morale of England's subject populations in Asia, an issue especially important during and around the First World War. Just before the war,

Malays were coming in record numbers to perform the pilgrimage, with this community rising to 10 to 15 percent of all pilgrims present in the Hejaz at the outbreak of hostilities.[53] The British Consul in Batavia, for example, wrote to his superiors just after the conflict ended that one of the best ways of countering German influence among the Arab community in the Indies would be to resume the Hajj in 1918. He even suggested combining religious and economic concerns by allowing British Muslim Southeast Asian subjects to carry sugar on their ships to Port Said, which could then be transshipped to Britain with the pilgrim ships afterward returning back to Asia with other goods on board.[54] The head of the army in Singapore was in some agreement but cautioned:

> I personally would much like to see an opportunity given to Muhammadans in the Malay Peninsula to participate in any pilgrimage from the NEI if it were possible. Local Muhammadan feeling, while sound in most places, needs a slight fillip in some localities where the shadow of suppressed disaffection due to ignorance still lurks … the great majority of Muhammadans of all races in the Malay peninsula are thoroughly loyal, and any efforts to obtain special facilities for the resumption of pilgrimage which might be made on their behalf would, I feel sure, be appreciated and regarded as a recognition for loyalty … But it is wholly out of the question to use a British ship for this purpose."[55]

A subsequent memorandum on this topic asked policy planners what they hoped to get out of this scheme from both political and pecuniary points of view.[56] Yet it was clear that the British had an eye on the "big picture" of the Hajj, and that reimposing an official presence in the Hejaz was important as the war drew to a close. This was certainly in part to keep an eye on Britain's political rivals. The British consul in Cairo wrote to London that the French, Italians, and Dutch were all in the process of reappointing consuls and legates to Jeddah, in some cases under false pretenses. The new Dutch envoy claimed that he was in Jeddah because of his health, "in which connection it may be stated with certainty that he is the first European who has found a health resort in the notoriously bad climate of Jeddah. It is clear, now that the pilgrims have all left, that he is being kept at Jeddah by his government for other purposes other than pilgrimage questions, and in order that he may act as Dutch representative, and report on the political situation."[57]

In the interwar years, the British continued to surveil the Southeast Asian Hajj in the Hejaz through a number of different indices. One of the most important was financial: London wanted to know exactly how much the Hajj cost for different Muslim communities globally, and what this meant for them, and how many people could afford to actually make the trip. Copies of Meccan newspapers such as the daily *Umm al-Qura* were therefore circulated between different branches of the British government when issues contained data of this kind; a clipping preserved in the India Office Library of one issue from November 1926 includes a small section earmarked specifically for Javanese pilgrims.[58] Translations were also made from the Arabic for the official Hejazi tariffs on the pilgrimage for any given year. Quarantine dues, inspection committee fees, portage rates, house rental prices, municipality dues, gratuities for the mutawwifs, water charges, camel hire, and tent costs all were listed. So, the British had a clear idea of how much pilgrims were expected to pay and at what points along their journeys.[59] London also kept very accurate statistics not only on its own Southeast Asian Hajj shipping from Singapore and Penang and outlying ports but also from the rest of the region and the entire Muslim world.[60] These statistics passed from the British envoy in Jeddah to his superiors in London, and templates were also drawn up to organize annual additions to longitudinal data. This involved writings on prices and shipping, customs, religious policies, and shaykhs, as well as pilgrim data on every imaginable group and subgroup of people, including annual runs of Hajjis from such seemingly innocuous and out-of-the-way places as Sarawak in British Borneo.[61] One scholar has calculated that even though Malays were going in smaller and smaller absolute numbers that Indonesians or Indians, as a percentage of available Muslim travelers inside the colony, they were actually performing Hajj in very high proportions. So, the collection of all of this data was deemed crucial by the colonial state.[62]

Not all places and themes were equal in the official British mindset of pilgrimage surveillance, however. Because London had a global political presence, certain political issues were treated as more potentially dangerous than others. The growth of Communism as an ideology on the world stage was one of these, as it bled into Hajj surveillance. Tsarist Russia and, after 1917, the Soviet Union were seen as hotbeds of such ideological contagion, so much so that when Soviet pilgrimage parties came to the Hejaz, they were closely watched, such as one cohort of nearly ten thousand pilgrims who came from Odessa in 1927.[63] The reasons for surveillance here were clear, according to the Acting British Consul in Jeddah in his report to London:

> The advantages of Mecca and the Hejaz generally as a headquarters for anti-European agitation in the Near and Far East need hardly be dwelt upon ... In Mecca malcontents from Morocco can meet refugees from Syria, and agitators from India can compare grievances with their sympathizers from Java and Sumatra ... The atmosphere of the Hejaz is different from that of ordinary countries. The air does not blow freely here. There are no free newspapers, no easy means of communication with the outer world; the Hejaz is an enclosed space in which prejudice (reigns) ... The climate of the Hejaz foster men on whose sharpened nerves the suggestion of Islam in danger from the West would produce jarring chords with immeasurable reverberations ... There is, then, excellent ground here for suggestive propaganda. The question is what use the present Soviet Agency have made of it.[64]

These links between Communism and Islam were not wholly imagined. In 1920, the PKI (or Communist Party of Indonesia) was formed, and it was quickly criminalized by an anxious Dutch colonial state in Batavia. This did not escape the notice of the British in the Hejaz, who exchanged secret letters with their own consul in Java as to the nature of the links between local communist cells there and pilgrim ships arriving in Jeddah. Several of these letters survive and they paint an entrancing picture of surveillance in action—missives shuttling back and forth across the length and breadth of the Indian Ocean, tracking the confluence of a decades-old ideology and a thousand-year-old religion, entwined as one as a threat to European rule.[65]

Secret
No. 100.

British Consulate-General,
Batavia.
July 25th, 1927.

Sir,

I have the honour to enclose herewith a translation of a letter, copy of which has been kindly furnished to me, under the pledge of secrecy, by the Chief of the Political Intelligence Service of the Dutch East Indian Government.

2. Though it is not so stated, the letter is evidently from the Dutch Consul at Jeddah, and is no less evidently addressed to the Governor-General of the Netherlands East Indies. It reports the activities of two communist organizations recently formed at Mecca for the purpose of conducting propaganda among the pilgrims arriving there from this country. As you will observe, six of the leading members of these organizations were arrested by King Ibn Saud. They have since been dispatched to Dutch India, where they have been taken into custody by the authorities.

3. In my confidential dispatch No. 66 of May 17th last, I had the honour to report the departure from Java for Mecca of Haji Agoes Salim, one of the leaders of the local Mahomedan association known as Sarikat Islam. I have received from the Chief of the Political Intelligence Service here a note (translation enclosed), stating that this man is reported to have been in contact with the Soviet representatives in the Hedjaz. His return to Java is expected before the month of October next. The Chief of the Intelligence Service will be grateful for any information which we ourselves be able to supply to him regarding the doings of H. A. Salim in Arabia. I am communicating this request to His Majesty's Consul at Jeddah, to whom also I am forwarding a copy of the present dispatch.

I have the honor to be,
With the highest respect,
Sir,
Your most obedient,
Humble Servant,

Copies to: -

His Majesty's High Commissioner in Egypt.
His Excellency The Governor of the Straits Settlements, Singapore.
The Secretary to the Government of India in the Foreign and Political Department, Simla.
His Majesty's Minister at The Hague.
His Majesty's Consul at Jeddah.
The Director of the Political Intelligence Bureau, Singapore.

Source: 1927 Letter, Sarekat Islam and Communism, British Consul Batavia to FO, July 25, 1927, #100, Secret, PRO, London.

Confluence—real or imagined—was one thing, but being able to act on this union was quite another. Ships were vital to this calculation in the Southeast Asian case because pilgrims relied on European vessels and would always be at the mercy of Western surveillance. In 1938, however, it came to the attention of the British security apparatus in the Hejaz that pro-independence groups in the Dutch Indies were trying to fund and build their own large-scale shipping lines, the express purpose of which was to shuttle Indies Hajjis on indigenous-owned ships. The vernacular press in the Indies announced that this was being done under the auspices of the Muslim political party Muhammadiyah, with the object of bringing the pilgrim traffic to Arabia wholly into native hands. While the British and the Dutch ran the numbers on capital accumulation and profit ratios, other Malay-language newspapers in the Indies added more details to the story.[66] The *Pewarta Deli* in Sumatra, for example, stressed that the prime movers behind the idea were receiving help from Germans, who were trying to get the initial scheme off the ground using a chartered German vessel. Another newspaper said that there was a growing Indonesian tendency to regard Italy as the protector of Islam—with Italian colonial stations stretched along the Red Sea's southern littoral, this idea was taken very seriously—and that negotiations had begun with Japanese interests as well.[67] This entire story eventually came to naught because of a combination of European suppression and the onset of the instabilities of the Second World War. Yet it is not hard to see where the fears of this endeavor potentially succeeding were leading, or which bedfellows London and The Hague imagined Muhammadiayah would wake up within their attempt to make the Indies Hajj "indigenous." The fact that German, Italian, or Japanese ships were no more indigenous than British or Dutch ones meant little in the end. What was at stake was control over the movement of human beings and what these humans had access to over the course of their long voyages to the Hejaz, both from materialist and intellectual points of view.

The Second World War signaled the beginning of the end to the colonial supervision of the pilgrimage to Mecca, though this took longer than the six years of the war itself. A "new order" of the Hajj did not appear until well after the hostilities were over in 1945. When the war began, the numbers of Southeast Asian Hajjis who actually made it to Mecca or back to Southeast Asia from the Holy Cities dropped precipitously. The 1940 British pilgrimage report suggests that only fifty-four Hajjis made it to Mecca from Southeast Asia that year, though these were mixed between Malay pilgrims from the peninsula; Javanese, Sumatrans, and Indies Arabs from the Dutch territories; and a few itinerant "Jawa" who made the trek from Aden or Cairo, having already been in the Middle East when the war had begun.[68] Once the hostilities started, the real battle in terms of colonialism and surveillance was a propaganda one, as both the Allies and the Axis tried to "sell" Muslims under their control that their own brand of rule would be best for Muslim interests. For the British, this involved accommodating the Saudi government in the Hejaz far more than had previously been the case, including over the matter of information control, which had been a hallmark of British action in the Red Sea for many decades. They did so through film censorship, but also brochures, such as one document that laid out all of the stations of the Hajj in a large pictographic image, replete with Muslim travelers' sketches and descriptions of Hajj rites from the ages, all in flowing Arabic script.[69] The brochure was presented to those who were identified as "notable Hajjis" as a gift of the British government, in a goodwill gesture aimed at showing London's continuing tolerance of the pilgrimage as a vital institution of the Muslim faith.[70] When it came down to requisitioning ships to carry Asian pilgrims who wanted to get to the Hejaz in the closing months of the war, however, London remained firm. The Admiralty expressed understanding at the desire of His Majesty's Asian subjects wishing to perform the Hajj, but no ships were to be made available for these purposes until after the fighting was over.[71] War was war, after all, and commerce was commerce. Religion and its many exigencies was another matter entirely.

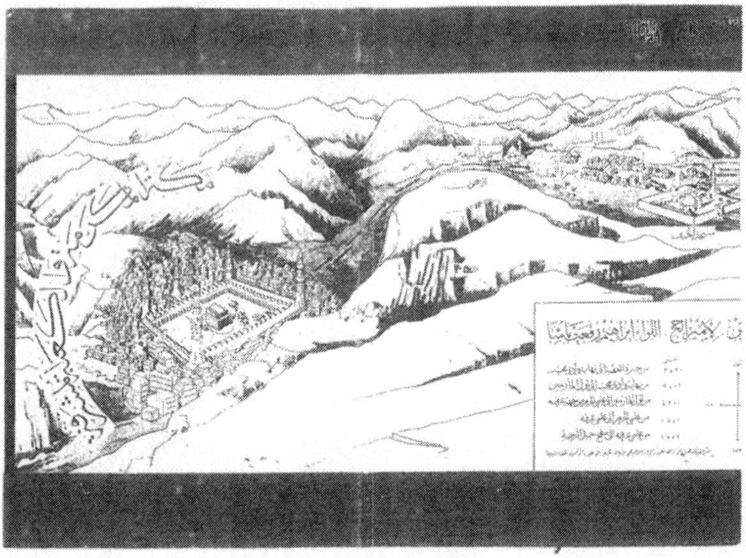

Credit: Fragment of a Large Map in CO/732/87/18; PRO, Kew, London

Conclusion

One of the many ways in which the West kept tabs on Islam as a "knowable" global phenomenon in the late nineteenth and early twentieth centuries was through the maritime surveillance of the Indian Ocean. Few aspects of surveillance were deemed as important as the collective European vision that was cast on the radials of the Hajj at this time. Though much of the annual pilgrimage to Mecca was seen as relatively harmless, the political implications of a growing Pan-Islamic movement lent a dangerous tinge to some of these proceedings as well. Paris, London, and The Hague—among other European capitals—equated the Hajj with a potential of dangerous rebelliousness against the status quo, alongside a raft of other negative conceptions that became stock Western images of this huge transnational flow of human beings.[72] In this, the Hajj was part and parcel of a larger civilizational discourse that was being constructed, one that took in places of Islamic learning such as the Al-Azhar in Cairo, Mecca, and Medina as nodes of potential subversion, as well as sites of religious authority and dissemination.[73] In this worldview, prevalent among policymakers and much of the

European general public, the sacred and the profane mixed in the Hajj, and necessitated close supervision of this annual religious exercise by the secular regimes of the Western world.

The surveillance extended over the pilgrimage to Mecca was part of larger structures of European vision that were being enacted in large parts of the world at this time. Much of this process ultimately had to do with the mechanics of criminalization, as "acceptable" forms of behavior were legislated in colonial cities for much of the planet's population. In Asia, this took on many forms: from sanitary surveillance in British colonial Singapore to the birth of policing regimes in Dutch, Spanish, and French Southeast Asia, or what is now Indonesia, the Philippines and Cambodia, and Vietnam.[74] In China, split between a variety of Western powers, the forms of criminalization and surveillance could be diffuse, often adjoining and abutting different forms of European authority all within the confines of a single city, such as cosmopolitan Shanghai.[75] In India, where only one foreign power was master by the mid-nineteenth century, regimes of control were more uniform, encompassing the acts and behaviors of "dacoits" (bandits), "thugi" (thugs), and so-called "dangerous castes," all into one system of supervision ultimately ruled from London.[76] What all of these modes of criminalization had in common was the aim of knowledge, legality, and coercion working hand in hand toward more complete systems of European control. The global Hajj became part of this larger paradigm in the late nineteenth and early twentieth centuries. Pilgrim traffic from Southeast Asia—almost exclusively confined to ships and passing along Western-dominated sea-lanes—was subsumed into these structures of long-distance surveillance and carefully-channeled movement. Part of this disciplinary whole, the pilgrimage to Mecca was a vital component of these ongoing dynamics.

Endnotes

* An earlier version of this essay has appeared as Chapter 8 in my book, *The Longest Journey: Southeast Asians and the Pilgrimage to Mecca* (New York: Oxford University Press, 2013), and appears here with permission.

1. See Christopher Dandeker, *Surveillance, Power and Modernity: Bureaucracy and Discipline From 1700 to the Present Day* (New York: St. Martin's Press, 1990), p. 32. His treatment of this topic is an elaboration and reinvigoration of Anthony Giddens' classic critique of paternalistic regimes.
2. Barry Hindess, *Discourses of Power: From Hobbes to Foucault* (London: Blackwell, 1996).
3. See for example M. Saddik, "Voyage a La Mecque" *Bulletin de la Societe Khediviale de Geographie du Caire*, 1, 1881: 5–40; S. Soubhy, "Pelerinage a La Mecque et a Medine" *Bulletin de la Societe Khediviale de Geographie du Carie*, 4, 1894: 45–88; 105–144.
4. Muhamed Bel Khodja, *Le Pelerinage de la Mecque* (Tunis, 1906); Zadeh H. Kazem, "Relation d'un Pelerinage a La Mecque" *Revue du Monde Musulman*, 19, 1912: 144–227.
5. See A. d'Avril, *L'Arabie Contemporaine, avec la Description du Pelerinage a La Mecque* (Paris, 1868); G. Cordier, "Un Voyage a La Mecque" *Revue du Monde Musulman*, 14, 1911: 510–513; E. Dinet and S. Baamer, *Le Pelerinage a la Maison Sacree d'Allah* (Paris, 1930); M. Gaudefroy-Demombynes, "Notes sur la Mekke at Medine" *Revue de l'Histoire des Religions*, 77, 1918: 316–344; D. Kimon *La Pathologie de l'Islam et les Moyens de le Detruire. Etude Psychologie* (Paris, 1897); B. Schnepp, *Le Pelerinage de La Mecque* (Paris, 1865).
6. From the inscriptions in the front covers of some of these books still kept in the Bibliotheque National, for example, or in the Bibliotheque SciencesPo in Paris, we can see the linkages between a number of these people (such as one book given to the French Ambassador to Syria by a Muslim Lebanese doctor, who had written on what he termed the "psychology of the Hajj"). Modern French scholars such as Laurence Husson have categorized and explicated some of these trends, including how French scholars imagined the Southeast Asian Hajj over time. See Laurence Husson, "Les Indonesiens en Arabie Saoudite pour la foi et le travail" *Revue Europeene des Migrations Internationales* 13, 1, 1997: 125–147.
7. R. Bayly Winder, *Saudi Arabia in the Nineteenth Century* (New York: St. Martin's Press, 1965).
8. Thomas Marston, *Britain's Imperial Role in the Red Sea Area, 1800-1878* (Hamden: Shoestring Press, 1961), p. 64 passim.
9. Priya Satia, *Spies in Arabia: The Great War and the Cultural Foundations of Britain's Covert Empire in the Middle East* (Oxford: Oxford University Press, 2008), p. 23 passim, p. 59 passim, p. 165 passim.
10. For the relevant diary entries, see KIT, Daniel van der Meulen Dairies, Dagboek, January 11, 1926 to June 13, 1927 (pp. 38–39); Dagboek,

Tweede Z.W. Arabie Exploratie, February 2, 1939 to May 21, 1939 (p. 1); Dagboek, Makassar to Jeddah, January 4, 1941 to May 7, 1941 (p. 1–6); Dagboek, Jeddah, February 4, 1942 to January 11, 1942 (p. 15); Dagboek, Saudi Arabia, December 15, 1944 to February 14, 1945 (p. 1); Dagboek, Arabia Reis met Bram Drewes, January 1, 1952 to March 31, 1952 (p. 2).

11. For van der Meulen's relevant publications on the Hajj, see "De Bedevaart naar Mekka en haar beteekenis voor Nederlands-Indie" *Zendingstijdschrift De Opwekker*, 86, 1, 1942: 474–486; "The Mecca Pilgrimage and its Importance to the Netherlands Indies" *The Moslem World*, 31, 1941: 48–60; "The Revival of the Pilgrimage to Mecca" *Niewsblad voor de Residentien Palembang, Djambi, en Banka*, September 14, 1937; "The Revival of the Pilgrimage to Mecca" *De Telegraaf*, October 2, 1937; "The Return of the Mecca Pilgrims to the Dutch East Indies" *Deli Courant*, March 25, 1938; "The Pilgrimage to Mecca" *Palembanger*, June 18, 1938; "The Mecca Pilgrimage" *Palembanger*, 1938 (n.d.—clipping).
12. The Italian archive at the *Istituto Italiano per l'Africa e l'Oriente* in Rome is a great center for this kind of period scholarship written in Italian. To see several period maps produced in 1885 and 1911, respectively, see F. Garbolino, "Carta del Mar Rosson e Teatro di Guerra in Africa" (Firenze: Benelli e. Co, 1885); Istituto Geografico Militare "Mar Rosso e Costa Orientale dell'Africa (foglio C2)" (Firenze: IGM, 1885); Istituo Geografico de Agostini, "Mar Rosson e Possedimenti Italiani in Africa" (Novarra: De Agostini, 1911). For textual sources, see G.B. Licata, "L'Italia nel Mar Rosson" *Boll. Sez. Fiorentina della Soc. Africana d'Italia*, March 1885, p. 5; A. Mori, "Le Nostre Colonie del Mar Rosso Giudicate dalla Stanley" *Boll. Sez. Fiorentina della Soc. Africana d'Italia*, May 1886, p. 84.
13. G. Mangano, "Relazione Riassuntiva di un Viaggio di Studi nell 'A.O., India, Ceylon, Malacca, e Giava" *L'Agricoltura Coloniale* 4/5, 1909, pp. 272 and 313; A. Mori, "Il Problema Coloniale nei suoi Rapporti con le Scienze Geografische e l'Attivita dell'Istituto Coloniale Italiano nei Primi Quattor Anni di Vita" *Congresso Geografico Italiano Palermo 1910* (Palermo, 1911), p. 478; R. Almagia, "Relazione dull'Esplorazione Geografica delle Nostre Colonie in Rapporto allo Sfruttamento delle Loro Risorse Economische" *Atti Convegno Nazionale per il Dopoguerra delle Nostre Colonie* (Roma, 1919), pp. 350–364.; F. Santagata "La Colonia Eritrea nel Mar Rosso Davanti all'Abissinia" *Libreria Internazionale Treves di Leo Lupi*, Napoli, 1935, p. 229; V. Zoppi, "Civilita Fascista" *Il Mar Rosso*, 1935, p. 321; A. Pirzio Biroli, "Il Mar Rosson e l'A. O. I." *Rivista delle Coloniale Italiane*, 1936, p. 1426.
14. See, for example, the letters of G. Bianchi to M. Camperio (6-6/1879); G. Rohlfs to M. Camperio (3-30/1880); G. Casati to M. Camperio (8-30/1883

and 9-5/1883) and M. Camperio to G. Casati (4-15/1889), all reproduced in Cesira Filesi, *L'Archivio del Museo Africano in Roma: Presentazione e Inventario dei Documento* (Roma: Istituto Italiano per l'Africa e l'Oriente, 2001).

15. D. Odirizzi, "Studio Storico della Provincia Arabica dello Jemen e Sulle Relzioni Etniche con l'Eritrea e l'Etiopia" *Atti Congresso Coloniale Italiano di Asmara* (Asmara: 1905), p. 323.
16. D. Odirizzo, *Note Storiche sulla Religone Mussulmana e Sulle Divisioni dell'Islam in Eritrea* (Asmara: Tip. Fioretti, 1916); E. Cerulli, "Note sul Movimento Musulmano in Somalia" *Riv. Di Studi Orientali* 10, 1, 1923, p. 1; E. Massara, "Islamismo e Confraternite in Eirtrea: I Morgani" *L'Ilustraz. Colon.* 8, 1921, p. 306.; R. Cantalupo, *L'Italia Musulmana* (Roma: Casa Editrice Italiana d'Oltremare, 1929).
17. N. Puccioni, "L'esplorazione Antropologica delle Colonie Italiane" *Atti I Congr. Studi Colon.*, Vol III. (Firenze, 1931), p. 309; R. Corso, "Per l'Etnografica delle Nostre Colonie" *La Rivista d'Orientale* 1934, p. 73.
18. Again, see P. Vigoni to G. Casati (8-2/1891); U. Ferrandi to P. Vigoni (3-24/1894); P. Vigoni to G. Casati (2–1/1895); G. Carerj to G. Casati (3-21/1895) and E. Bencetti to G. Casati (6-1/1895), all reproduced in Cesira Filesi, *L'Archivio del Museo Africano in Roma: Presentazione e Inventario dei Documento* (Roma: Istituto Italiano per l'Africa e l'Oriente, 2001).
19. See Puuhena, "Historiografi Haji," p. 413.
20. ANRI, Resident Besoeki to Gov Gen NEI, February 23, 1856, #541, in K23. Daftar Arsip Besuki (1819–1913). This and all of the following ANRI cites are from the Gewestilijke Stukken Archive.
21. ANRI, #4369 Semarang: Sea Passes enclosed in #4362–4370 "Stukken Inzake de Bedevaart naar Mekka" in K10. Semarang, (1816–1880)
22. ANRI, Regent Tegal to Resident, Tegal, June 5, 1857, #571 in K8. Tegal (1790–1872).
23. ANRI, Resident Tegal, Opgave der Uitgereiktepassen voor de Bedevaart naar Mekka voor 1856, January 2, 1857 in K8 Tegal (1790–1872).
24. ANRI, "*Rapporten Dari Perkara Hadji Hadja njang Minta Pas dan njang Baru Datang dari Mekka, 1860/61/62/63/64*" in same.
25. ANRI, "Rapport, Residentie Tagal, #27" in "Laporan Pergi dan Pulang Haji," #196/5, in K8. Tegal (1790–1872).
26. ANRI, Regent of Tegal to Resident of Tegal, June 5, 1857, #571 in K8 Tegal (1790–1872).
27. ANRI, May 18, 1914, Resident Batavia to Assistant Resident Tangerrang, in "Stukken Betreffende Mohammedanaansche Zaken, o.a. Mekkagangers, 1913–1914" in K2. Tangerrang.

28. See the documents around this newspaper clipping in ARA, "Arabie: Onlusten te Djeddah" *Handelsblad*, December 31, 1878, in "A" Dossiers, #74 "Correspondentie over woelingen, slavenhandel en slavernij in de Hedjaz 1872–1936."
29. ARA, W.H. Read, Dutch consul, to Count de Bylandt, Dutch Minister, March 19, 1881, in same.
30. ARA, UK Gov. Weld, Singapore, to Gov Gen NEI, May 13, 1881, Confidential, in same. See Michael Laffan, "A Watchful Eye: The Meccan Plot of 1881 and Changing Dutch Perceptions of Islam in Indonesia" *Archipel* 63, 2002: 79–108
31. See Eric Tagliacozzo, *Secret Trades, Porous Borders*, pp. 149–151; 171–175
32. See "De Bedevaart naar Mekka, 1919/10" *Indische Gids*, 1910, 2, pp. 1637–1638. For a larger view on Islam, danger, and the pilgrimage at this time, see Michael Low, "Empire and the Hajj: Pilgrims, Plagues, and Pan-Islam Under British Surveillance, 1965-1908" *International Journal of Middle Eastern Studies*, 40, 2008: 269–290.
33. See *Koloniaal Verslag* 1878, pp. 120–121; 1881, pp. 104–105; 1884, pp. 102–103.
34. *Consulaat-General der Nederlanden te Singapore, Verslag*, 1872 (p. 354); 1874 (p. 544); 1875 (p. 490). See also *Consulaat-General der Nederlanden te Penang, Jaarlijksh Verslag*, 1904 (p. 971).
35. The number of *mailrapporten* dealing with the Hajj and "dissident Islam" and surveillance is too large to list in full here, but the most important files that I have made us of include: MR 1872, #820+; MR 1878, #474; MR 1879, #668+; MR 1881, #259+; #563+, 709+, #839+; #860; #1107; #1139+; MR 1883, #252+; #1075+; #1173; MR 1885, #638+.
36. See ANRI, Residentie Bangka, Politiek Verslag 1872, and Algemeen Verslag, 1890; Residentie Billiton, Algemeen Verslagen 1874, 1880, 1885, and 1890; Residentie Lampong, Politiek Verslagen 1864, 1867, 1886, 1887, 1888, and 1890; Residentie Ternate, Diverse Stukken 1892; Residentie Riouw, Administratief Verslagen 1867–1874, and Residentie West Borneo, Algemeen Verslagen, 1875, 1886, and 1891 for details. Residentie Borneo Zuidoost, Algemeen Verslag 1889/1890 has a particularly good table on local Hajjis en route to Mecca for the entire decade of the 1880s from southeastern Borneo.
37. The Political Reports from the Outer Islands (*Politieke Verslagen van de Butengewesten*) give us a huge arc of reporting on Dutch visions of Islam across the outer edges of the Indies archipelago in the *late* nineteenth and early twentieth centuries. For the northern half of Sumatra, we have reporting on the ongoing insurgency from Aceh; armed "Muslim gangs"

in Tapanuli; the spillage of Muslim violence into the plantation districts of East Sumatra; and "troublemaking" of Muslim chiefs such as Djandi Radja, whose attacks solicited the response that "our prestige demands that we make an end to this matter." See Gov. Atjeh G. Van Daalen to Buitenzorg, 4 June 1907, Telegram #608; "Extract uit het dagboek van het Controleur van Toba, 10 June 1906;" Resident, Sumatra OK to Buitenzorg, 3 December 1904, Telegram #117; and Resident Tapanoeli to Gov Sumatra WK, 9 November 1901, #7502. In the southern half of Sumatra, the reporting is often similar: the necessitated redrawing of political contracts with the sultan of Riau; the need to strengthen the colonial military apparatus in Jambi and Palembang because of a Muslim rebellion in the highlands; and attacks and general hatred against the Dutch by the local population in Lampung, reported as "*slechte geest onder de bevolking van afdeeling. Depoetih, en tegenwerking van het bestuur.*" See "Verslag van den aan den Sultan van Lingga, Riouw, en Onderhoorigheden Verleende Audentie, 9 Mei 1903;" Gov Gen NEI to Min Kol, 16 February 1901, #327/3; "Kort verslag omtrent den stand van zaken en het personeel in de residentie Palembang over de maand Januari 1915, #2194/23;" "Residentie Lampongsche Districten, Mailrapport 1906/7." Finally, for Borneo and Eastern Indonesia, there is reporting on murders in the vicinity of Sambas in West Borneo; more murder upstream from the Dutch controleur in Berau, East Borneo; attempts by the Boni Sultanate in Sulawesi to exercise sway over non-Muslim upland populations, and cross-border troubles (including more murders) between Ternate and its maritime Muslim neighbor of Mindanao in the southern Philippines. See "Kort verslag der Residentie Westerafdeling van Borneo over de maand November 1899;" Resident ZO Borneo to Gov Gen NEI, 26 May 1899, #5278/1; "Kortverslag van het Gouvernement Celebes en Onderhoorigheden over de maand Juni 1898;" and "Extract out de rapporten van den Commt. Van H.M. vaartuig "Edi," 15 August tot 28 September 1898."

38. *Memories van Overgaven* from West, Central, and East Java tell us of the context of Muslim "fanatacism" as revealed in Banten; of the situation of Indies Arabs in urban places like Semarang, Pekalongan, and Tegal; and the growth of Sarekat Islam alongside the nascent nationalist parties, among other things. See West-Java, MMK 1, Hardeman, J.A. (resident) Memorie van Overgave (1906); Midden-Java, MMK 40, Gulik, P. J. van (Gouverneur) Memorie van Overgave (1931); Oost-Java, MMK 83, Hardeman, W. Ch. (Gouverneur) Memorie van Overgave (1931). In Sumatra, we can glean information on the ostensible connections between

Islamic disturbances against the state and communist uprisings in places such as Idi on the east coast of Aceh; on the weaponry of jihadists on the west coast of Sumatra; and on the large differences in Muslim "dissent" between the Jambi uplands and the adjacent lowlands. For these subjects, see Sumatra (Atjeh), MMK 158, Goehart, O.M. (Gouverneur) Memorie van Overgave (1929), p. 2; Sumatra Westkust, MMK 163, Heckler, F.A. (Gouverneur) Memorie van Overgave (1910, p. 6); and Sumatra, Jambi, MMK 216, Helfrich, O.L. (Resident) Memorie van Overgave (1908), pp. 7–8. In Western Borneo, residents reported on the conversion practices of Dayaks to Islam, and in Southeastern Borneo on how many indigenes can actually speak and use Arabic, as well as the importation (again) of Sarekat Islam after 1911; see Borneo West, MMK 261, Vogel, H. de (Resident) Memorie van Overgave (1918), pp. 18–19; and Borneo Zuidoost, MMK 271; Rickmans, L.J.F (Resident) Memorie van Overgave (1916), p. 58. Finally, in Eastern Indonesia, material can be gleaned on Islamization in the highlands of Sulawesi and on the nature of violence —Muslim and otherwise—in outstretched residencies like Ternate. See Celebes, MMK 281, Swart, H.N.A. (Gouverneur) Memorie van Overgave (1908), p. 21; and Ternate, MMK 329, Sandick, L.W.H. can (Gouverneur) Memorie van Overgave (1926), p. 9.

39. Bijblad, August 19, 1902, #5741; Staatsblad, January 17, 1923, #15.
40. Bijblad, June 15, 1928, #11689; Bijblad, July 27, 1909, #7130.
41. Staatsblad, April 29, 1906, #236; Staatsblad, October 25, 1912, #531.
42. Bijblad, May 16, 1911, #7469; Staatsblad, November 18, 1932, #554.
43. Staatsblad, January 26, 1931, #44.
44. ARA, Djeddah Archives, 1.2.6 Politieke Aangelegenheden, Fiche #175: Dutch Vice Consul (Widjodjoatmodjo) to MvBZ, August 22, 1933, #1183 Secret; Fiche #193: Minister of Foreign Affairs, Mecca, to Dutch Consul, Jeddah, February 15, 1938; Fiche #192: Dutch Consul to GGNEI, May 10, 1940, #619/B-10. For a good overview of the consuls, see Sarah Searight, "Jiddah in the Nineteenth Century: The Role of European Consuls" in Janet Starkey, ed., *People of the Red Sea* (Oxford: British Archeological Reports Series, 2005), pp. 109–116.
45. See Putuhena, "Historiografi Haji," pp. 419–422.
46. ARA, Djeddah Archives, 1.2.6 Politieke Aangelegenheden, Fiche #182: Dutch Consul to MvBZ, February 18, 1932, #10/P42; Fiche #197: Dutch Consul, Jeddah, to MvBZ, January 7, 1941, #9/P-8.
47. ARA, Djeddah Archives, 1.2.6 Politieke Aangelegenheden, Fiche #188: Dutch Consul to MvBZ, June 8, 1937, #497/P-105; Fiche #200: Dutch Consul, Jeddah to MvBZ, April 27, 1929, #695/98.

48. ARA, Djeddah Archives, 1.2.6 Politieke Aangelegenheden, Fiche #199: Dutch Consul, Jeddah to GGNEI, April 26, 1931, #511/H; Fiche #201: Adviser for Internal Affairs, NEI, to GGNEI, August 14, 1939, #1048/K-1.
49. ARA, Djeddah Archives, 1.2.6 Politieke Aangelegenheden, Fiche #202: Dutch Consul, Bombay to Dutch Consul, Jeddah, November 22, 1944, #2754; Fiche #203: "Memorandum on Terms of Employment." For context, see Tom van den Berge, "Indonesiers en het door hen Gevolgde Onderwijs in Mekka, 1926–1940" *Jambatan* 7, 1, 1989: 5–22.
50. Robin Bidwell, *Travellers in Arabia* (London: Hamlyn, 1976).
51. J. G. Lorimer, *Gazeteer of the Persian Gulf, Oman, and Central Arabia* (Calcutta: Government Printers, 1915).
52. See Eldon Rutter, *The Holy Cities of Arabia* (Vols I) (London: G.P. Putnam's Sons, 1928), p. 14.
53. Mary McDonnell, "Conduct of the Hajj," pp. 626–628.
54. UK Consul, Batavia to Gov't Secretary, India, May 15, 1918, #79, in IOL/L/PS/11/137 P 3174.
55. IOL, Gen. Commanding Troops, Singapore, to UK Consul, Batavia, July 2, 1918, #12920 in IOL/L/PS/11/137 P 3174.
56. Memorandum of Observations on Batavia Despatch #79, in IOL/L/PS/11/137 P 3174.
57. PRO, UK Consul, Cairo, to Arthur James Balfour, London, January 28, 1917, #18, in FO 141/668/1/
58. IOR, Extract of *Ummal-Qura*, #100, November 12, 1926, #100, preserved in Gov't Secretary India to Gov't of India Dept. of Education, Health and Lands, December 30, 1926, #1840, in IOR/R/15/2/1439)
59. IOR, "Translation of the Official Tariff Published by the Hejazi Government: Dues and Transport Charges Imposed on Pilgrims for the Pilgrimage Season of AH 1351 (1933)" in IOR/L/PJ/8/783/Coll 125/7B.
60. IOR, UK Consul, Jeddah, to FO, August 16, 1938, #1800/402/203 in IOR/L/PJ/7/789.
61. IOR, UK Consul, Jeddah, to FO, August 9, 1937, #E4922/201/25.
62. See McDonell, "Conduct of the Hajj," pp. 631–635. McDonnell postulates that in the first half of the twentieth century Malays made up some 7 percent of total Hajjis, as compared to 15 percent from the Dutch Indies and 20 percent from British India. But as a percentage of available Muslims to go, she says that Malays actually were leaving in ten times the numbers of the other two groups.
63. FO, UK Consul-General Batavia to FO, March 29 1927, E 1793/323/91 Secret in FO 371/12248, "Records of the Hajj."

64. FO, Acting British Agent to FO, March 18, 1927 in FO 371/12248 "Records of the Hajj."
65. See for example the two fascinating letters enclosed in British Consul, Batavia to FO, July 25, 1927, #100 Secret, in "Records of the Hajj."
66. IOR, UK Consul, Batavia, to FO, March 14, 1938, #75E in IOR/R/20/B/1454.
67. IOR, UK Consul, Batavia, to FO, September 21, 1938, #260E, in IOR/R/20/B/1454.
68. IOR, Pilgrimage Report for 1940 in UK Consul, Jeddah, to FO, September 28, 1940, #71 Confidential, in IOR/L/PJ/8/755 Coll. 125/1A.
69. IOR, Under-Secretary of India to UK Consul, Cairo, January 22, 1941, #F.9 (34)-G/40; FO to R.T. Peel, Esq., 3 September 1936, P/3041/128/150 Confidential; British Board of Film Censors to India Office, July 9,1936, all in IOR/L/PJ/8/127/Pt. Vi.
70. PRO, Ministry of Information, London to CO, April 10, 1943, #FP 39/12 in CO 732/87/18.
71. PRO, Head of Military Branch I, Minute Sheet Comments, August 3, 1944, P.O. 21240 in Admiralty 1/12119.
72. Syed Muhammad Khairudin Aljunied, "Western Images of Meccan Pilgrims in the Dutch East Indies, 1800–1900" *Sari*, 23 (2005): 105–122.
73. Holger Warnk, "Some Notes on the Malay Speaking Community in Cairo at the Turn of the Nineteenth Century" in Fritz Schulze and Holger Warnk, *Insular Southeast Asia: Linguistic and Cultural Studies in Honour of Bernd Nothofer* (Wiesbaden: Harrassowitz Verlag, 2006): 141–152.
74. See Brenda Yeoh, *Municipal Sanitary Surveillance, Asian Resistance and the Control of the Urban Environment in Colonial Singapore* (Oxford Geography Research paper #47, 1991); and for colonial Indonesia, the Philippines, and Indochina, see the relevant chapters in Vincente Rafael, ed., *Figures of Criminality in Indonesia, the Philippines and Colonial Vietnam* (Ithaca: Southeast Asia Program Publications, 1999).
75. The best extant source for this is Frederic Wakeman, *Policing Shanghai, 1927-1937* (Berkeley: University of California Press, 1995).
76. See for example, Anand Yang, ed., *Crime and Criminality in British India* (Tucson: University of Arizona Press, 1985); for Bengal in particular see Ranjan Chakrabarti, *Authority and Violence in Colonial Bengal: 1800-1860* (Calcutta: Bookland Private Ltd., 1997), and Arun Mukherjee, *Crime and Public Disorder in Colonial Bengal, 1861-1912* (Calcutta: K.P. Bagchi and Co., 1995).

4

Little Men between Big Empires

Muslim Cosmopolitanism in the Age of Imperial Expansion

Seema Alavi

In the late eighteenth century, Muslim reformists responded to the political crisis caused by the establishment of British rule in Northern India by writing religious texts that offered ways of coping with the changing times. These Mughal legatees, trained as Indo-Persian scholar gentlemen, wrote in Persian, Arabic, and the North Indian vernacular, Urdu. The print culture of the early nineteenth century made their Urdu texts easily accessible to people. Their books drew the attention of readers to the Arab tradition as represented in particular in the Koran and the Hadith. They advised them to self-interpret religious scriptures so as to find their own solutions to the political crisis.[1] Influenced by the new reformist learning that streamed in from the Arab world, they too hoped that this normative literature, with its stress on the individual, would unite Muslims globally.

The turn to Arab learning at the end of the eighteenth century was a fallout of the Mughal political crisis and the efforts of its intellectual elites to readjust to British rule. By the mid-nineteenth century, the normative ideals of Urdu reformist literature were cannibalized and used by religious scholars in self-driven ways. This gave a new spin to the Arabicist tradition and made it a far cry from the one encased in the normative texts. The emphasis in the texts on self-interpretation rather than reliance on religious figures of authority gave newfound agency to the individual.

This essay shows that the turn to Arabic, both linguistically and culturally, reflected the coming of age of the multilingual Indo-Persian gentlemen. Many of them, along with their followers, began to migrate away from Hindustan into the northwest frontier region. Here, away from the glare of British India's officials, they strategized on how best to adjust to the loss of Muslim political sovereignty. Others used their intellectual expertise and outreach beyond Hindustan to stretch out their networks from the Indo-Persian Hindustani society to the Arabic-speaking Ottoman world. In the aftermath of 1857, as the British clampdown on them intensified, many escaped to the Ottoman cities: Cairo, Mecca, and Istanbul. They responded to the "official nationalism," that imposed territorially rooted subject identities and borders in British Asia, in unique ways.[2] From their new locations, they used their linguistic expertise and cashed on imperial fault lines to create an intellectual niche for themselves. They produced their mantra for Muslim unity in the interstices of empires. The essay views their efforts to formulate a universalist conduct to unite Muslims across empires as a form of cosmopolitanism.

This cosmopolitanism was partly 'traditional' in that it derived from the Koran precepts and the Hadith (Traditions of the Prophet) prescriptions; it invoked the Islamic principle of consensus to reconcile cultural differences among Muslims; and it positioned itself in the 'Islamicate' centers of Cairo and Istanbul and in the Islamic heartland of Mecca. It built on an Ottoman imperial vision as articulated in the global aspirations of Caliph Abd al Hamid, who was the patron of many of these Indian émigrés. And it used the printing press and the Ottoman intellectual repertoires that were articulated by the reformist bureaucrats and moderate ulema that advocated political and moral reform in sync with contemporary ideas of science, reason, and rationality. These moderate reformists, ousted from the core of the empire by Abd al Hamid, who had little patience with them, located themselves in its Arab provinces where most Indian émigrés landed. At the same time, Muslim cosmopolitanism also remained dependent on British imperial webs, transport, and modes of communication and information dissemination. The cosmopolitanism between empires was articulated as a universalist Muslim public conduct based on consensus in matters of belief, ritual, and forms of devotion.[3] The networks forged by Muslim cosmopolitans shaped and acquired a momentum of their own as individuals harnessed both their Indo-Persianate gentlemanly expertise and the long tradition of commercial and intellectual contacts between Hindustan and the Middle East to the new imperial highways of communication and print capitalism.

The essay foregrounds the individual and his ability to negotiate the imperial assemblage of the nineteenth century in its study of Muslim cosmopolitanism. It puts the spotlight on the cosmopolitanism forged between empires by two Muslim reformist scholars who arrived in Ottoman Mecca as fugitives convicted for their role in the 1857 uprising. It discusses the careers of Rahmatullah Kairanwi and Imdadullah Makki, two people who constituted the Muslim bridgehead that connected the Indian Ocean and the Mediterranean societies. They used imperial networks to spread their reformist doctrine and get connected to intellectual hubs in the Mediterranean area. As trans-imperial subjects, they forged a vast cosmopolis between Empires where they articulated their cosmopolitan vision. Their careers show that Muslim cosmopolitanism was entrenched in the challenges and opportunities offered by nineteenth-century imperialism. Firmly rooted in the Islamic tradition of consensus to reconcile cultural differences within Muslims, it was constituted of individual attempts to reconfigure these imperialisms so as to better align them with self-driven particularistic interests.

Rahmatullah Kairanwi (1818–1892)

Rahmatullah Kairanwi was a noted scholar of reformist Islam from the Kairana region of Meerut in North India. Trained by teachers from the Delhi reformist tradition of Shahwaliullah that emphasized self-interpretation of scriptures, he soon became famous for his religious public debates in Delhi and Agra with the German evangelical priest C.G. Pfander. By the mid-nineteenth century, he was a well-known figure in Delhi's political and intellectual circuits. Not surprisingly, in the aftermath of the 1857 uprising, the police hounded him for his anti-British activities. He had an arrest warrant issued for him and an award of Rs 1,000 was announced for anyone who gave information about him.[4] With the police hot on his heels, he disguised himself, changed his name, and left on foot from Kairana, near Meerut, for Delhi and then toward Surat. From there, he took a sailing boat to Jeddah. In Kairana, his huge estate, where his family and workers lived, was confiscated by the British and put on auction. He died in Mecca.

In Mecca, he connected with like-minded scripturalists in the Ottoman Arab provinces. He introduced his Indic eclecticism, which brought the Shariat and the Naqshbandi Sufi orientation together, to the Arab lands. Kairanwi tapped imperial networks and exploited political rivalries to gain access to the Mediterranean intellectual hubs. At the same time, he cashed also on the long history of intellectual contact between the Indian and Meccan intellectuals.[5] His career shows how the imperially embedded and individual-driven Muslim cosmopolis articulated a unique cosmopolitanism that had the scriptures as its core and an Ottoman Tanzimat-style 'modern' outlook. This cosmopolitan remained intimately linked with Muslim politics within India.

Kairanwi made his mark in Mecca by the establishment of his madrassa for *muhajirs* (immigrants) in the heart of the holy city. Known by the name of Madrasa Saulatiya, it became a perfect fit in the reform initiatives of exiled Ottoman reformists and moderate ulema in the Arab provinces of Syria, Lebanon, and Egypt. Like them, he too forefronted the scriptures and was happy to add to them knowledge of science and rationality that had the legitimacy of tradition. Indeed, the Delhi Naqshbandiya Sufi *silsila* of Shahwaliullah that laid out Islamic heritage in similar ways became the base of the madrassa's curriculum. His madrassa was unique in the Hijazian context because its syllabus followed the pedagogy perfected in the seminaries of India. Particularly noteworthy was the emulation of the course structure of the Firangi Mahal at Lucknow, which combined religious studies with scientific and rational sciences. The rational sciences oriented *Dars-i Nizamiyya* education format popularized by the Firangi Mahal became the educational base of Madrasa Saulatiya as well.[6]

The eclectic intellectual base of the madrassa became its most striking feature. This reflected the carryover to Mecca of the Naqshbandiya Sufi legacy, which was known for its spirit of accommodation and compromise. In Delhi, it had combined the individual-centric movement—*sirat-i-mustaqim*—meaning 'the right path' or adherence to the Koran and the Sunnat, with the significance to the sheikh as the moderator of prescriptive practice. Kairanwi became the conduit via which the intellectual legacy of the Delhi Sufi Shahwaliullah of the Naqshbandiya Sufi silsila and his disciple Sayyid Ahmad Shahid, which framed Sufism within scriptural prescription, found its way into the heart of the Arab world. He was able to introduce the Naqshbandi tradition in the education system because the region had a familiarity with this Indic stream of thought.[7] But he was the first to institutionalize this legacy as the pedagogical base in his madrassa. At its inauguration itself, readings were done by Kairanwi and his companion Imdadullah Makki from the *Bukhari Sharif* and the *Masnavi Sharif*—both popular in Hindustani religious circuits that combined monism with Sufi tasawwuf but were relatively less known in the Arab world.[8]

In line with the Firangi Mahal tradition of introducing rational sciences in the madrassa curriculum, he too made the syllabus broad and inviting, with a view to bring the 'enlightened' ummah together. He integrated the study of scriptures with the commentaries on law and lessons on the *Ilm-i-Hayat* or a knowledge of life that focused on astronomy and the planetary sciences. The madrassa's intellectual energy was in tune with reformist Islamic currents, notably the Salafi ideas, sweeping the late nineteenth-century South and West Asia. Keeping pace with the late nineteenth-century Ottoman and Arab liberal reformist stress on combining religion and technical education, he introduced technical entrepreneurial skills such as craftsmanship or *dastakari* in the madrassa. He also introduced modern disciplines and knowledge, such as *Ilm-i-mubahisa* or the art of debating, *Ilm-i-mantaq* or logic, *Ilm-i-falsafa* or philosophy, and *Ilm-i-falkiat* or astronomy.

In contrast to the tradition in Arabia, where the syllabus focussed mainly on the Mu'atta of the legist Imam Malik, he introduced the teaching of a Hadith written by the Shaifite legist Imam Bukhari, called the *Bukhari Sharif*, in his madrassa. In Hindustan, this Hadith is still regarded as the most authentic because it claims to be a compendium of only those sayings and observations of the Prophet that were narrated directly by him to his close companions and were not passed on via several layers of interlocutors. The introduction of this text was even more interesting given the fact that Kairanwi himself claimed to be a Hanafite. Indeed, Kairanwi broadened the scope of learning and introduced a sprinkling of learning from all the four Islamic legal schools of thought. It clearly reflected the South Asian seminary tradition of never pronouncing as wrong any of the four schools of laws prevalent in India even as one could claim allegiance to only one of them. In the Hijaz, this eclecticism proved particularly useful, as the idea was to introduce a curriculum that would have trans-Asian appeal. Kairanwi's audience was the muhajirs of all countries who spoke different languages. He pledged to take care of their religious and material requirements. He also included texts like the *Masnavi Sharif* in the curriculum to take care of his diverse clientele. His associate and pupil Maulvi Imdad-ul-mulk delivered hugely popular lectures on this text.

The madrassa maintained a steady supply of books from Hindustan. And thus, a vibrant print ecumene underpinned the madrassa and made it the hub of the trans-Asiatic Muslim network. Books like the *Ruh Nisar* and those penned by Muhammad Ali Monghyri arrived at the madrassa from India. The *Azaltah Alaawaham*, produced in India, was also taught here.[9] Literature from India stamped the accommodative Indic seal on the nineteenth-century Arab liberal reform that emanated from the Ottoman provinces in the Middle East. Indeed, it was a momentous day when he began his *dars* on Shahwaliullah's book *Hajutullah al baligha* (Detailed Discussion), which talks about the wisdom of the Islamic Shariat and its accretive potential. He also lectured at length on astronomy and Ibn-Khaldun's literature.[10]

Also noteworthy was the inclusion of his own books published in India and Istanbul that encouraged a dialogue between Muslims and the Christian world. Thus, his own masterpiece book, *Izharul Haq*, which compiled his debate with the Evangelical priest Pfanders and alluded to the exceptional intellectual heritage of Islam, was on the syllabus.[11] His madrasṣa also received books printed in Cairo and Istanbul. These reached Mecca using imperial networks and the rivalries that energized them.

Even as he depended on imperial networks to sustain his discursive Muslim civilizational space between empires, he never let go of the older forms of Islamicate connectivity. Thus, for instance, the universalist

Islamic connectors: the *fann tajveed* or the mode of pronunciation, *hifz* or memorizing, and *qira'at* or Koranic recitation became the focus of his attention at the madrassa. He appointed an Egyptian *qari*, (orator) who had been chosen in the time of Abd al Hamid Pasha as the best orator out of 500 contestants, to teach his Hindustani students the art of Koranic recitation or *qira'at*. The students picked up the skill quickly. One of his Hindustani students, Qari Abdulla, was certified by the Egyptian teacher as 'being the best in the Arab world'.[12] Ashraf Ali Thanawi, of the Deoband fame, exercised his qira'at with guidance from Qari Abdullah. He became so good by regular practice that when he recited the Koran crowds collected below his window and people could not make out whether it was his voice or that of Qari Abdullah. The madrassa soon became a center that encouraged students from all over the world to perfect the art of qira'at and use it as a global connector.[13] Most qaris in Lucknow, Bhopal, Deoband, Multan and other parts of India who are known for this talent owe their training to his madrassa.[14]

Madrasa Saulatiya and the Making of Muslim Cosmopolitanism

Kairanwi's cosmopolitanism had the scriptures as its base and a very Tanzimat-inspired pragmatic and scientific outlook. It offered a readymade template for attracting Muslims, as it stretched as a discursive civilizational space between the British and the Ottoman Empires. It was sustained by intellectual ideas, disseminated via books and energized by Madrasa Saulatiya. As we saw above, it became the nodal point from where books written in India circulated in the Hijaz and the Ottoman Arab provinces. They continued their onward journey to Southeast Asia via itinerary teachers and students who linked the madrassa to the larger Asian world outside. Alongside books, students played a critical role in the formation of this brand of cosmopolitanism. Kairanwi's students included his own brother's grandson, Sayyid, who he groomed to take charge of the madrassa after his death.[15] But his ambit was not confined to family members. It included learned alims from Egypt, such as Qari Ibrahim Saad, a specialist in the Koran who attended the lectures on the *Bukhari*

Sharif with rapt attention and taught the Koran to the students at the madrassa.

His notable students who fanned out into the world included Sheikh Alqara, Hazrat Qari Abdullah Makki, and his brother, Qari Abdul Rahman Allahabadi.[16] Javanese scholars from Southeast Asia attended his lectures, studied at the madrassa, and went back home to set up madrassas that were similarly oriented.[17] Aboe Bakar Djajadiningrat, the informant and close associate of the Dutch orientalist Snouck Hurgronje, and who had been deputed in the Hijaz area by his government to study the relationship of the Hijaz to the Javanese, was a Naqshbandiya Sufi who had been educated in the tradition of Kairanwi via one of his students Abd Allah Zawawi.[18] And he had many Javanese students who were similarly trained. A range of Javanese scholars in Mecca were students of Kairanwi's intellectual peer and reformist scholar Dahlan. Many others from the archipelago were influenced by Kairanwi's scholarship during their stint at Cairo, where he was well-known because of his students in the city.[19]

Indeed, many of Kairanwi's students, such as Shaikh Abdulla Siraj and Shaikh Ahmad Ali Hasan, became muftis, qaris, and teachers in the Ka'aba and other mosques and madrassas in Mecca, Taif, and in the madrassas in North India and port cities like Karachi.[20] Branches of the Saulatiya madrassa were also established in Eastern India. In fact, Begum Saulatiyah, a wealthy Bengali zamindar's wife and the chief donor of the madrassa, went back to Bengal after her haj and established a branch of the madrassa in her village in the district of 24 Parganas. She allocated a part of her estate as waqf property to look after the financial deals of the madrassa and the mosque attached to it.[21]

Significant financial networks underpinned much of this trans-Asiatic intellectual energy. There were always many Indians with property and money in the Hijaz who had influential contacts with Muslim notables back home. Indeed, notables such as the Nizam of Hyderabad and the Begum of Bhopal owned houses in the Mecca–Medina region. They were ever-willing donors. Thus, for instance, the learned scholar Imdadullah Makki, an important student and companion of Kairanwi who also taught at the Madrasa Saulatiya, was offered a house to stay in Mecca by the Hyderabad State, which owned several properties in the area. Help generously flowed from other sources as well. He eventually decided to take up the offer of one of his Indian disciples who bought a house for him in the residential area called Hartah Albab.[22] And of course, every year hajis from India who flocked to Mecca, made donations and exchanged religious and political news with the alims of the madrassa. Imdadullah once hosted a feast for a large contingent of ulema from Hindustan.[23]

Kairanwi viewed India as integral to his cosmopolitan world carved between empires. The links with India were not merely because of his interest in the anticolonial struggle. Rather, Indian financial, intellectual, and emotional resources were critical for the conceptualization of the embracive Muslim civilizational space across empires. Kairanwi was always worried about the future of Indian Muslims and toyed with different ideas about the best way they could cope with their new British rulers. Very much like his contemporary Arab and Ottoman reformists, who fanned the winds of intellectual change while in exile, Kairanwi too saw education as the way to both resurrect and energize the accretive civilizational heritage of Muslims. He pledged to make this legacy the core of his brand of cosmopolitanism, even as he depended on important imperial networks to sustain its vast edifice. This sentiment was behind the expansion of the Madrasa Saulatiya.

Kairanwi firmed up his cosmopolis by investing in seminaries in India. From 1866, he was very instrumental in the establishment of the famous madrassa at Deoband, in North India. He maintained close ties with the Deobandi ulema: Maulana Hazrat Abid Husain, Maulana Muhammad Qasim Nanatawi, Maulana Zulfiqar Ali, and others. Maulana Yaqub Nanatawi—the first president of the madrassa—was his mentor. Imdadullah Makki, his associate in Mecca, sent one rupee per month to the madrassa.[24]

Kairanwi also maintained a continuous correspondence with the ulema of Deoband participating in all their intellectual discussions and urging them to stay put in India as their "initiatives for the community *(ijtimai kaam)* were more valuable than their migrating and living in Mecca." In a letter to Abid Husain at Deoband, he reiterated the value of the Deoband initiative: "It is in your interest to stay on in Deoband and serve the madrassa in the way Allah wants you to do."[25] At the same time, he was always eager that the Deoband and Saulatiya madrassa, at Mecca, should work in intellectual camaraderie and have student exchanges. He invited the son of Maulana Nanatawi, Maulana Hafiz Muhammad Ahmad, to come over and enroll at Madrasa Saulatiya for further education[26].

Madrasa Saulatiya and the trans-Asiatic networks that emanated from it always created alarm in British circles. The British Foreign Office saw the literary productions and print ecumene of Kairanwi not just seditious but also politically lethal. In 1888, Colonel Henderson said that his spy confirmed that Kairanwi was summoned a second time by the Pasha to Istanbul, "and was instructed to again distribute seditious books among the pilgrims." He also reported that the Sultan advanced him money to establish a press for printing such books.[27]

British complaints on Maulana Kairanwi reached Istanbul regularly. And he made several visits to the city to offer his explanations. During his meetings with the Caliph, he narrated the general state of affairs of the Muslims in India, especially the details on their indictment by the British government in the 1857 mutiny-rebellion.[28] It is in the course of these discussions in Istanbul that in 1864 the Caliph expressed a desire that Kairanwi pen his experiences and discussions with the German evangelical priest Pfanders in the form of a book. The Turkish administration offered to translate and publish the book in different languages once it was written. Kairanwi agreed. And thus was produced the *Izharul Haq*—The Truth Revealed. He began to write this book in 1864 in Istanbul. He lived in the city until he finalized the book, in a record period of six months, and presented it to the Pasha Khairuddin.

The book lays out Kairanwi's use of the Koran as the exceptional connector and the most accretive platform on which Islamic internationalism is showcased. *Izharul Haq* is a major effort to demystify the Koran by highlighting not just its revealed wisdom but also the Prophet, who was its chief recipient. It underlines the relevance of the Koran by placing it in this worldly evidence that is subject to historical scrutiny. The focus on the individual and the worldly context (*dunyadari*) even while acknowledging the exceptional powers of Allah and the Prophet offered immense flexibility in interpretation.

Izharul Haq reveals Kairanwi's use of the 'modern' norms of authorship and scientific objectivity to frame religious writing. This methodology exemplified the crux of his literary format that was simultaneously heeled in the scriptures and sustained by imperial networks and the Ottoman Tanzimat-inspired modern vision. Like the Tanzimat impacted Ottoman reformists, Kairanwi too saw the "modern" norms as Islamicate and not European in origin. He uses the Islamic reformist language of the Salafi intellectuals of the Ottoman Arab provinces, who stressed reason, logic, and scientific wisdom to scrutinize the religious literature of Christians, Jews, and Muslims. He concludes that judged by such an Islamic yardstick of "modernity," the Koran outshines all other religious literary productions.[29]

Izharul Haq lays out the blueprint of Muslim cosmopolitanism. Its production via Ottoman patronage itself revealed how dependent this cosmopolitanism was on imperial networks. In the period he finalized his book, he stayed in Istanbul for a year and was honored with numerous exalted titles by the Pasha in recognition of his writings. During this stint, he interacted with a range of Turkish ulema and religious scholars. He intellectually responded to their concern that the new generation doubted Islamic knowledge because of the influence of Western education. In 1865, on their request, he wrote a book on issues of divine message and Prophethood. This book was called *Tanbihat.* This was also published in Istanbul with the orders of Khair al-Din Pasha. His deft play of diplomacy was evident when he continued to enjoy royal patronage despite dedicating the book to the Arab Sherif of Mecca. His high intellectual stance in Istanbul notwithstanding, he returned to Mecca, which remained his home and the pivot of his cosmopolis until his death.

Imdadullah Makki (1817–1899)

Kairanwi was not the only Indian scholar-fugitive in Mecca. Imdadullah Makki, his associate and student, also escaped to Mecca after being declared a suspect in the 1857 mutiny-rebellion. He too used his new location in the Hijaz, tapped its long history of connections with South Asia, and exploited the late-nineteenth century "imperial moment" to fashion his cosmopolitanism as an urbane civility based on universalist Muslim virtuous conduct. He fashioned a cosmopolitanism that aspired to unite the Muslims via advocating a form of public conduct that derived from the tradition of consensus as laid out in the Koran and the Hadith. His cosmopolitanism underlined the salience of the *murshid* or guide and leaned also on the Ottoman reformist vision that combined Islamic tradition with a scientific outlook. Imdadullah showcased Muslim virtuous disposition to manufacture a form of urbane civility that was in sync with the fast-changing material world.

Indeed, Imdadullah Makki's formula that combined devotion to and the celebration of God (*zikr*) with the act of following the right Islamic path (*sirat-i-mustaqim*) became the trans-imperial political formula for the unity of all Muslims living under European influence. This produced a system—*nizam*—that offered a way of life to be followed by Muslims living under foreign occupation. Imdadullah urged them to interpret religion for guidance. His message was to make religion central to everyday life rather than shun it altogether. He underplayed Muslim reliance on self-judgment and co-opted the Sufi way of seeking guidance from a sheikh in matters of interpreting normative religion. He emphasized that without the moderator, who he called *murshid*, one should not follow the ritual of *azkar*, or repeatedly praising God, or undertaking any form of devotion. He equated the *murshid* to the physician. He argued that just like medicines should not be taken without the guidance of the physician, the *murshid* be consulted in all spiritual matters.[30] He clarified that "the sufi way is useful only when it is applied in a certain way in the correct proportion."[31] Thus, the company of the spiritual guide, or *sohbat sheikh*, became the signature of what came to be regarded as his brotherhood—*Silsila Imdadiyah*.[32]

He wrote eight very important books in Urdu, Arabic, and Persian that laid out best his blueprint of cosmopolitanism. Some of them, written in British India, such as his commentaries on the *Masnavi Maulana Rum* and *Ghiza-i Ruh*, read like Sufi texts that aim at uniting different Muslim sects. They aim to forge trans-imperial bonds by pitching Islam as an inclusive philosophy of harmony.[33] Writing in Urdu for a larger audience in Hindustan, he talked to people about Satan and his dealings (*satan kei wasawa*), the defects of the spirit (*nafs kei mughalte*), and the consequences of ignorance and backwardness (*jihalat kei natayaj*). He emphasized the significance of spirituality that enables one to transcend differences and unite people.[34]

The book that made him very famous was written in Arabic while he was located in Mecca. Titled *Faislah Hafte Maslah* (Verdict on Seven Issues), it focussed on issues of custom and ritual that were mooted and caused friction between different sects of Muslims. He identified seven such issues—five practical or *amli* and two intellectual or *ilmi*—that divided Muslims. The practical issues included *milad* or celebration of the Prophet, *fatiha* or prayer for the dead, *murawwaja* or a package of customs, *urs* or the celebration of the cult of the saint, and *sama*, which was collective singing known as *qawwali*. The *ilmi* ones were *Imkaane Nazeer* and *Imkaane Kazab*. The former was about the revealed truth on the exceptional status of the last Prophet, and the latter dismissed the idea of the uniqueness of Allah's singular existence. Tired of Muslims quarreling on these issues, he tried to establish a consensus to forge their unity.[35] He was of the view that all these practices can be easily accommodated within Islam as they had a long history in Islamic societies. With a view to minimize disagreements, he offered truce by saying that his opponents were not false but needed to provide more evidence for their claims to be taken seriously.[36]

One of the most significant issues of the book was the new definition of *bid'a* or heresy. It was no longer defined only as deviation from the singular path of belief in one God or *tauhid*, and the performance of rituals and customs that were unacceptable in Islam. Rather, it integrated local customs and offered them religious legitimacy. For instance, the book defined any ritual that focused on the celebration of Allah and the Prophet as integral to religion. This opened up space for accommodating local customs. Imdadullah did not spell out his definition of nonreligious. But given his disinterest in politics, it is very likely that he alluded to the mix of religion in politics when he talked of the nonreligious sphere. According to him, politics that used religion would make the perfect case for *bid'a*.[37] The book was a far cry from the Hindustani reformist literature of the early nineteenth century. It reflected far more flexibility and outreach in uniting different sects of Muslims than the efforts of the Naqshbandis of the eighteenth century who had settled in Mecca.

If *Faisalah* laid out the contours of his cosmopolitanism, it was his book *Zia-ul Qulub* (Light of the Heart), also penned during his Mecca stay, that lent it a universalist public conduct. Imdadullah authored the *Zia-ul Qulub* in 1862. It is a sixty-four-pages-long text originally titled *Marghob Dil*. It articulates a form of Muslim public conduct as an urbane civility based on virtuous disposition. The guide or murshid played a pivotal role in fashioning this conduct as a form of inclusive cosmopolitanism. Imdadullah projects the murshid as the exemplar of Islamic virtuous conduct viewed as a form of urbane civility that is universal in its reach. According to him, Islamic public conduct as modeled on that of the murshid, should be embracive and inclusive within the theological frame.

The *Zia-ul Qulub* breaks new ground in Muslim intellectual history as it begins with the idea of diluting the late nineteenth-century trend toward individuation of prescriptive religion: individual interpretation of the Koran and Hadith and self-moderation in forms of devotion. And yet does not discard it entirely. Indeed, the text reaches a middle ground in bringing different Sufi silsilas and sects of Muslims together.[38] According to Imdadullah, he was persuaded to write such an inclusive text by Hafiz Muhammad Yusuf, who was of the Chishti sect.[39] However, Imdadullah extended his brief. He not only struck a middle ground between Sufi sects but also improvised on both his Shahwaliullah Naqshbandi as well as his Deobandi legacy.

The Delhi Naqshbandi silsila of Shahwaliullah, with its Arabicist worldview, had encouraged individuation of religion, even as it borrowed from the Sufi organizational format of the hospice (*khanqah*) and adopted the practice of the oath of allegiance to its leader (*bai'at*). Its notable legatees, such as the reformist Sayyid Ahmad Shahid, continued with the Sufi emphasis on initiation to the silsila with the oath of allegiance to the leader (khalifa/murshid). The oath of allegiance to the leader did not stop Sayyid Ahmad from encouraging his followers to model their lives in accordance with the Koran, Hadith, and the life of the Prophet alone (*tariqa-i-Muhammadiya*). And this emulation was to be a very private individual affair. He shunned as *bid'a* or heresy any public form of devotion centered on leaders: pir, murshid, or khalifa. The leader was never the center of the reformist way of life.

In contrast, Imdadullah argues that when God wishes to give someone direction, the blessed one shuns all his sinful acts and turns toward Him. But a guide or leader should mediate this relationship with God as the individual himself is incapable of forging a direct relationship with Him. And thus, he should hand himself over to some *murshid kamil* or perfect guide. Very much like the medieval Indo-Persianate political theorists who invoked the analogy of the ideal physician to define the perfect king, Imdadullah too compared the perfect guide to the best of the physicians. He refers to the guide as the physician of the soul (*dil kaa tabib*).[40] And advocates individual forms of devotion (*saluk*) as prescribed by him. According to him, the perfect guide should take care of the internal (*batini)* well-being of the individual very much like the physician who cures the physical ailments of his patients.

Imdadullah forefronts urbane civility that is framed in Islamic virtuous conduct as the essential requirement for the murshid. This has universal appeal. Thus, he argues that the murshid should be an epitome of good conduct. He should uphold the Shariat and tradition. (*shariat aur tariqat ka jamaih ho*) and follow the Koran and the Sunnat in his handling of individuals. (*batini amraz kei ilaj kei liyei Quran va Sunnat kei irshadat va hidayat ka paband ho*). According to Imdadullah, the guide, like the physician, has to first cure the inner diseases of jealousy (*hasad)*, pride (*kibr*), hypocrisy (*riya*), and envy (*kina*). Only when these are substituted by good conduct (*akhlaq-i-hasina*) that the blessings of God will arrive (*wasul ali Allah*).[41]

Imdadullah enhances the role of the murshid, making him the mediator not just between God and the individual but also between the local and the global. The text projects him as the agent who makes localized renditions of devotion connect to universal standardized norms of conduct without entirely making them lose their particularistic veneer. For instance, the role of the murshid in arriving at a consensual format on culturally and regionally diverse forms of *zikr* to unite the ummah brings out his role as a moderator very well. Imdadullah projects himself as the ideal murshid and his *Zia-al Qulub* as the guidebook to shape readers into perfect Muslim gentlemen.

Alongside the murshid, the Islamic notions of consensus *(ijma)* and mutual trust (*i'temad*) are the other two referents critical to forge the unity of the ummah around a standard form of virtuous public conduct. Imdadullah describes the varied prescriptive formats for devotion (*zikrs*) offered by different Sufi silsilas: *akhyar ka tariqa, ashab mujahidat va riyazat ka tariqa, Shatariya tariqa*. Imdadullah forefronts the murshid as the pivot who synthesizes these diverse forms of devotions and arrives at a consensual prescriptive conduct. Via this search for consensual unity on Muslim virtuous conduct, Imdadullah hoped to unite the ummah based on tolerance and recognition of internal difference. He was able to pursue this as he, like many others of his peer group, had multiple initiations in Sufi silsilas. He had been initiated into the Naqshbandi silsila by his pir Nasiruddun Dehlavi, and into the other three by his pir Mian Nur Muhammad Jhanjhanwi. And thus, the book has chapters on all four Sufi tariqas, albeit with the aim of generating trust and bringing them on a common meeting point.

The text begins with discussions on the Chishti prescriptions on ideal public conduct. It describes the bodily comportment in taking the oath of allegiance (bai'at), and in the performance of different forms of devotion: *ashghal, azkar, and muraqabat*. It elaborates the varied forms of *zikr* via expressing devotion to Chishti saints: *zikr ism zat, zikr nafi va asbat, shaghal Sultana nasir, and so on.*[42] With a view to bringing different Sufi silisilas together, it lays down their comparable prescriptions on forms of devotion (*ashghal*). It talks about prescriptions on *zikr*—like *ism zat*—and the meditational feats (*muraqabat*) of the Qadiri silsilas.[43] It ignores the reformist doctrines of the Naqshbandis and instead focuses on prescriptions that overlap with the other Sufi silsilas: meditation (*muraqabat*), augury or reliance on omens (*istikharah*), forms of *zikr*, like the *zikr jarub*, the rituals for concluding the devotion to revered elders (*Khatm Khwajagan*), and the rituals to be observed at the Prophet's tomb (*ziyarat nabi*).[44]

It focuses on the universal norms and etiquette on the recitation (*tilawat)* of the Koran and the bodily comportment to be followed during prayer (namaz). These forms of appropriate bodily etiquette are projected as a type of Muslim virtuous public conduct that unites the culturally diverse ummah.[45]. The prescriptive etiquette to be followed on a visit to the Prophet's tomb (ziyarat) constitutes another set of standardized norms of conduct that unite the sects. He projects this standard form of public conduct as the mark of the community's ability to arrive at a consensus on such matters.[46]

Throughout the text, he picks up many other mooted rituals and forms of conduct that traditionally divide the Muslims and attempts to build a consensus: the public conduct centered on the Muslim fasting (*roza),* prayers (namaz), recitation of the Koran (tilawat), pilgrimage (haj), and jihad. The book standardizes a specific kind of etiquette (*akhlaq*) for all Muslims: it urges the individual to give up undesirable acts (*aadat-i-zamima*) and adopt a desirable conduct and pleasing etiquette (*akhlaq-i-mamida*). Finally, he reaches out to his reformist colleagues by approving also of the individual self-driven way to reach God. In a significant deviation from his signature focus on the murshid he urges people to shun the austerity and abstinence (*riyazat*) as prescribed by some and get into individuated forms of devotion that are self-driven: like reciting the name of God to mark ones devotion—*zikr.*[47] In the conclusion, Imdadullah invokes the scriptures to legitimize this consensual public conduct and uses their universal appeal to market it far and wide. He invokes also his Deoband legacy, which upheld such scripture-driven reformist Islam.[48]

The text is significant because here the focus shifts from the self and the individual to the murshid as a moderator of virtuous conduct. More importantly, the moderator mediates not only between the individual and God but also between the local and the universal by setting standardized universal formats of devotion. The book reaches out to both the regional flavors of Sufi silsilas as well as to the Koran and the Hadith, which have a global appeal. This mixed bag of the local and the global constitutes the formula of ideal public conduct as a standard norm that would connect Muslims globally and unite them internally. This model of standardized Muslim virtuous conduct is a form of cosmopolitanism that also constitutes a theologically framed form of urbane civility.

The making of the Zia-ul Qulub

Even though written in Mecca, the language of the original text of *Zia-ul Qulub* is Persian. An indicator perhaps of the caution Imdadullah exercised in initially limiting the text to only a select audience. And restraint was the need of the hour in writing an eclectic text from the Arab heartland of Mecca. This was a city where even after the fall of the Wahhabi control (1819) and the establishment of Ottoman rule the climate of religious scholarship was heavily stamped by reformist Sufi doctrines. Both the Middle Eastern Salafi, as well as the South Asian Naqshbandi reformists, had created a niche for themselves in the city. Both relied heavily on individual interpretation of doctrinaire texts to reach out to the world outside and diluted the reliance on mediator guides and public devotions to them. They forefronted the individual and urged him to turn to the Koran and the Prophet to connect to the world outside. In contrast, in the *Zia-ul Qulub*, Muslim trans-imperialism was a kind of cosmopolitanism that was exemplified in a universalist public conduct that was moderated by the murshid or guide who regulated devotion to God and the reading of the Koran. It was, as we saw earlier in this chapter, interactive, inclusive, and based on consensus within the theological frame.

Imdadullah's temporal and spatial location gave him access to both the older repertoires of connectivity constituted by itinerant traders, litterateurs, and pilgrims, as well as new forms of connections offered via the imperial networks of steamships, telegraph, and print capitalism. He made the best use of both these networks to write the *Zia-ul Qulub*. His letters to Hindustan indicate how visiting scholars, publishers, traders, and pilgrims played the intermediaries in carrying the manuscript of the book back and forth from Mecca to Hindustan for intellectual inputs. Imdadullah sent the manuscript to Maulvi Rashid of Deoband for a thorough review before he finalized it. He explains to Rashid that the manuscript is a compilation of forms of devotion (*azkar va ashghal*) of the Chishti and other Sufi silsilas that came to his notice via the elderly wise men of the Qadari and Chishti silsila. Rashid was given a free license to edit it and bring the corrected version to his use.[49] He sent the manuscript via Haji Ismael Saharanpuri, a private press owner, who had visited him in Mecca. The book was published in Meerut by the notable maulvi, Abdul al Hakim, who was the brother of Abdul Karim Rais and Shaikh Ilahi Baksh *thekedar* of Meerut. This wealthy publisher family had offered to publish it free of cost. Imdadullah took their offer and requested Maulvi Qasim to personally take the manuscript to Meerut and hand it over to Munshi Mumtaz Ali, who would oversee its publication in their press[50]

Imdadullah also wanted people in the arabophone world to read his book. And thus, an Arabic translation was urgently required. He organized this via his well-known reformist friend Ashraf Ali Thanawi, who got it translated and printed in Hindustan. He also arranged for its export to Mecca. Imdadullah's wide contacts enabled him to publish and disseminate, in multiple languages, various editions of the *Zia-ul Qulub* in the Arab provinces of the Ottoman Empire, which were heavily impacted by the reformist religious atmosphere of the earlier Wahhabi regime.

In a letter to Thanawi, he underlines the urgency of the Arabic version reaching the Ottoman world of Arabia, Egypt, and Dagestan as the people there did not know Persian or Hindustani.[51]

He asks him to get at least 100 to 200 copies published and promises payment at the earliest. He asks him to take particular care of the paper and the quality of binding. He wants that he should be consulted in case any clarification is required.[52] In subsequent letters, he continues to inquire about the status of the publication and reiterates the urgency of sending the Arabic version quickly to the Hijaz (*Maulvi Muhammad Husain sahib Allhabadi ko tehrir karein keh agar Zia-ul-Qulub Arabi tabah ho gayi ho to bahut jald matlah karein*). He stresses the urgency of obtaining the copies because 'people of Arab, Syria, and Istanbul will be able to access it and that will make him happy (*aksar masanih Arab va Sham va Istanbol ... faqir bhee dekh kar khush hoga*)'.[53]

Conclusion

Historians have contested the view that cosmopolitanism is a melting pot ideology that is incompatible with religions like Islam.[54] They have argued that there is no necessary incompatibility between it and the religious traditions.[55] In the context of Islam, Kress sees it as a kind of Muslim engagement with the world as opposed to a more local and region-specific way of life. Ottomanists view this global outreach as a Caliph-centric form of Pan-Islam that was driven by the domestic and foreign compulsions of the late nineteenth-century empire. Selim Deringil focuses on the "crisis of legitimacy" in the Hamidian era that triggered a Pan-Islam that aspired for global legitimacy for the Caliph.[56] Cemil Aydin views this Pan-Islam as Tanzimat inspired and driven by its principles of equality and justice to all.[57] And given its eclectic stance, it was eager to tie up with Pan-Asian aspirants from Japan.[58] And for a later period, Selcuk Esenbel has shown Pan-Islamism across the board as the "history of international relations of nationalism" that fitted with the Asiatic political ambitions of imperial Japan.[59]

South Asianists have studied the global aspirations of Indian Muslims in the context of nineteenth-century religious reform.[60] Barbara Metcalf and Ulrike Stark show how the new print culture of the nineteenth century was quickly used by reformist Muslims charged with new socially oriented religious zeal to form transnational connections in novel ways.[61] Ayesha Jalal has discussed the issue of Muslim internationalism via Muslim normative thought and its careful balancing of Muslim particularism with universalism. This enabled the individual to carve out identities in innovative ways.

More recently, Muslim global networks, seen as a form of cosmopolitanism, have been viewed in tandem with the growth of nineteenth-century industrial and capitalist cultures. In India, Nile Green shows the making of Bombay cosmopolitanism as integral to its growth as an urban metropolis and industrial hub.[62] And Indian Ocean studies have focused on the urban port cities—their early contact with English education that produced a particularistic cosmopolitanism.[63]

This essay has shown that Indian Muslim cosmopolitanism, as it evolved between empires, was unique. Its protagonists were not Caliph-oriented. Neither were they conditioned by the British Raj in the manner of their anglicized port-city brethren. Instead, they were products of the Indo-Persianate world: Urdu literate, persophone, and arabophone. They wrote simultaneously in Urdu, Persian, and Arabic. They had an encyclopedic knowledge of the world combined with a religious education that made them gentlemen. Many of them were men of religion trained in the Delhi Naqshbandi Sufi Shahwaliullah's tradition with its emphasis on unity and inclusivity based on scriptures. Their differences with port city anglicized intellectuals notwithstanding, they too were impacted by the nineteenth-century economic, cultural, and intellectual challenges posed by the politically ascendant Europe. They saw Europe more as a civilizational and spiritual challenge rather than a territory-bound political one. And they conceptualized the Muslim space that they carved out between empires also as an intellectual and civilizational zone that transcended empires and territory. It is here that they hoped to weld Muslim unity around virtuous conduct and meet the Western challenge.

Kairanwi and Imdadullah's careers show that Muslim cosmopolitanism benefitted from the "imperial moment" when the post-1857 British Empire tightened its noose on Muslims and the post-Crimean War (1856) Ottoman Empire, hurt by its marginalization from the European imperial club, began to project a pro-Muslim image to garner internal sympathy and external support. Sultan Abd al Hamid (1876–1909) projected himself as a just and benevolent Muslim sovereign with an eye to a place in the Western League on the strength of his influence in the Muslim world.[64] This political moment created the ideal context in which Muslim cosmopolitanism as an inclusive trans-imperialism could be produced at the cusp of empires and exported globally from an imperial cross-section like Mecca.

Notes and References

1. See Khurram Ali, *Nasihat-I-Muslameen*, reprint Lucknow, 1999.
2. For the "official nationalism," as sponsored by the British government in India, see M. Goswami, *Producing India: From Colonial Economy to National Space*, Chicago, 2004. Identities were imposed via the passport, census, legal, and consular regimes.
3. E. Simpson and Kai Kresse, *Struggling with History: Islam and Cosmopolitanism in the Western Indian Ocean*, Columbia, 2008, Lambick's foreword, p. xix. I borrow this idea from Kresse and Lambick, who use the concept of urbane civility as a form of comportment that bonded port-city societies together as cosmopolitan centers.

4. Maulana Asir Adravi, *Mujahid Islam: Maulana Rahmatullah Kairanwi*, Delhi, 2004, p. 288–289.
5. Azumardi Azra, *The Origins of Islamic Reformism in South East Asia: Networks of Malay-Indonesian and Middle Eastern Ulema in the Seventeenth and Eighteenth Centuries*, Honolulu, 2004, pp. 13, 21.
6. For a discussion on the making of the Dars-i Nizamiyya in Awadh, see F. Robinson, *The Ulama of Farangi Mahall and Islamic Culture in South Asia*, London, 2001, pp. 46–55.
7. Ibid., pp. 240–251.
8. H.M.A. Zafar, *Rahmatullah Kairanwi Aur Un Kei Muasareen*, Lahore, 2007, pp. 472–473.
9. Zafar, *Rahmatullah Kairanwi*, p. 483, citing the *Safar-i-Hijaz* of Maulana Sarf-ul Haq.
10. Ibid., p. 517.
11. Ibid., p. 484.
12. Ibid., p. 482.
13. Ibid, pp. 482–483.
14. Ibid., p. 521. See list of fourteen qaris. These include Qari Abdul Rahman of Allahabad, Maulvi Suleiman of Bhopal, Qari Mizan Shah of Nadwat ul-Ulama, Lucknow, and Qari Abdul Malik of Madrasa Furqania in Lucknow.
15. Ibid., p. 484.
16. Ibid., p. 473.
17. M. Laffan, *Islamic Nationhood and Colonial Indonesia: The Umma below the Winds*, Routledge, 2002, pp. 20–21.
18. Ibid., p. 61. He was the son of the famous Qadi of Jeddah, Muhammad Salih Zawawi.
19. For Jawanese scholars in Mecca and Cairo, and the Arabic-press reportage on their Arabic and scholarly potential, see Michael Laffan, 'Another Andalusia'. Images of Colonial South East Asia in the Arabic Newspapers', *Journal of Asian Studies*, Vol. 66, No. 3, 2007, pp. 689–722.
20. Zafar. *Rahmatullah Kairanwi*, p. 518–520. See list of names of his students and their placements.
21. Zafar, *Rahmatullah Kairanwi*, pp. 474–475. He converted it into an English middle school. It soon became a government school. At different times, several Muslim luminaries of Bengal, such as Sufi Qadri Muhammad Mustaqim, remained associated with it. Begum Saulatiya set up other schools and cheap hotels for poor Muslim students of Calcutta. She helped in spreading the knowledge of the Koran and Arabic learning in the region.

22. Basir Ahmad, *Tazkira Haji Imdadullah Makki*, Delhi, Kitab Bhawan, reprint 2005, p. 50.
23. Ibid., pp. 51. Financial networks, between Indian Muslims and the Palestine waqfs as well as between trusts of Indian royalty and Shia ulema of Iraq and Iran have been documented by Omar Khalidi and Meir Litvak respectively. See Omar Khalidi, ' Indian Muslims and Palestinian Awqaf', in *Jerusalem Quarterly*, 2009–10, No. 40, pp. 52–58; Meir Litvak, 'Money, Religion, and Politics: The Oudh Bequest in Najaf and Karbala, 1850–1903', in *International Journal of Middle East Studies*, Vol. 33, No. 1, Feb. 2001, pp.1–21.
24. Ibid., p. 53.
25. Nisar Ahmad Faruqi, *Marqumat Imdadiyah*, Delhi, Maktab Burhan, 1979, p.77.
26. Zafar, *Rahmatullah Kairanwi*, pp. 502–503.
27. Col. P.D. Henderson's note, July 21, 1888, Foreign Dept., Secret I, Proceedings June 1889, Nos. 1-8, R/1/1/98.4.
28. Zafar, *Rahmatullah Kairanwi*, p. 306.
29. See discussion on this text in Seema Alavi, *Muslim Cosmopolitanism in the Age of Empire,* Cambridge, Mass, Harvard University Press, 2015, pp. 197–207.
30. Ibid, pp. 76–77, 101–102.
31. Ibid., p. 102.
32. Ibid., pp. 113–115.
33. Ahmad, *Tazkira,* pp. 121–142.
34. Ibid., p. 130.
35. Imdadullah Makki, *Faislah Hafte Maslah. Tausihhat wa Tashreehat*, Urdu Tr. by Mufti Muhammad Khalil Khan Barkati, Delhi, 1974, p. 49.
36. Ibid., pp. 128–129.
37. Ibid., p. 43.
38. Imdadulaah Makki, *Tazqiat-ul-Qulub*, translated into Urdu by Syed Abdul Mateen as *Zia-ul Qulub*, Delhi, 1346 Hijri, p. 3.
39. Ibid., pp. 2–3.
40. Mateen, *Zia*, p. 5.
41. Ahmad, *Tazkira*, pp. 124–125.
42. Ibid., p. 125; Mateen, *Zia,* pp. 8–50.
43. Mateen, *Zia*, pp. 50–59.
44. Ibid., pp. 59–75; Ahmed, *Tazkira*, p. 126.
45. Mateen, *Zia*, pp. 75–107.
46. Ibid., pp. 83. Urges people to bathe, put perfume, and imagine the Prophet sitting in front of them.

47 Ibid., p. 5.

48 Ahmad, *Tazkira*, p. 127.

49. Hazrat Ashraf Ali Thanawi, *Marqumat-i-Imdadiya* (Writings of Imdadullah), Delhi, Maktab Burhan, 1979, p. 55. Henceforth, *Marqumat*.

50. Ibid., p. 130. It was translated in the lifetime of Imdadullah itself into Urdu as *Tasfitah Alqalub* by Maulana Nizamuddin Ashaq Kairanwi and Maulvi Muhammad Beg. The Urdu version was, however, published from Delhi after his death in 1910, and since then, has had several editions.

51. *Maktubat-i-Imdadiya*, (letters written to Asharaf Ali Thanawi), Lucknow, Academy of Islamic Research and Publications, 1915, letter no. 8, no page numbers. Henceforth, *Maktubat*.

52. Ibid.

53. Ibid., letter No. 11.

54. For the profane ideal of cosmopolitanism, see K.A. Appiah, *Cosmopolitanism: Ethics in a World of Strangers*, London, 2006, pp. 137–147.

55. For the blend of the religious and the profane in the idea of the cosmopolitan, see S. Bose, *A Hundred Horizons: The Indian Ocean in the Age of Global Imperialism,* Cambridge, MA: Harvard University Press, 2006; E. Ho, *The Graves of Tarim*, Los Angeles, CA, California University Press, 2006; T.N. Harper, "Empire, Diaspora and Languages of Globalism, 1850-1914," in A.G. Hopkins, ed., *Globalization in World History*, London, W.W. Norton & Co, 2002; M. Frost, "'Wider Opportunities': Religious Revival, Nationalist Awakening and the Global Dimension in Colombo, 1870-1920", *Modern Asian Studies* 26, 4, 2002, pp. 937–967.

56. Deringil, S., "Legitimacy Structures in the Ottoman Empire: Abd al-Hamid II 1876-1909", *International Journal of Middle East Studies*, 23, 3, 1991, pp. 345–359.

57. C. Aydin, "The Muslim World as a Site of Global Intellectual History, 1839-1924," manuscript copy, 2010.

58. C. Aydin, *The Politics of Anti-Westernism in Asia: Visions of World Order in Pan- Islamic and Pan-Asian Thought*, New York: Columbia University Press, 2007.

59. S. Esenbel, "Japan's Global Claim to Asia and the World of Islam: Transnational Nationalism and the World Power, 1900-1945", *American Historical Review*, Oct., 2004, pp. 1140–1170.

60. Janet L. Abu Lughod, *Before European Hegemony: The World System A.D. 1250–1350*, New York, Oxford University Press, 1989; F. Robinson, "The Islamic World: From World System to Religious International," in

A. Green and V. Viaene, ed., *Religious Internationals in the Modern World*, London, Palgrave Macmillan, London, 2012.

61. B.D. Metcalf, *Islamic Revival in British India. Deoband, 1860-1900*, Delhi, 2002; U. Stark, *An Empire of Books: The Naval Kishore Press and the Diffusion of the Printed Word in Colonial India*, Ranikhet, Permanent Black, 2007, pp. 285–291.
62. N. Green, "Saints, Rebels and Booksellers: Sufis in the Cosmopolitan Western Indian Ocean, Ca. 1780-1920," in Simpson and Kresse, eds, *Struggling with History*, pp. 125–166.
63. M. Frost, "'Wider Opportunities': Religious Revival, Nationalist Awakening and the Global Dimension in Colombo, 1870-1920", *Modern Asian Studies*, 26, 4, 2002, pp. 937–967.
64. Aydin, "The Muslim World as a Site of Global Intellectual History, 1839-1924". He argues that Abd al Hamid's desire for global status in the Western league of empires made the cosmopolitan sinews of the old Empire the template for Islamic unity: Tanzimat-driven ideas of equity, justice, rule of law, and protection of minority rights became the key principles in the modernizing and centralizing agendas. Later, in the 1870s and 1880s, however, domestic problems and international defeats would make sultans like Abd al Hamid turn this image into more traditional roles like being the Caliph of the Muslim world. See also S. Deringil, *The Well-Protected Domains: Ideology and the Legitimation of Powers in the Ottoman Empire 1876-1909*, Oxford and New York, I.B. Tauris, 1998.

5

Revolutionaries, Maulvis, Swamis, and Monks

Burma's Khilafat Moment

Sana Aiyar

Bahadur Shah Zafar, the last Mughal Emperor, died in Rangoon in 1862 where he had lived in exile for five years. He was buried near the Shwedagon Pagoda, an imposing pre-colonial landmark that was one of the most sacred Buddhist sites in the region. With his burial in an obscure, unmarked grave, the colonial government intended to permanently erase the Mughals and their authority from South Asia, pensioning off Zafar's descendants to keep them in Rangoon in "poor plight" and "powerless to act." By 1903, it appeared that the British had succeeded in this mission. Zafar's grandson, Jamshed Bakht, who was born in Rangoon, was dependent on his government "pension," while his great-grandson, Moazzam Sultan, Bakht's nephew, worked as a clerk for an advocate in the city.[1] More poet than king, Zafar had had a premonition of this fate in his own lifetime as he wrote:

When death has fallen, on my tomb
O Zafar! Can any prayers repeat;
When worn out marks no longer loom,
Erased by numerous passing feet2

Many feet did, indeed, pass through Rangoon, far from the Mughal capital of Delhi. Burma's Lower Delta along the Irrawaddy river came under British rule in 1852 after the second Anglo-Burmese war, and it took another war in 1885 for the British to defeat the Burmese King, Thibaw Min, and exile him to Ratnagiri in western India, far from the royal capital of Mandalay that had been established just months before the 1857 rebellion.[3] During this time, Burma became a province of

British India, with Rangoon as its capital. From a population of about 98,745 in 1872, Rangoon boasted of a population of 230,000 residents in 1901. There were approximately 40,000 Muslims in Rangoon, amounting to 18 percent of the capital's population; by 1921, 68,000 Muslims came to live in the city, the majority of whom were migrants from India.[4] Contrary to Zafar's prophecy, far from being wiped out by obscurity and poverty, the Mughals and their descendants formed the nucleus around which the growing migrant population of Muslims and Hindus lived, worked, and worshiped.

In June 1921, Jamshed Bakht died. His funeral procession included thousands of Muslim mourners led by Abdulla Misri Khan, an itinerant maulvi from the United Provinces who was mobilizing Hindus and Muslims in Rangoon to join the Khilafat/non-cooperation movement that had been launched a few months earlier by the Indian National Congress.[5] Close to 5,000 of those present were members of the Anjuman Tahzib-ul-Akhlaq, the volunteer corps of a temperance and boycott movement Misri had organized. The picketing of liquor shops was led by Swami Parmanand, a priest associated with the Arya Samaj in Rangoon, and it was volunteers of the Anjuman who attended a large meeting of over 8,000 people at the Shwedagon Pagoda a month later to protest against the imprisonment of U Ottama, a Burmese Buddhist *pongyi* (monk) who was found guilt of sedition. Misri was one of the most prominent speakers at the protest meeting at the Shwedagon Pagoda leading the crowd of Muslims, Hindus, pongyis, and Burmese women in hailing "Mahatama Ottama ki jai."[6]

What brought the maulvi, the swami, and the pongyi together in Rangoon? This essay examines the genealogy of the postwar protests in Burma, when Muslim concerns over the Khalifa, anti-colonial Gandhian satyagraha, and Buddhist Burmese non-cooperation coalesced for a brief moment that has been all but forgotten in South Asian historiography. Islam, Sugata Bose and Ayesha Jalal contend in the introduction to this volume, is the ocean. Steam and print transformed oceanic Islam over the long nineteenth century, accelerating the pace of travel, both literally and imaginatively, for Muslims.[7] The universalist Muslim ecumene that emerged from the circulation of people and ideas across the Indian Ocean encountered, accommodated, and challenged territorial assertions of sovereignty by both European empires and their twentieth century nationalist counterparts. Among the most well-known expressions of this Islamic universalism is the Khilafat movement, which scholars regard as a critical conjuncture in South Asian history and historiography, a turning point marked on various scholarly registers. Historians have examined the Khilafat movement to interrogate the religious and political consciousness of Muslims in India and argue, on the one hand, that in this moment, with the deployment of religion into politics, we can trace the beginnings of Muslim separatism from nationalist mobilization that foreshadowed the demand for a separate homeland. Others have noted that it was, in fact, the Khilafat cause that facilitated the successful launch of an "Indian" national anti-colonial movement. The scope and scale of the Khilafat movement has also been studied to reveal the ways in which transimperial and transnational Islamic networks and consciousness framed very specific local demands and politics among Muslims in India, that both complemented and competed with other strands of communitarian mobilizations.[8] Building on this, historians have moved beyond the national framework to excavate the unfolding of regional iterations of the Khilafat agitation in Bengal and the United Provinces, for example.[9] Despite this rich and diverse scholarship, Muslims in Burma are not included in any of these discussions of Islamic universalism, anti-colonial nationalism, and communitarian separatism.

Indeed, Burma itself is left out of South Asian historiography, despite its being a province of British India till 1937. This scholarly oversight is largely due to two interconnected teleological arguments that map religion and nationalism on to historiographical frames of analysis. Pointing to the large presence of Indian labor and capital in Burma in the 1920s and 30s, Burmese nationalists within the Legislative Council and in the local press argued that their country was colonized twice over—by Britain and by India and Indians.[10] In demanding the separation of Burma from India, these nationalists invoked their religious, civilizational, and racial distinction in imagining and defining Burma as a Buddhist nation whose temporal and spiritual sovereignty was under threat from the millions of Muslim and Hindu migrants who were changing the demographic core of their country. This conflation of race on to place is reflected in Burmese historiography as Burma's history is cast as "Buddhist," and scholars have been overwhelmingly engaged with interrogating Buddhism and ethnicity in Burma.[11] In so doing, much like the Burmese nationalists who demanded the separation of Burma from India, historians have been both implicit and complicit in arguing that the inclusion of Burma in British India was an artificial, colonial "accident," and that unlike Pakistan and Bangladesh, Burma was never part of India, and by extension, South Asia.

The ongoing Rohingya crisis, however, has pulled the veil off any historical or historiographical claim Myanmar can make to either religious homogeneity or Burma's separation from South Asia. The expulsion of the Rohingya from the Arakan (Rakhine state) has made tragically visible the deeply entangled history of imperial and national assertions of territorial sovereignty; contestations over claims to homelands and citizenship; and the pursuit and persecution of oceanic and riverine mobility across the Bay of Bengal. The connections made by these entanglements and circulations go back more than a century. Steam and print enabled Muslims to "redefine the geography they inhabited, on both concrete and conceptual levels." As a result, "travel and translational contacts delivered content to movements whose social and cultural foundations [were] found at home."[12] Burma's Khilafat moment emerged at one such intersection of oceanic Islam, Burma's increasingly Buddhist Irrawaddy Delta, and Rangoon's Hindu and Muslim enclaves inhabited by migrants from the Indo-Gangetic plains.

While much of the discussion about the Indian presence in Burma in historical works has revolved around the tropes of exploited migrant labor and exploitative capital and moneylenders in the interwar years, this essay looks at Muslim merchants, intellectuals, and reformers who mobilized the large migrant community in Rangoon a decade earlier. Connecting the individual biographies of itinerant revolutionaries, swamis, maulvis, and pongyis in Burma, this chapter makes visible the networks and solidarities that converged in the everyday encounters on the streets of Rangoon and the oceanic circulations of intellectuals, emissaries, and political activists. In so doing, I argue that far from being bounded by a religiously, racially, or territorially defined community, Burma's postwar political ecumene emerged from the shared concerns of Hindus, Muslims, and Buddhists. Crossing the ocean, rivers, and deltas over which the British empire was continually asserting its temporal sovereignty, these concerns ranged from the mundane to the sacred, bringing together the maulvi, the swami, and the monk in the densely populated capital of Rangoon to challenge such imperial assertions. This was Burma's Khilafat moment.

Rangoon and Its Mughals

"Rangoon owes its history to two factors, the Shwe Dagon pagoda and the River." This is the opening sentence of the first "History" of Rangoon written by B.R. Pearn for the "Corporation" of the city in 1938, a piece of work commissioned by M.M. Rafi, who served as the mayor of the capital in 1936.[13] The hill on which the pagoda stood, Pearn continued, was an "obvious" place for worship as it rose "high above the level flats of the Irrawaddy Delta," while the river was "a natural highway from the fertile hinterland of Burma to the sea."[14] The city of Rangoon was developed into a port in 1755 by Alaungpaya, the founder of the Konbaung dynasty whose rule ended with Thibaw's exile to India in 1886. In 1852–1853, immediately after the Irrawaddy Delta had passed into British hands, Lord Dalhousie oversaw the redevelopment of Rangoon, pointing to its river bank as the obvious place to situate the "new town" due to its growing importance as a port and commerical city.[15]

Close to eleven million acres of land came under rice cultivation in the Irrawaddy Delta between 1896 and 1926. More than a million tons of this rice went to India, and just under two million tons was shipped elsewhere.[16] After being sowed, planted, and reaped, paddy reach rice mills, from where the grain was prepared for shipping. Approximately 5/6th of Burma's entire trade went through Rangoon port, making it among the busiest in the world, well beyond Dalhousie's prediction.[17] As business on the port grew, so did the city itself and its inhabitants. The government built numerous wharves along the river, adjacent to which business houses set up warehouses where grain and other exports were kept ready to load on to ships that docked in Rangoon. These warehouses were concentrated on the east of the river along the Strand, a grand street that crossed the breadth of the city. Rangoon's commercial hub, the aptly named Merchant Street, ran parallel to the Strand to the south of it, and to its north lay Dalhousie Street. Beyond Dalhousie lay Canal Street; northwest of Canạl was marked off as the cantonment where the colonial administration, with its military and European administrators, lived close to the Shwedagon Pagoda. A series of narrower streets ran perpendicular from the Strand to Canal Street, forming a complex grid.

While most of these streets were simply enumerated for nomenclature, one, in particular, was given a name, allegedly by Dalhousie himself "during the consumption of after-dinner port" because it was among his favorite in the city.[18] This was Mogul Street, named after the Muslim merchants settled there, that ran parallel to 29th Street and perpendicular to Merchant Street. In the absence of a rice stock-exchange, the cost and profits of over 3 million tons of this grain were traded on along Merchant and Mogul Streets, making this area, quite literally, the heart of Burma's political economy.[19] In 1911, out of a population of about 293,000, almost 80,000 people lived in these narrow streets that covered less than a dozen blocks, the majority of whom were migrants from India. These few square miles that they inhabited comprised of the entire spread of Alaungpaya's mid-eighteenth-century Rangoon that had been a "small island" in the river that flowed into the Irrawaddy.[20]

In 1872, about 15,000 migrants from India lived in Rangoon. A decade later, they constituted more than half of the population of a hundred thousand residents in the new colonial capital.[21] While Muslims initially outnumbered Hindus, by 1893, 58,000 Hindus and 29,000 Muslims came to live in this compact grid of blocks.[22] Some of the earliest residents of Mogul Street were likely among those who had been part of Bahadur Shah Zafar's entourage in exile.[23] By the early twentieth century, however, it was Burma's booming rice-industrial complex that attracted moneylenders and seasonal migrants from India, who constituted the bulk of Rangoon's population.

Chettiar bankers from Madras, already operating in the rice industry in the province and supplying credit in Ceylon and Malaya, moved in to provide capital to Burmese cultivators. By the 1870s, Chettiar moneylenders had established firms in the main towns of the Irrawaddy Delta, including Rangoon and Moulmein. Initially, they provided loans to local moneylenders who, in turn, extended credit to cultivators in the countryside. As the worldwide demand for rice increased and cultivators increasingly grew paddy for the market, the Chettiars offered agricultural credit directly to farmers and tenants. By the 1880s, Chettiar firms had opened branches in large villages and towns along the main rivers and railway lines of the delta. In 1910, about 350 firms operated in Burma, and over the next two decades, more than 1,650 Chettiar agencies supplied credit to small- and large-scale cultivators across the expanding rice frontier.[24] By 1930, Chettiar capital provided close to 60 percent of all crop loans and about 45 percent of long-term agricultural loans, amounting to approximately 500 million rupees.

The heavy lifting in this rice-industrial complex, quite literally, was done by unskilled migrant labor from across the Bay of Bengal who worked as seasonal agricultural labor in the countryside during the harvest, in rice milling factories after the harvest, and as porters on the Rangoon wharf carrying rice and other cargo on to the ships. As the scale of migrant sojourners increased, laborers themselves became part of the cargo on ships, and capitalists from Madras, Bombay, and Bengal ventured into the shipping industry, buying ships that carried deck passengers and modest amounts of cargo across the Bay of Bengal.

Chettiar capital and seasonal unskilled labor migrants have framed histories of Burma, especially as the 1930s were bookended by anti-Indian riots in Rangoon, and studies have conflated class, race, religion, and location into the flattened out figure of the Indian migrant.[25] But between the Chettiar's "venture" capital and the sweat and toil of coolie labor, migrants in Rangoon were busy going about their everyday, mundane lives, eating, praying, shopping, sleeping, and teaching, and it was to provide for these services that Tamil Muslim shopkeepers known as Chulias, Muslims merchant from Gujarat known as Suratis, and a large number of butchers, barbers, bookkeepers, commissioning agents, *darwans* (doormen), teachers, and preachers from the

Indo-Gangetic plains, especially the United Provinces and Bengal, arrived in and around Mogul Street and set up shop.[26] From the mid-nineteenth century onward, it was these Muslim, and not only the much written about and lamented Chettiar capitalists, who left their mark, quite literally, on the city, by buying property, building mosques, schools, and bazaars, and establishing rice mills.

Ebrahim Ali Mulla, for example, was the largest property owner in all of Rangoon in 1910. His father came to Burma from Rander, in Surat, and set up two rice mills covering 41 acres. Business was so profitable that the family built a private residence on the Ridge that covered nearly 29 acres.[27] Ebrahim took over his family business in 1862 and became Rangoon's municipal commissioner in 1871—a position he held for 37 years. In 1868, he founded the Surati Bazaar Company Limited that managed Surati Bazaar, located on Mogul Street, the most valuable property in Rangoon by the turn of the century by some accounts. Surati Bazaar, established around 1853, was spread over four blocks with more than 3,000 stalls where everyday goods and foodstuff were bought and sold. Ebrahim was one of several Muslim merchants from India who laid claim to Rangoon from the mid-nineteenth century onwards. The numerous mosques built around half a dozen blocks were patronized by other merchants who became self-appointed leaders of the community in the public realm. These included the Sunni Jamah Bengali Masjid built in 1862, the Chulia Jama Mosque established in 1856, the Mogul Shia Mosque erected in 1854, and the Surati Sunni Jama Masjid that opened around 1871.[28] With the exception of the Surati Masjid, all these religious sites were given to the community by the government as holdings that were exempt from taxation and purchase-price, generating nearly two lakh rupees for the city in sales within two years of its redevelopment.[29]

By the turn of the century, Rangoon was hailed as a quintessentially "modern" city, with a "rapidly developing … hybrid civilization" that welded together "the beneficient essentials of two enlightments … oriental and the occidental."[30] As a Sikh visitor described it in 1910 in a fitting analogy: Rangoon river's "muddy and murky" waters over which steamers brought passengers into the city gave way to a well-developed harbor "lit with thousands of incandescent electric bulbs." The wharf shed light on the "heterogenous" population of Buddhists, Hindus, and Muslims who "jostle against one another" on the streets scattered with mosques, temples, and churches. And it was in this "cosmopolitan" city that the wealthy, propertied Muslims formed public associations to assert their claims over the city as its respectable citizens and make themselves visible to Muslim intellectuals and activists in Bengal and the United Provinces.

An early expression of this came in 1895 in a letter to the editor of the *Muhammadan Observer and Moslem Chronicle* published in Calcutta. Titled "Rangoon Muhammadans," the writer, A.H. Chanea, complained that only two madrassas existed in the city to educate young boys of the community, among which was the Madarsa-i-Islamia that had been established in 1888 by two merchants and the Madarsa-i-Salamat. Bemoaning those who "squander their money in marriages and feastings," Chanea's note ended in an appeal: "O Muslims of Burma! Are you still asleep? How long are you going to remain in utter darkness? Do you not know your bretheren the Indian Muslims are striving hard to overthrow the veil of ignorance? ... Awake! Awake! and send your children to Madrasa and schools for the acquirement of knowledge [sic]."[31] In June 1899, a "Bengal Mohammedan Association" was established in Rangoon to "cultivate the principles of unanimity and fraternity among its members." The association met on the first Sunday of every month. Within a year, it rented a permanent space on Dalhousie Street that could accommodate up to 300 people.[32] Approximately 800 people attended the public meetings of the Bengal Muhammadan Association. The parochial title of the association was, however, misleading. Speeches were delivered in Urdu, Hindustani, Bengali, and English, and maulvis from the Indo-Gangetic plains as well as the local Surati and Bengali masjids were prominent participants at the meetings and ceremonies at the madrassa where students were offered the "title of Hafiz."

It was because of this large and visible Muslim community that lived, worked, studied, and worshiped in Rangoon that the colonial government worked so hard to marginalize the Mughals, confining the royal family to the cantonment area, northwest of the commercial hub, at the foot of the Shwedagon Pagoda. In 1872, Bahadur Shah Zafar's son built a mosque near his quarters. The mosque lay to the east of Rangoon Central Jail. It was moved and rebuilt by prisoners within the garden of the jail compound a couple of times to accommodate the expansions of the prison. After his parents' death, Jamshed Bakht repeatedly laid claim to being the rightful heir of the mosque and the land around it. The government refused to issue him the land grant, claiming that there was no record of the original title to the site, nor any mention of the mosque in the demarcation plans for the jail garden that was built in 1896–1897.[33] Poverty and obscurity, the government believed, would prevent Zafar's descendants from assuming a public profile. But the last of the Mughals continued to be held in "high veneration" by a number of Muslim intellectuals in India and Burma.[34]

In 1903, Abdul Salam Rafiqi, a "well-known writer in Urdu and Persian" from Nurpur, Kangra, arrived in Rangoon "anxious to discover traces of Bahadur Shah Zafar and his descendants."[35] Rafiqi applied to the government to establish himself as a *waqaf*, but he was turned down. He then found employment as a commissioning agent for the many Muslim business houses that operated out of Mogul Street. Shortly thereafter, Rafiqi located the land where Zafar and his Begum, Zinath Mahal, had been buried in 1862 and 1886 respectively, in the compound of a house within the military cantonment area, wedged between a tennis court and horse-training circuit. "Distressed" by this "insult to the memory of the last of the Mughals and the Muhammadans of India," Rafiqi launched a press campaign in Burma and India. On behalf of the Muslims of Rangoon, he requested that private individuals be allowed to purchase the strip of land enclosing the grave to put up "a monument worthy of the memory of Bahadur Shah." He wanted to create a space that would accommodate Muslims who "may wish to pay their respects to the last King of Delhi," who was revered not just as a royal but as a Sufi saint and poet. A local businessman in Rangoon, C.S. Ahmad Islamabadi, was willing to finance the project. Rafiqi demanded that the government "mark the resting place of the ex-King" in a manner that would befit "the last of the proud line of the Mughals" and recover the grave from its current "unsung" and "dishonoured" state. The king-emperor, Rafiqi argued, was "said to rule over a larger number of Musalmans than any other sovereign."[36] Despite Queen Victoria's pardon extended to the rebels of 1857, he lamented, "Zafar could not escape calumny even after death; the ashes have to suffer contempt for the supposed guilt of the once living body." Rafiqi went on to reason that even if his grave "may not be preserved as befits a king and compeer of the British throne, it ought to be preserved as a tribute to the memory of Zafar, the charming ... and celebrated poet."[37]

On the eve of his departure from India as Viceroy in 1905, Lord Curzon turned down this proposal, agreeing with the opinion of the Governor of Burma that "it would be very inappropriate" for the government to "perpetuate or pay respect" to Bahadur Shah's memory. More significantly, they feared that rescuing his grave from obscurity would risk the tomb becoming "a place of pilgrimage."[38] Rafiqi continued his public campaign, eventually meeting with some success. Curzon's successor in 1907, the Earl of Minto, acquiesced to placing "a plain stone slab" over the tomb and to building an iron railing around it. Although the new Viceroy had "no wish to do honor to the memory of the ex-King," he acknowledged that the grave "should not be lost sight of," suggesting a simple inscription to be carved on the slab: "Bahadur Shah, Ex-King of Delhi, died at Rangoon November 7th 1862 and was buried near this spot."[39] An additional inscription was subsequently included that read, "Zinath Mahal wife of Bahadur Shah who died on the 17th July 1886 is also buried near this spot."[40] On the face of it, this seemed a victory for Rafiqi, but he requested a few changes to the proposed engraving. He asked that two separate graves be built for the poet and his wife, and that the phrase "near this tomb" be removed. He also requested that the mausoleum be given to the Muslim community in Rangoon, and that a Persian inscription be included along with the English. Perhaps it was Rafiqi's insistance that the exact sites of Zafar and Zinath Mahal's burials were identified by "several people alive to-day who were present at the death and burial of these two" that caused the government to turn down these requests, as Rafiqi was likely refering to the Mughal's descendants, especially Jamshed Bakht. He accused the government of deliberately "misleading" Muslims into thinking that the potentially sacred site had been lost in time by including the words "near this spot" in the inscription.[41] In fact, visitors would be standing at the exact spot where their late-emperor had been buried; this place of pilgrimage, as Rafiqi envisioned it, would be an eternal reminder of the loss of Mughal—and Muslim—sovereignty, which made it all the more urgent for the government to retain complete control over.

On August 26, 1907, about 300 "leading Mohammedans" of Rangoon gathered to thank the government for having erected a "permanent memorial" over the grave.[42] Ahmed Mulla Dawood presided over the public meeting at which Rafiqi moved the resolution of gratitude to the government. Dawood's father, Mulla Dawood Hussain, had moved to Rangoon from Jamnagar, in Kutch, in 1860. Hussain established a firm of merchants and millers, Mulla Dawood, Sons and Company, in Rangoon at Merchant Street, to oversee his large business acquisitions, which included two rice mills, oil presses, ginneries, and a large number of commissioning agents, not just in Rangoon but across the province. Dawood was born in 1866 in Medina. Dawood began to work in the firm in 1889 and took over the Rangoon business from his father in 1903, which he ran with his son, M.H. Mucky Mulla Dawood.[43] Dawood was as much a businessman as he was a community leader. In 1910, he served as the Secretary of the Rangoon Rice Merchants' Association and simultaneously held the position of President of the Rangoon Mohammedan Association, which had supported Rafiqi's campaign to rescue Bahadur Shah Zafar's mosque from obscurity.

As a devout Muslim and patron to the community, Dawood associated himself with Zafar's descendants, including Jamshed Bakht. An Irish convert to Islam who was born in Scotland in 1874, Yehya-en-Nasr (John Parkinson), spent two years in Burma, 1908–1910, during which time he published widely on matters relating to his faith.[44] Three monographs, *Muslim Chivalry*, *Essays on Islamic Philosophy*, and *Outward Bound*, were published in Rangoon, influenced, quite likely, by conversations Parkinson had had with leading Muslim intellectuals in the city. He joined Rafiqi and Dawood's campaign to restore Bahadur Shah Zafar's tomb, and dedicated his 1909 publication, *Essays on Islamic Philosophy*, to Rafiqi "as a token of esteem."[45] In 1911, Parkinson edited, published, and circulated "Inversion of Times," a pamphlet written by Rafiqi in 1906 as part of his ongoing campaign to erect a "tomb due an emperor" that would "perpetuate the memory of the royal poet and the last line of the mightiest dynasty the world had ever seen."[46] On his departure from Rangoon, forty-one "Muslim Gentlemen of Rangoon," hosted a banquet for Parkinson. Dawood was the "chairman" of the banquet. Seated at the center of a photograph commemorating the event was Jamshed Bakht, with Dawood to his right and Parkinson, the guest of honor, to his left.[47] Evidently, for Muslim merchants and intellectuals in Rangoon, the exiled royals remained at the center of elite Muslim networks and public shows of respectability.

The public thanksgivings and banquets hosted by the "Muslim gentlemen of Rangoon," however, obscured the emerging political consciousness of men like Rafiqi and Dawood who found themselves at the center of oceanic and riverine revolutionary networks at the outbreak of the First World War. In the aftermath of the Swadeshi movement, Rafiqi's own politics came under government notice in Burma, where he spent about a decade. In 1907, the Criminal Investigation Branch of the Burma police took notice of "seditious" articles that he carried on a train in Rangoon. These included copies of the revolutionary paper, "Indian Socialist" printed in London, and a supplement to *United Burma*, a journal edited by Vyavaharik Madanjit. Rafiqi and Madanjit were part of a wider oceanic network of Swadeshi activists. Madanjit had arrived in Burma from South Africa, where he had enlisted in M.K. Gandhi's Indian Ambulance Corps during the Boer War in 1899–1900. Madanjit was a close associate of Gandhi's and had founded the *Indian Opinion* in Natal three years before moving to Burma. *United Burma* had a modest circulation of about 550 subscribers.[48] The supplement that Rafiqi was carrying featured a photograph of Lala Lajpat Rai, who had been deported to Mandalay, without trial, for his involvement in the Swadeshi movement. The page carried the title "Vande Mataram," the rallying slogan of Swadeshi activists, and described Rai as "the first deported Martyr."[49] Rafiqi was also involved in Muslim educational initiatives in the United Provinces and collected close to Rs 8,000 for Aligarh College from Rangoon's merchants and traders. He did not, however, send this money to Aligarh, and left Burma in 1912 when this was discovered by a professor from the college who visited Rangoon.[50] From Burma, Rafiqi went on to Singapore, Tokyo, Batavia, and Medan. His political itinerary placed him at a "crucial juncture in Ghadar transoceanic communications," suggesting a revolutionary political pilgrimage that began in Rangoon and ended, as far as the archival record is concerned, in Kupang.[51] It is likely that the money he collected in the name of education reform was used to finance revolutionary activity.

In March 1915, the Government of Java arrested Rafiqi for printing Urdu pamphlets that urged the people of India to "rise and seize the opportunity" provided by the First World War, especially the "successes" of Germany and Turkey, to "rid this sacred country of the unclean barbarian English."[52] Later that year, Rafiqi's associates in Rangoon, Ahmed Mulla Dawood, Madanjit, and a dozen other mostly Muslim merchants of Rangoon, were also interned on suspicion of being involved in the Ghadar conspiracy. Although Dawood and Madanjit were "rendered innocuous" and released at the end of the war, their fellow-detainee, Ali Ahmed Siddiqi, was tried under the Defence of India Act of 1915. Ali was found to be the "most vicious conspirator" and sentenced to death for preaching sedition, advocating rebellion against the King-Emperor, and trying to create a "rising among Burmans."[53]

Ali Ahmed Siddiqi and the Mandalay Conspiracy Case of 1917

The outbreak of the Balkan wars in 1912–1913 threatened Ottoman sovereignty and mobilized Muslim intellectuals in the United Provinces, especially students and faculty of the Aligarh College, to join the Red Crescent Society to express the "deep sympathy and goodwill" of Muslims in India toward their "co-religionists" in Turkey.[54] Maulana Mohammad Ali's paper *Comrade* and Maulana Abul Kalam Azad's *Al-Hilal* took the lead in publicizing the events taking place in Turkey, expressing concern and support for their spiritual leader, the Khalifa. Dr Ahmad Mukhtar Ansari took a medical mission to the Balkans in December 1912 that included five doctors, seven dressers, and ten nurses and ambulance bearers. The mission was given a public and emotive send-off by Mohammad Ali, while Azad gave a moving eulogy to the "proud and affectionate Muslims" on their departure, advising them to take care of the Turks and their wounds "softly and with great care… since those wounds are not the wounds of the Turks alone but are the scars of Islam itself."[55]

Ali Ahmed Siddiqi, who was 18 years old at the time, joined the mission as a compounder.[56] He was one of these twenty-two men who spent about six months in Turkey, stopping briefly in Egypt before returning to India.Siddiqi was born in Shahzadpur, Faizabad district, in the United Provinces in 1899. He was one of three brothers and passed his matriculation examination from Allahabad University. One brother joined government services in Rai Bareli, while the other set up a meat shop in Rangoon. On his return to India, Siddiqi went to Burma, initially to Nyaunglebin. He tried to return to Europe as an ambulance volunteer at the outbreak of the First World War, but his request was turned down by the government. He then joined his brother in Rangoon, tapping into the city's large Muslim community in and around Mogul Street to find work and company. Mulla Ahmed Dawood employed Siddiqi as a clerk and introduced him to other firms. In December 1914, he got a job as a twine department clerk in Abdul Gany Beg Mahomed's firm, where he was tasked with weighing rice bags for three hours every morning and two hours in the evenings. Three months later, Siddiqi was fired from this job for oversleeping.[57]

Siddiqi lived with his brother, Nisar Ali Ahmed, above a tobacco shop on 25th Street in a room they rented from the shopkeeper, Zain Ali. Ali was also from the United Provinces and had qualified as a teacher in Lucknow. He come to Rangoon from Lucknow in 1909 to serve as a schoolmaster of the Shokut Islam School, later becoming its headmaster for five years. He was then appointed Honorary Superintendent of the Jamal Moslem Girls' School, a position he held while also attending to his shop. Between March and December 1915, Siddiqi was out of work and spent his days in and around his brother's meat shop on 26th Street, expanding his network of acquaintances in the city. Among these were Rafiq-ul-Haq, a school teacher from the United Provinces who taught in the Shokut Islam School; Mohsin Ali, headmaster of the Memon Jamat Academy; M.M. Naidu, assistant teacher at the academy; and Sheikh Juman, a contractor who had been living in Rangoon for 18 years and owned an eating house. Siddiqi also got close to Mahbub-ul-Rahman, a tobacco shopkeeper who came to Rangoon to meet his uncle who taught at the Surati Masjid. Siddiqi joined a Quran reading group that Rahman attended on Thursday evenings.[58]

Siddiqi had several visitors from the United Provinces in early 1915, many of whom were connected with his travels in Turkey. Among them were Abdul Hamid, a student leader at Aligarh, and Shah Jilani, who had served in Dr Ansari's medical mission with him. Jilani was accompanied by Niaz Khan of Bhopal and Fahim Ali of Muradabad, both of whom had spent time in Cairo before coming to Rangoon. Fahim Ali, whom Sidiqi had met in Turkey, stayed in the city for five months between January and May 1915, employed as a preacher in the Isha'at-i-Islam society. Nizamuddin Qureshi, a follower of Khwaja Hasan Nizami of Delhi, also came to Rangoon in March 1915 and met Siddiqi. Qureshi worked as an editor of a local newspaper and taught at the Madarsa-i-Islamia mentioned in the previous section. He lived on Mogul Street until he left Rangoon for Delhi in November 1915.[59]

The First World War, the future of Britain, the history of India and India's Muslims, and their experience in Turkey during the Balkans war were the main intellectual, political, and social concerns that the preachers,teachers, and traders whom Siddiqi befriended discussed at length on Mogul Street and in the mosque, schools, and shops adjoining it. Siddiqi engaged his new acquaintances in long discourses on the Turks, his travels in Constantinople and Egypt, his impressions of Dardanelles, and his perspective on colonial education, the British government in India, and the war itself. His time in Turkey had made a deep impact on Siddiqi. He was impressed with the Young Turks, particularly Enver Bey, whom he met with Dr Ansari and his volunteers.[60] He talked to Naidu, Rahman, Juman, Mohsim Ali, and Zain Ali about the military education given to the rich and the poor by the Young Turks, who, he believed, were very strong and had great sympathy for Muslims in India. These Turkish revolutionaries, Siddiqi assured his friends, regarded Indian Muslims as "very dear to them." He closely followed the events at Dardanelles during the war, claiming that the Turks would be successful in defending their straits from the

British. Siddiqi reported to Juman that the British had lost thirty-five ships and eight lakh men at Dardanelles and told Zain Ali that "one Turk could seize two white men and bang their heads together." He would often include a poem in these eulogies to the Turks, warning the Europeans, especially the British, that they would now realize the consequences of killing Turks during the Balkan wars.[61]

Siddiqi's admiration of the Young Turks was juxtaposed to his disillusionment with the British. At their Thursday Quran reading group, he told Rahman that after his time in Turkey, he no longer "had the same respect" for the English. Siddiqi spoke to Naidu, Haq, and Zain Ali at length about the injustice of British education in India. This education, he concluded, kept Indians in slavery. Taking examples from government school books that the teachers used in their classrooms, Siddiqi pointed to the portrayal of Indian fathers as agriculturists plowing their land, the mothers grinding corn, and the children carrying implements of husbandry. Rather than teaching students about "horses and swords and riddles" to make them "brave and enthusiastic," the colonial curriculum "disheartened" students, Siddiqi complained. He was particularly critical of the "Hunter History of India," the textbook assigned to teachers for their qualifying examination. This textbook, he complained to Zain Ali, glorified the British and cast Muslims as degenerate, especially since Aurangzeb's time. He criticized the British for paying higher salaries to Europeans over Indians and pointed to the plague in India as an example of English injustice that had left his compatriots so poor that they had to burn dried cow dung instead of coal to cook their food, causing disease and pain. The British, Siddiqi concluded, had to be removed, and he talked about raising money to send to the Turks and Germans to ensure their victory over Britain during the war, and "kick" the British out of India.[62] He soon got the opportunity to put his thoughts into action.

On February 15, 1915, about 900 Indian soldiers of the 5th Light Infantry, a predominantly Muslim regiment, mutinied in Singapore.[63] The British considered this part of the Ghadar conspiracy originating in the United States. Within days of the uprising in Singapore, two Ghadar activists, Hussein Khan of Punjab and Mujtaba Hussain from the United Provinces, arrived in Rangoon.[64] Between February and

July 1915, several other revolutionaries entered Burma from Siam. They rented a room in a house that had hitherto served as a coolie barrack. Located east of Mogul Street, near the warehouses and the docks, 16 Dufferin Street became the Rangoon headquarters of the Ghadar Party.[65] The revolutionaries hoped to pass unnoticed in the immigant enclaves of the capital among the thousands of seasonal laborers who worked in the warehouses and wharves along the river.

Hussein Khan had lived in Hong Kong at the turn of the century. In Rangoon, he had a chance meeting with an old acquaintance from China—Harbaj Rai. Rai had gone from Hong Kong to Canada in 1907 and moved to Rangoon in 1915 to teach in St Gabriel's School. Rai befriended another teacher in the city, Rafiq-ul Haq, who had been listening closely to Siddiqi. His impassioned political discussions had resonated with Haq. On a mission to recruit Rai, Khan brought Mujtaba Hussain with him to Juman's eating house in March, where Rai was joined by Haq. Hussain talked to them about the need for Indians to get higher education, of Mazzini and the improvements he had made in Italy, and of India as a "golden sparrow" that they should "not let slip." Although he failed to recruit either, in Haq's words, Hussain made a "great impression" on him and he took him to meet his "friend" Siddiqi who "spoke the same way."[66] Haq brought Hussain to Siddiqi's house on 25th Street, and with this introduction, Siddiqi became the epicenter, in Rangoon, of revolutionary networks in across the Indian and Pacific oceans that came together to fight the empire created by the little island in the Atlantic ocean.

Having recruited Siddiqi to their cause, Mujtaba Hussain and Hussein Khan left Burma for Siam, promising to send him Ghadar papers and pamphlets for distribution, and arms and ammunition to put into action their plans to assassinate European officials. In June, they put together a bundle of revolutionary literature that were sown into a mattress in Rehang, Siam. From Rehang, the papers arrived in Mae Sot, on the border of Siam and Burma, where they were taken out of the mattress and put into a bundle to be sent to Rangoon by a trusted Ghadar recruit. Meanwhile, Sohan Lal, another revolutionary, brought about 1,000 copies of Ghadar papers from into Burma. He, too, stayed at 16 Dufferin Street and met Siddiqi before proceeding to Pyawbwe, where a large number of Sikh soldiers were stationed. Before their departure, Siddiqi had introduced Hussain and Khan to Fahim Ali. Ali revealed that he was deputed by the Turkish government to "spread sedition" in Burma. Together, they took an "oath" written by Sohan Lal, a paper "that was regarded as the Koran." Ali and Siddiqi distributed the Ghadar papers at the Surati and Bengali masjids in Rangoon.[67] In May 1915, however, fearing arrest, Ali left for Moradabad, where he was subsequently arrested.[68] Siddiqi's other visitors from the Red Crescent Society, Niaz Khan, Shah Jilani, and Nizamuddin Qureshi, were also arrested in India for their "pro-Turkey," "anti-British" activities.[69] But Siddiqi continued his activities in Rangoon, staying under the radar among the many thousands of migrants in the city. He deployed his large network of intellectuals and traders around Mogul Street to recruit teachers and merchants to his cause that had traversed the Indian Ocean and made its way from the Indo-Gangetic plains to the Irrawaddy Delta, making it simultaneously a comunitarian and universalist one that was anti-colonial and revolutionary, and concerned both India and Burma.

A month after meeting with Mujtaba Hussain, Hussein Khan, and Sohan Lal, Siddiqi went to the Memon Jamat Academy, where M.M. Naidu, a Tamil Hindu teacher he knew, taught English. He spoke to Mohsim Ali, the headmaster of the academy, with "great prolixity" about the need for Muslims to follow "Sikhs, Hindus and Punjabis" who were "keenly alive to their national greatness." Muslims, he lamented, were "striking into oblivion without retrieving the tottering power of the past."[70] Siddiqi suggested starting a society in Rangoon to help Turkey and thereby subvert British rule, telling both Naidu and Ali that he had "promised" the Sultan of Turkey to organize a "mutiny" in India. Ali framed the rules and objectives of the society, which included a written oath to initiate members and promises not to betray one another if they were arrested, to spy on police moves to avoid arrest, and to give pecuniary aid in the event of a member's arrest. Other members included Nizamuddin Qureshi, the itinerant scholar from Delhi; Munshi Abdul Shakur, who owned a gramophone store; Wally Mohammed, who had a furniture shop; Ebrahim Gora Bawa, a merchant and contractor who had employed Naidu as a clerk; Maulvi

Mohammed Ahmed; Maulvi Fani; Sheikh Juman; and Mohammad Salim, who lived with Juman. Significantly, Siddiqi also tapped into Abul Salam Rafiqi's network of intellectuals and community leaders, bringing some of them into the society. These included Vyavaharik Madanjit and Ahmed Mulla. Independent of Siddiqi, Dawood had been in touch with the Singapore revolutionaries. In January 1915, a Muslim merchant in Singapore wrote a letter to Dawood claiming that the soldiers of the Malay States, who were predominantly "devout" Indian Muslims, were ready to "fight for the Sultan" of Turkey, and asked Dawood to arrange for a Turkish warship to be sent to Malaya to take them to the war front.[71]

Siddiqi, Bawa, and Mohsim Ali administered the oath to members, who used the password "Mohammed" to identify one another.[72] Siddiqi was tasked with collecting firearms, raising money, and spreading sedition along with Ali Ahmed Saad, Wally Mohamed, and Qureshi. At the conspiracy trial in April 1917, Naidu claimed that the society had distributed between 10,000–20,000 Ghadar papers during this time. Ali Baksh was tasked with converting soldiers to their cause, while Munshi Shakur, whose gramophone shop was a front to smuggle opium and cocaine, was put in charge of acquiring arms and ammunition. Madanjit, who was an active member of the Burma Provincial Indian National Congress, was to tap into the Hindu community in Rangoon to raise subscriptions and recruit members, while Naidu was to recruit Chulia shopkeepers, approximately 40,000 of whom lived in Rangoon at the time, to the cause and circulate Ghadar papers.. Bawa acted as treasurer, keeping track of money and distributing funds for the members' activities.[73]

The entire group came together at the Memon Jamat Academy and at Madanjit's and Shakur's houses; individual members also met one another in and around Mogul Street in their homes, shops, and mosques. Siddiqi gave Mohsim Ali Ghadar papers and pamphlets, which he had translated from Urdu into English, for Naidu, who, in turn, reproduced the material in Tamil to distribute among the Chulia. In July 1915, an Afghan named "Rasul" visited Rangoon and met Siddiqi, Dawood, Naidu, and Bawa. He accompanied Siddiqi to the Surati Masjid to distribute Ghadar papers and gave Naidu some money for the society's activities. Shakur had procured at least half a dozen pistols by then and was expecting a larger consignment of arms. A month earlier, A.M. Ghose (alias Bose) arrived in Rangoon from Calcutta and met Naidu and Siddiqi at Madanjit's house. Ghose gave a bomb-making formula to Siddiqi, and Madanjit suggested that he travel in Upper Burma disguised as a pongyi to avoid arrest. The group also decided to use a monk's disguise to recruit Burmans to their cause by finding a relation of the Burmese royal family to join them.

By this time, the police had uncovered Mujtaba Hussain's activities in Singapore leading up to the mutiny there and had begun tracing his movements in Siam and Burma with the help of his brother, Mustafa Hussain, who was employed in Gorakhpur, and with whom Mujtaba had been corresponding. In October 1915, Tassadaq Hussein, the police inspector in the United Provinces appointed to find Mujtaba, located the bundle of Ghadar papers he had put together for Siddiqi in Siam which included two letters addressed to Siddiqi and Fahim Ali. Hussein went undercover to Rangoon and gave these to Siddiqi, using the letters as proof of his revolutionary credentials. Siddiqi kissed the letter on receipt.[74] Bakr Id fell on October 19 in 1915, a few days after Siddiqi got his marching orders from Hussain. Siddiqi immediately convened a meeting at the Memon Jamat Academy with Ali, Naidu, Madanjit, Bawa, Shakur, and Dawood, where they resolved to start a "mutiny" on Bakr Id.[75] Dawood promised Rs 20,000 for the cause; Bawa contributed Rs 500; and Madanjit had collected approximately Rs 600. The first plan of action was to shoot Europeans at Montgomery Street. The "rising," however, was postponed to December because of inadequate ammunition, giving the police a little more time to gather evidence against Siddiqi, Naidu, and Ali.

In November 1915, the police in Rangoon recruited Maung Po Thein, a Hindustani-speaking Burmese paddy and general broker who had spent two months in Siam in August 1915, to go undercover into the group. Thein approached Naidu on the pretext of wanting him to teach English to his children, meeting him almost every day until his arrest. He told Naidu that he had heard about the Ghadar party during his time in Bangkok and indicated that he wanted to support the cause, claiming that he knew how to locate members of the Burmese royal family. Naidu sent Thein to meet Siddiqi, suggesting a "chance" meeting at a Chulia reading room or Juman's eating house, places that Siddiqi frequented. Naidu eventually sent Siddiqi to Thein's house directly.[76] Thein was just the man Siddiqi needed to expand his thus far predominantly Indian and Muslim revolutionary network to the Burmese. Emphatically stating that it was "time to wipe all white men out of our country," Siddiqi asked Thein to locate for him a pongyi *kyaung* (Buddhist monastery) where he could keep arms and revolutionaries hidden away from the police. Thein took him to the Thein Byu Kyaung Dike in Stockade Road and promised to introduce him to the head pongyi of the monastery to influence Burmans to rebel.

In the first week of December, the government arrested several Sikh military policemen at Pyawbwe who had collected firearms and explosives following Sohan Lal's visit earlier in the summer.[77] Worried that the arrival of this ammunition would activate the Rangoon group into action, the governor ordered their arrest. On the 7th of December 1915, Siddiqi, his brother Nisar, who had actively criticized Siddiqi's politics to their neighbors, Dawood, his son M.H. Mucky Mulla, Madanjit, Munshi Shakur, Mohsim Ali, Naidu, Sheikh Juman, Ali Baksh, Bawa, Wally Mohammed, and Abdul Hamid were arrested and sent to Cheduba Island in Kyaukpyu district on the Arakan coast.[78] Two weeks later, the governor successfully petitioned the Government of India to include Mandalay, Rangoon, Amherst, and Yamathein under the Defence of India Act of 1915—an emergency wartime legislation passed to deal with revolutionaries.[79] The Act armed the government to take into preventive detention and detain without trial individuals suspected of threatening the security of the empire, and to set up special tribunals to fast-track specific cases as needed in different provinces.

A total of 127 people were detained in Burma under the Defence of India Act.[80] In April 1916, Ali Ahmed Siddiqi was tried at Mandalay along with Mujtaba Hussain and two other Ghadar revolutionaries. They were accused of waging war against the King-Emperor to "deprive him of the sovereignty of British India."[81] The trial lasted three months. Siddiqi denied all charges, dismissing as "false" the evidence of his

Rangoon circle, including Huq, Rahman, Juman, Zain Ali, Naidu, and Hussein Khan (both of whom turned approvers) and the accounts of Tassadaq Hussein and Maung Po Thein. His lawyer, a Bengali Hindu R.B. Mukerjee, argued that Siddiqi was not a Ghadarite but a member of a "local revolutionary society" that was a separate association. The Special Tribunal Judge, however, concluded that although the society was formed in Rangoon, its objectives were "identical" to those in the Ghadar network. He also pointed that at the very least, Siddiqi was considered a "leading Gadarite" in Siam as he was entrusted with the "important duty of distributing literature on a large scale." Finally, the judge argued that the reestablishment of "the vanished glories of the Mahomedan empire" was "the bait" for Muslims to be recruited to the Ghadar cause, "just as the restoration of the Burmese rule was for Burmans." Significantly, despite his young age, it was Siddiqi's aspiration to "create a rising among Burmans" which, if even "partially successful would have had awful results," that led the judge to sentence him to be "hanged by the neck till he be dead." Mujtaba Hussain received the same punishment.[82] It was the potentially explosive intersection of the temporal assertations of oceanic Islam and riverine Buddhist sovereignty that so threatened the colonial state that it moved quickly and violently to silence such a challenge.

In December 1917, Siddiqi and Hussain succeeded in having their sentences commuted to transportation for life. They were sent to Andaman Central Jail in February 1918. A year later, with the end of the war, the British government extended clemency to those detained under the Defence of India Act in 1915 unless they had committed violent crimes, including murder. In response, the governor of Burma, Reginald Craddock, noted that Siddiqi was a "dangerous Pan Islamist conspirator," turning down his clemency plea in May 1920 on the grounds that "the conspiracy was a recent and exceedingly dangerous one."[83] In November 1921, Siddiqi was transferred to Naini Central Jail in Allahabad, where he met Pandit Krishnakanta Malaviya, later a member of the Central Legislative Assembly, who was also incarcerated there.[84]

Siddiqi's wife, Musamat, whom he had married in November 1915, just seventeen days before his arrest, petitioned the government in July

1924 to extend clemency to Siddiqi on the grounds of his youth at the time of his arrest, arguing that he had fallen into "the evil company" who "appealed to him in the name of patriotism" and in whose hands he "became a tool". In view of the "changed political situation" in India, Musamat requested Siddiqi be released from jail "in the name of humanity and mercy," concluding that she had been living like a widow since her marriage, and was "young and helpless, with no one to support her."[85] Although the governor of Burma did not reply to her, Malaviya took up her cause with another member of Legislative Assembly, Diwan Bahadur T. Rangachari, claiming that Siddiqi had "suffered" and "repented," and was willing to be released "on any condition." Rangachari put pressure on the government, suggesting that it would be a matter of "great satisfaction to the public" if Siddiqi were released.[86] On July 20, 1925, Siddiqi's clemency petition was accepted. The superintendent of police and home department noted that although his crime had been a serious one, he had not in fact done anything except distribute Ghadar literation in 1915. Having served eight years in jail, local officials found him a "suitable case for clemency" under the following conditions: that he would not return to Burma, would not participate in any form of political activity, and would report his residence to the police every three months. Siddiqi willingly agreed to these conditions, promising to do "nothing unconstitutional," expressing his plans to "do social service for my country," but outside of politics, which had caused him to "suffer" and lose his "health."[87]

Although Siddiqi was the only one of the Rangoon circle to be tried and convicted after their arrest in December 1915, his trial in Mandalay had made it clear that Dawood, Baksh, Mohammed, Ali, Bawa, Shakur, Madanjit, and Naidu were "active seditionists prior to their internment."[88] In August 1916, the District Magistrate at Kyaukpyu recorded statements of those arrested. Naidu turned approver and was allowed to go to Madras after the trial. The others were detained as a "precautionary measure" to render them "innocuous" until the end of the war, when they were released.[89] While Siddiqi renounced politics in 1925, by the time Dawood and Madanjit were released after the war, the political milieu in Rangoon had shifted, taking Siddiqi's political concerns beyond the small group of Muslim intellectuals and merchants to a large number of Hindus, Muslims, and Buddhists in the city who launched a Gandhian satyagraha involving the boycott of government schools, the picketing of shops selling foreign cloth and liquor, and demanding the restoration of the Khalifa.

Khilafat, Non-cooperation, and Mass Mobilization across the Bay of Bengal

The Defence of India Act of 1915 armed the government to detain not just revolutionaries but anyone it identified as a threat to Britain and her empire. Mohammad Ali and his brother Shaukat Ali, who had consolidated the support of Muslim students at Aligarh for Turkey during the Balkan wars, were arrested and confined to a remote corner in Central India to limit their reach among Muslims in the country. Before their internment, the Ali brothers had found a spiritual mentor in Maulana Abdul Bari of Farangi Mahal, Lucknow, with whom they kept in close contact. Bari headed the Anjuman-i-Khuddam-i-Kaaba, an association concerned with protecting the holy places of Islam, especially as Turkish sovereignty—the seat of the Khalifa—was under threat.[90] Keenly aware of this anxiety, the British government made several proclamations between November 1914, when they went to war with Turkey, and January 1918, as the hostilities was nearing its conclusion, to reassure Muslims in India that their conflict was a political one, with the Ottoman government, and not a religious one. Lloyd George pledged that Muslim holy places would not be attacked and that Constantinople would remain in Turkish hands. The decisive defeat of the Ottoman empire in October 1918 was watched closely in India, as it became clear that the British would not necessarily keep their pledge. Dr Ansari, who had led the Red Crescent Society medical mission that took Siddiqi to the Balkans, chaired the annual Muslim League meeting in December 1918 in Delhi, welcoming into its fold the ulema, especially Bari. Ansari publicly criticized Britain's policy regarding the Khalifa, indicating the increasing ambivalence of Indian Muslims toward the government. "The Indian Musalmans take a deep interest in the fate of their co-religionists outside India," he stated, warning that the "collapse of the Muslim powers of the world is bound to have an adverse influence" on his community.[91]

The immediate aftermath of the First World War created a "unique historical conjuncture" that accommodated Bari, Ansari, and the Ali brothers' Islamic universalism with their local, political assertions. In March 1918, Bari and Ansari met Gandhi, successfully convincing him to join them in their campaign to release the Ali brothers.[92] A year later, Gandhi began to lead sporadic satyagraha protests against specific events in March–April 1919. The Rowlatt Bills introduced in March extended into peacetime many provisions of the Defence of India Act. Gandhi responded by calling for a nationwide hartal (strike). On March 30, 1919, his followers urged shopkeepers in Delhi to observe the hartal, resulting in a skirmish during which the police opened fire, killing a number of Hindus and Muslims. A week later, on April 13, 1919, a large group of unarmed men, women, and children gathered at Jallianwallah Bagh in Punjab to protest against continuing government repression. Military troops opened fire, killing close to 400 and injuring more than 1,000 people. Led by their religious leadership, these atrocities mobilized large numbers of Hindus and Muslims to join Gandhi's satyagraha, pushing him, in turn, to bring together these sporadic protests against specific wrongs into a sustained movement of non-cooperation, a move that Gandhi shied away from at the time. Among these were Ansari, Bari, and Swami Shraddhanand, an Arya Samaj leader whom Gandhi had met in 1915 through C.F. Andrews.

Bari linked the Rowlatt satyagraha directly with the Khilafat issue, presenting this connection as a scheme for Hindu–Muslim unity to Gandhi, offering to put a stop to cow slaughter in return for his support. While Gandhi rejected such a quid pro quo, in September 1919, he joined the ulema in their campaign.[93] A month later, Bari, the Ali brothers, Ansari and others formed an All-India Khilafat Committee and declared October 17 as Khilafat Day along similar lines to Gandhi's Rowlatt satyagraha—through hartals, prayers, public meetings, and fasts. Khilafat Day was a huge success, drawing more than 50,000 to a meeting in Delhi where Ansari and Bari shared the stage with Shraddhanand, who had emerged in the spring of 1919 as an unlikely ambassador of Hindu–Muslim unity.[94] A few months earlier, during the Rowlatt satyagraha, Shraddhanand hailed the victims of the Delhi police shooting as martyrs and attended a memorial for them at the Jama Masjid on April 4. Addressing the gathering from the pulpit of the mosque, Shraddhanand invoked "O God of the Hindus and Muslims," concluding that the "innocent blood" of Hindus and Muslims would not "flow in vain … May we be prepared," he emphatically stated, "to sacrifice ourselves for the freedom and progress of our country."[95] The October meeting in Delhi emphasized Hindu–Muslim unity and was followed by another Khilafat Conference in November where Bari urged his followers to refrain from cow slaughter because "we are children of the same soil." In January 1920, a "Khilafat delegation" wrote to the viceroy emphatically arguing for the preservation of the Khalifa as the "Warden of the Holy Places" of Islam. The signatories included, along with Shaukat Ali and Bari, Shraddhanand and Gandhi.[96] Two months later, the Central Khilafat Committee, of which Gandhi was a member, prepared for non-cooperation. From the early months of 1920, leaders of the Khilafat Committee and delegation focused on mobilizing the ulema, students, and other volunteers to the movement, and raising funds. This mobilization brought Hindu and Muslim emissaries from India to Burma in the summer of 1920.

Muslims in Burma, particularly those in Rangoon, where a Khilafat Committee was formed, had been closely following the question of the Khalifa, the campaign of the Ali brothers and Bari to restore the holy places of Islam to the Turkish Sultan, and Bari's schemes for Hindu–Muslim unity.[97] In December 1917, for example, in a public address to the Viceroy, who was in Burma at the time, Chulia Muslims expressed their deep gratitude to the British government for declaring that they would hold "the Holy places of Islam in respect and not allow them to be polluted."[98] In Rangoon's crowded immigrant enclave that comprised the grid of congested streets around Mogul Street, the slaughter of cows on Bakr Id in close proximity to Hindu temples had been a bone of contention among Hindus and Muslims since the early 1890s.[99] In August 1920, however, Bakr Id passed with a "remarkable decrease" in cow slaughter indicating the seriousness of the community's commitment to Bari and his cause.[100] In October 1920, Shraddhanand arrived in the province to celebrate the anniversary of the Burma Arya

Samaj, which was founded in Mandalay in 1897. A Rangoon branch of the Arya Samaj was set up two years later. Shraddhanand spent more than a month touring the province to collect funds for his *gurukul* in Haridwar while delivering public speeches on non-cooperation.[101] More than 10,000 people gathered around Rangoon wharf to greet Shraddhanand.[102] The bridge to the jetty was lined with men wearing sashes of green, red, and yellow, invoking Hindu–Muslim unity, and a red flower and broach "emblazoned with the sign of the motherland." Shraddhanand was welcomed not only by members of the Arya Samaj but also by the local Khilafat Committee and the Burma Provincial Indian National Congress. They included Madanjit, Mohsin Ali, K.B. Banerji and a person identified as Parmanand in the newspapers, quite likely a priest associated withthe Arya Samaj. Amidst cries of "Bande Mataram" and "Hindu Mussalman ki jai," Shraddhanand was garlanded and carried by a dozen volunteers to the house of Dr P.J. Mehta, who, like Madanjit, was a close associate of Gandhi from his South Africa days. Shraddhanand's visit energized the large Indian community in Rangoon, including three detachments of volunteers who took part in a public procession.[103] One group comprised of durwans (doorkeepers), who were on foot, and twelve men on ponies led by Mathura Singh, a contractor employed in the Rangoon Public Works Department. The chief inspector of police, Rangoon found this volunteer corps, which consisted of former army and policemen armed with lathis (batons), to be "distinctly hostile and turbulent." The second group, amounting to over one hundred men, was commanded by Dr Ganpat Rao. His subordinates, Lakshmi Chand and Bechar Lal, acted as subalterns. These volunteers were predominantly Muslims who had actively taken up the Khilafat issue in Rangoon. A third unit consisted of twelve schoolboys from the Gujarati Anglo-Vernacular School recruited by V.D. Mehta.[104]

A day after his arrival from Calcutta, Banerji welcomed Shraddhanand "on behalf of the citizens of Rangoon" in a public address that emphasized the Swami's political, rather than religious, stature. Banerji began with an acknowledgment that "the Indians are living in harmony with the liberal-minded sons of the soil." He talked at length about Shraddhanand's work in promoting national education in his gurukul through vernacular education, which made students into "manly men to fight the battle of life and produce in them love for [the] service of humanity." Next, Banerji highlighted one of Shraddhanand's crowning achievement as being "the first Hindu" to preach from the pulpit of the Jama Masjid in Delhi on "the National doctrine of Hindu Muslim unity… the real keystone to Swaraj." Finally, Banerji expressed admiration for the Swami's success in taking up the Khilafat cause and the campaign for cow protection "as the preservation of cattle is not only essential to the agricultural and industrial prosperity of India and Burma but is also vital to the health and vigour of the people."

From Rangoon, Shraddhanand went to Mandalay, where he was met by thousands at the train station who welcomed him with the slogans, "Shraddhanandji ki jai, Hindu Musalman ki jai."[105] Haji Wally Mohammed Peer escorted Shraddhanand in his elaborately decorated car from the station to the Arya Samaj premises, a journey that took an hour because of the large procession that accompanied them. In their welcome speech, the Mandalay Arya Samaj members expressed their "deep gratitude" to Shraddhanand. "In welcoming you in the once metropolis of Burma and giving you our loyal devotion," they proclaimed, "we are really honoring those shining ideals which clearly mark out oriental civilization from the purely material occidental culture." Shraddhanand next went to Myitnge to the workshops of some large English firms where thousands of Hindus and Sikhs were employed.[106] More than 5,000 attended his public meeting, where he arrived in procession in a chariot. He delivered an hour-long lecture insisting not only on Hindu–Muslim unity but including Buddhists in his satyagraha.[107] This inclusion was no accident.

The end of the war brought into the public not only instances of Hindu and Muslim protests against the government in India but also of many other Burmese groups in Burma. These included Burmese Buddhist monks, students, and an emerging political leadership belonging to the General Council of Burmese Associations (GCBA), an organization formed in March 1920 to lobby for constitutional reforms that Burma had been left out of under the Government of India Act of 1919.[108] The GCBA worked closely with U Ottama, a Buddhist monk, to mobilize Burma's large number of pongyis into political action.

U Ottama was born Paw Tun Aung in Akyab in 1880, where he attended an English primary school before joining a Buddhist vernacular school led by Saya Ledaung. In 1895, he was ordained a priest at the age of fifteen at Saya Shwe Zedi's monastery in Sittwe.[109] Tun Aung Gyaw, a clerk in the Bombay Burma Trading Company, a public company dealing in teak set up by Scottish businessmen, in which Indian merchants had substantial equity, financed his education in Calcutta, where Ottama went to study metaphysics and Buddhism.[110] Between 1895 and 1918, U Ottama spent more than eight years in Calcutta and less than three in Burma. During this time, he traveled to England, the United States, France, and Japan, where he became a professor of Pali at Nishi Hongonji, a Buddhist University. The Japanese defeat of Russia, the Swadeshi movement in Bengal, during which he taught Pali at the Bengal National College, the Home Rule Movement, and Madam Cama's *Bande Mataram*, the journal of Indian revolutionaries living in self-exile, left a deep impression on U Ottama, who increasingly turned to overtly political rather than steadfastly apolitical *sasana* (spiritual) concerns of his fellow pongyis. He sought inspiration and exchanges in India as his attempts to induce the Buddhist *sangha* (monastic community) in Burma into discussing mundane, political issues were unsuccessful until 1918.[111]

Nineteen eighteen marked an important milestone in Burma's political history. Just as the Khilafat issue gave political expression to the universalist ecumene of oceanic Islam, the sanctity of their sasana mobilized Buddist monks and laymen across the Irrawaddy Delta into political action. Pongyis, who hitherto had ignored U Ottama's calls for political engagement, catapulted into the public political realm over the issue of shoe-wearing at the Shwedagon Pagoda. Hitherto, Europeans and government officials had been exempted from removing their shoes when entering pagodas.[112] In April 1918, U Ottama attended several meetings to discuss the removal of the exemption notice posted at the pagoda.. At these meetings, he took the opportunity to move the discussion beyond shoe-wearing and lectured his audience on the Swadeshi movement and Home Rule. At an all-Burma conference to discuss constitutional reforms, U Ottama expressed his satisfaction that his compatriots who had "not bothered their heads with how their country or any other country was governed" were now prepared to study "politics as their life work."[113] While Governor Craddock had proposed a reform scheme that "in the end" would give "self-government" to Burmans, having seen the hollowness of these promises during his years in Calcutta, U Ottama publicly proclaimed that this "end" would never come.

Between January and April 1919, U Ottama traveled across Burma delivering speeches on Home Rule, the boycott of foreign goods, and freedom. As his discourses became increasingly anti-government, the commissioner of police issued him a warning to refrain from making speeches that were "fostering sedition." Rather than be silenced, U Ottama left for Calcutta shortly thereafter, returning to Burma only a year later. He marked his return calling for the governor's removal in a public letter headlined "Craddock Get Out." U Ottama spent the next two months delivering lectures on Home Rule, urging Burmans to "unite and throw off the yoke they were bearing," and criticizing the British for their seventy-year occupation of the country, during which they and done nothing for the welfare of Burmans. As the government scrambled to find a way to censor him, he left for Calcutta once more, in August 1920, and stayed there for six months.[114]

Meanwhile, in December 1920, Rangoon College and Judson College students went on strike to protest a new university act passed by the government that increased the cost of education and emphasized a high level of proficiency in English, which would disadvantage students whose school education had been in Burmese.[115] The students accused the government of perpetuating a system of education that would keep the Burmese enslaved. They took shelter at the steps of the Shwedagon Pagoda and were joined in their strike by high-school students in Rangoon and Mandalay.[116] From Calcutta, U Ottama tried to wire a telegram of support to the students in Burma stating, "I am in entire accord with the action of the students. They should remain firm until their demands are conceded."[117] The local government censored the message. In response, U Ottama published his telegram and news of its censure in the local papers in Calcutta. The government's suppression of U Ottama's message "brought forth inspiration and encouragement and irritated the students more against the bureaucratic government of the day."[118]

Significantly, another source of inspiration to the students was Swami Shraddhanand, who was visiting Burma at exactly this time. Although it was mostly Hindus and Muslims who had gathered in large numbers in Rangoon, Mandalay, and Myitnge at his meetings, Burmese newspapers reported widely on the Swami's public engagements, reproducing his speeches that were read by the students in the midst of their boycott. In his speeches, beyond talking specifically about Hindu–Muslim unity, Shraddhanand denounced the "slave mentality" inculcated by colonial education. His talk of "national education," the principle along which he had organized his Gurukul, resonated among the students who had been objecting to the University Bill on the very same grounds.[119] Craddock worried so much about the impact of Shraddhanand's discourses that he claimed the student boycott was "undoubtedly the direct outcome" of the Swami's visit. Warning of the potential damage that could be caused by visits from other Indian "agitators" such as Gandhi, Maulana Azad, and the Ali brothers in Burma, Craddock repeatedly asked the viceroy for permission to use the Defence of India Act to prohibit them from entering the province. Craddock was particularly concerned about the reverberation of the politics of these emissaries among pongyis, who had "lost more to our rule than any other class" in Burma. As he put it, the "unrest the war has engendered has been far greater since its termination than it ever was while the conflict was in actual progress."[120]

Although Craddock was specifically worried about the "infinity of harm" that Gandhi and his "satellites" could unleash if they became more than "mere names" in Burma, he had no control over Gandhi's ideas that came into Burma with not only the swamis and maulvis but also with U Ottama. The monk returned to Burma in January 1921 and took up, in his words, active "propaganda work". He was accompanied by Madanjit, who had become a close associate and friend. Over the next two months, U Ottama delivered a series of lectures across the Irrawaddy Delta, capitalizing on his growing visibility and popularity in the aftermath of his call for Craddock to "go." His audience included students, monks, women, and cultivators. U Ottama had studied Gandhian ideas and strategies very closely and he actively courted arrest in his speeches, which contained three main themes: criticizing colonial rule, mobilizing the Burmese into political action, and offering strategies for protest. "Every nation has its own king and country," U Ottama lamented, "but Burmans have no king." This, he argued, was the root of their enslavement.[121] "Your land," he told his audience, "is occupied by another nation … It is time to get Burma back." As long as the "heathens" "robbed" and ruled "our land," U Ottama warned, neither Buddhism nor "national education" would prosper. "What we want," he emphatically stated at his public meetings, was "not Nirvana but freedom of [the] nation from slavery." If the 80,000 monks living in Burma made a "great push for nation freedom," he believed, "we are sure to get it."

Invoking Gandhian non-cooperation, U Ottama compared working for the government with "committing national suicide," noting that "if we are to work for the people, we must in all cases go against the government." This endeavor, he warned, would result in imprisonment. Forecasting that he too would be sent to jail "for the cause of the country," U Ottama goaded the government, claiming it "cannot put me to death". He offered boycott as a strategy for students and monks alike, and urged them to withhold taxes, boycott Burmans working for the government, boycott visits from government officials, and to stop buying foreign goods. Commemorating the university and school strikes of December 1920, U Ottama applauded the "wise" students for "brightening our eyes" by rejecting the colonial system of education that "would make them slaves" and demanding one that would "make them masters."[122]

On March 21, 1921, U Ottama was arrested and charged with sedition. On July 4, he was sentenced to imprisonment for one year.[123] The arrest and conviction only increased support for him among monks and political activists. Indeed, as an editorial in the Indian-owned *Rangoon Mail* put it, "the car of repression has been set in motion in Burma, the first victim to be struck down being Bhikku U Ottama … naturally the Burmese people will resent this act … it has caused a thrill of consternation throughout the length and breadth of this province."[124] Citywide hartals followed U Ottama's arrest as large numbers of men and women gathered at Rangoon wharf and the Shwedagon Pagoda in a show of support.[125] On the July 11, 1921, close to 8,000 people attended a meeting at the steps of the Shwedagon Pagoda to protest U Ottama's sentencing. Significantly, more than 6,000 were Indians, and it was an itinerant maulvi from India, Abdulla Khan Misri, who was working closely with the Khilafat Committee in Burma, who took the lead at this meeting.[126]

Maulvis, Swamis, and Pongyis

Maulvi Abdulla Misri of Mirzapur in the United Provinces and Hakim Abdul Mannan from Bihar arrived in Rangoon to work with the Khilafat Committee to organize a permanent volunteer corps in early 1921. Mannan took the lead in starting the Anjuman Tahzib-ul-Akhlaq, a society to "suppress immorality," recruiting more than 5,000 volunteers who were armed with Gandhi caps and Khilafat badges. Misri became president of the Anjuman and its members immediately began picketing the brothels and liquor shops around Mogul Street and its neighborhood.[127] The original non-cooperation plan of the Indian National Congress did not inlcude liquor and toddy shops, although Gandhi had long advocated for abstention. The purity campaign of uniformed volunteers emerged spontaneously in several parts of India and was retroactively adopted by the Congress.[128]

Misri publicly advocated non-cooperation, speaking in the mosques and streets of Rangoon, trying to convince the many traders and merchants who lived there to join his campaign. The administration considered him a "dangerous fanatic" and prosecuted him for causing public disturbances in April 1921. In court, Misri announced that he was willing to go to jail "without defending himself", and a large crowd of 4,000 volunteers gathered in his support.[129] Rather than send him to jail and risk "serious trouble," the magistrate served Misri with a notice to refrain from making public speeches.[130] The maulvi agreed, stating that until Gandhi gave the go-ahead for active civil disobedience, he would follow the court order, but noted that he would break the law as soon as the satyagraha allowed him to. Till then, he worked behind the scene with his volunteers, putting together a large network of prominent Muslims and Hindus sympathetic to the triad of concerns he had raised—the Khilafat restoration, non-cooperation, and temperance. Among those who worked closely with him were Dawood, who had been interned during the war, Dr Mehta, Banerji and Swami Parmanand, all three of whom had been prominent members of the reception committee welcoming Shraddhanand to Rangoon. Misri also worked with several members of the Khilafat Committee who were not involved in the Anjuman purity campaign. Among them were Abdul Sattar Ismail, a cloth merchant and secretary of the Rangoon Khilafat Fund Committee; Ayub Ali, another cloth merchant and committee member; and Ebrahim Hansa, secretary of the Khilafat Committee.[131]

Between March and September 1921, the enrollment of the Anjuman Tahzib-ul-Akhlaq grew. Misri met Parmanand soon after he took over the association at Mehta's house, where a group of lawyers had convened to discuss the boycott of foreign cloth and goods. Parmanand was a twenty-four-year-old Hindustani Buddhist priest. He lived with monks in a Buddhist monastery in Lanmadaw, west of the river, and was also active in the Arya Samaj in Rangoon.[132] Misri recruited Parmanand to his temperance campaign. When his "mouth was shut … by the 'Nadirshahi' order," as he put it in his own words, that is, Misri was debarred from making public speeches, Parmanand "took up his duties." Several police inspectors had been closely watching both Misri and Parmanand to find a way to censor them because of the "excitement" caused by their anti-drink campaign and the large crowds they commanded. On May 6, 1921, at seven in the evening, Parmanand was also served with the "Nadirshahi" order, preventing him from addressing the public because the "temperance meetings were being made a cloak for the discussion of politics." A few hours later, a large group of about 300 volunteers, walked from Mogul Street to Fraser Street, arriving at a liquor shop owned by a Chinese shopkeeper. The shop, which ordinary remained open till 10 pm, had closed in the evenings for the last five days under pressure from the Anjuman volunteers. On the sixth of May, the shop stayed open late but quickly shut down when the shop attendants saw the large crowd that, by police estimates, amounted to almost 5,000 people. In response, the volunteers tried to force the doors open, throwing stones and brickbats, hitting a European police inspector in the arm in the melee. The inspector and several other witnesses claimed that a group of men armed with lathis was led by Permanand, who was dressed in yellow robes. The Swami was charged with having caused the "riot."[133]

At his hearing, Parmanand denied the charge, bringing in Misri, Ismail, and Dawood as his witnesses. His testimony made it clear that Misri's house on 30th Street had turned into a hub for the Anjuman volunteers and Khilafat activists at dusk. Parmanand was staying with him, and it was here that the Swami was served with the "Nadirshahi order." In the court, Misri stated that on the evening of the May 6, after Parmanand had received the order, a group of volunteers came to his house claiming that the Chinese were arming themselves with sticks to assault the "anti-drink workers" in retaliation against the pressure they had put to force their liquor shop to close. Since Gandhi had "not yet preached the doctrine of force," after consulting with Dawood, Misri advised Parmanand to stay indoors and not address the volunteers. Instead, Misri sent another Hindu priest who was living in his house at the time, Swami Mohandas, to speak to the group.

Mohandas had come to Rangoon from India in March 1919. He met Parmanand and Misri in Syriam, where the latter had given a lecture on the boycott of foreign goods. He arrived in Rangoon on the May 3rd, and after spending a couple of nights at the Hanuman temple, he went to Misri's house on the morning of the 6th. He was present when Parmanand was served with the order that restricted his public appearances. Both Mohandas and Misri stated that it was Mohandas, and not Permanand, who went to address the crowd after the Anjuman volunteers informed them of the fracas. Their lawyer, A.B. Banerji, argued that because both the swamis wore yellow robes and had shaved their heads, it was likely that the witnesses had mistakenly identified Mohandas as Permanand.[134] The magistrate remained unconvinced and sentenced Parmanand to imprisonment for two years.

While Parmanand was incarcerated, Misri continued to lead the purity campaign and toured the province advocating non-cooperation. When Bahadur Shah Zafar's grandson, Jamshed Bakht, died in July 1921, Misri led his volunteers in a large funeral procession, in the midst of which a European municipal engineer was assaulted when he refused to stop his car to allow the mourners to pass. Seven members of the Anjuman Tahzib-ul-Akhlaq were sent to trial and four were convicted.

Again, a large crowd turned up at the hearings to demonstrate their support.[135] Two weeks later, on August 1, 1921, on the first anniversary of Tilak's death, the Indian National Congress finally launched its boycott of foreign goods. In Rangoon, the Khilafat Committee held several meetings to promote the boycott at which Misri, Mohandas, Tribhawan Sharma, a Hindu priest from India, and Hakim Abdul Mannan, who had organized the Anjuman, shared the stage. Misri traveled to Nyaunglebin, Pyuntaza, and Pegu. In his speeches, he lamented the "oppression and tyranny" of the British under which Indians had suffered, which, he argued would only be relieved through the attainment of Swaraj through non-cooperation. In October 1921, a group of four people including Mannan, Tribhawan Sharma, and Abdul Rahman Chulia toured across the length of Burma lecturing on Khilafat, Swadeshi and Hindi–Muslim unity and circulating the Delhi ulema's fatwa that forbade government service, especially in the army and police, among whose rank and file were large numbers of Muslims. In his speeches, Mannan exhorted his supporters to sacrifice "everything … even life itself" in their fight against the "enemies of Islam."[136]

Even as the expressions of the Khilafat/non-cooperation mobilization were infused with the language of Islamic universalism, the itinerant groups of maulvis and swamis reached out to Hindu and Muslim migrants from the Indo-Gangetic plains and Burmese Buddhists and Muslims to join their anti-colonial boycott. Significantly, Misri was among the main speakers at the mass meeting held at the Shwedagon Pagoda on July 11, 1921 to protest U Ottama's imprisonment. Approximately 8,000 people gathered at this meeting where speeches were delivered in Burmese, Hindi, and Urdu.[137] In his speech, Misri urged the Burmese to adopt non-cooperation, comparing the government with a "mast" (uncontrollable) elephant. It was U Ottama's ardent supporters—pongyis and women—who were present at this meeting, which closed with the slogans, "Mahatma Ottama ki jai" and "Mahatma Gandhi ki jai." Misri met with several monks in Rangoon, taking steps to organize the nonpayment of taxes, and pledged to collect money for a fund in U Ottama's name. In particular, Misri held discussions with politically engaged pongyis of the Thayettaw Kyaung Daik. This was the headquarters of the Burmese National Schools, with approximately 1,000 affiliated scholars, and among the monastery's frequent visitors, peior to his arrest, was Parmanand. Misri and the pongyis discussed Indo-Burman unity, the boycott of foreign goods, and the need for more monks to follow in U Ottama's footsteps. Reaching beyond his expertise in Islam, Misri also planned to deliver a lecture on the themes of Muslim–Buddhist unity and the "five precepts," of Buddhism on the steps of the Shwedagon Pagoda although this meeting did not eventually take place.[138]

Beyond the pongyis, U Ottama's arrest also mobilized the GCBA, which had hitherto been reluctant to take up non-cooperation. In August 1921, it passed a unanimous resolution to boycott foreign cloth and promote abstention from liquor. Much like the Tahzib-ul-Akhlaq's purity campaign that converged around the Khilafat leaderhsip, the GCBA reached out to Buddhist temparance initiatives in villages across the Irrawaddy Delta and brought them into its non-cooperation movement.[139] Over the next few months, several meetings were held across the province, including a three-day all-Burma conference of the GCBA and its affiliates in Mandalay in which over 5,000 people participated. After its conclusion, a small group including U Ba Pe and U Chit Hlaing, two leading members of the GCBA, embarked on a tour of Upper Burma to advocate for Swaraj and non-cooperation and were joined by Vyavaharik Madanjit.[140] At the same time, Mannan's group of itinerant Khilafat mobilizers also met with success in bringing Burmese Muslims to their cause in Mandalay, where about 500 people attended a meeting, the majority of whom were Zerbadi (those of Buddhist and Muslim parentage). Two Burmese speakers, Ba U and Ba Thi, addressed the meeting, supporting the boycott foreign goods and the Prince of Wales's impending visit to India and Burma, and calling for "a strengthening of the bond binding Hindus, Moslems and Burmans together."[141]

In September, the Ali brothers were arrested in India. The Anjuman Tahzib-ul-Akhlaq volunteers held demonstrations against this arrest, which ended in a confrontation between them and the police in Rangoon. On September 18, Misri addressed a large gathering at the idgah in Ahlone in a show of support for the Ali brothers. Despite being served with a second notice preventing him from making public speeches, Misri attended another meeting two days later at which his volunteers threw stones and shoes at the police. He was arrested and sentenced to a year's imprisonment for violating the notice. Shortly thereafter, five volunteers were arrested and convicted for stirring up a "riot" near the Sule Pagoda during a pro-Misri demonstration at which his supporters attacked a European deputy inspector with stones and lathis.[142]

The Khilafat campaign continued after Misri's arrest. In late November, 4,000 Muslims attended a meeting chaired by Maulvi Ali Ahmed of the Surati Masjid at the idgah in Ahlone, at which several resolutions urging non-cooperation were passed. The first confirmed that it was "against national dignity" and "unlawful", according to the sharia, to continue employment in the government. This was in keeping with an important fatwa issued in Delhi that had pronounced serving in government a sin. Several volunteers of the Tahzib-ul-Akhlaq, who had been circulating the fatwa for several weeks before this meeting, distributed copies among the thousands gathered. Another resolution included a pledge to organize a hartal when the Prince of Wales arrived in Rangoon. While this November meeting can be considered Burma's Khilafat moment, at which Muslims in Rangoon decisively threw in their lot with the Muslims of the Indo-Gangetic plains under the leadership of itinerant maulvis, this moment, in fact, emerged from a longer mobilization and circulation, of ideas and people. These included Mulla Dawood and Abdul Salam Rafiqi's campaign to restore Bahadur Shah Zafar's grave in the early 1900s to counter the threat to Islamic sovereignty posed by the British empire; Ali Ahmed Siddiqi's pro-Turkish discourses and his distribution of oceanic revolutionary literature at the Surati Masjid in 1915; and the invocations of Mughal sovereignty of volunteers who mourned Zafar's grandson, Jamshed Bakht's death in 1921. Moreover, while the Khilafat moment built on the city's prior entanglements with various expressions of oceanic Islam, it also expanded the horizons of Islamic universalism with a distinctly local ecumene in which Buddhist universalism was invoked by maulvis, monks, and swamis to join forces against the colonial assault on the temporal and sacred sovereignty of both the Indo-Gangetic plain and the Irrawaddy Delta.

Gandhi called off the non-cooperation movement after violence broke out among satyagrahis in Chauri Chaura in the United Provinces in February 1922. In Burma, however, it was at exactly this time that Gandhian strategies of boycott and non-cooperation were adopted by the GCBA, who were invigorated with U Ottama's release from prison. Once free, the pongyi picked up from where he had left off, touring the province to mobilize his compatriots, calling upon them to "break the law of the land" by joining the non-cooperation movement and taking the lead in gaining Home Rule for Burma. Toward this end, using Gandhian terminology, U Ottama gave the monks a "constructive programme" to go to districts, towns, and villages to "prepare people" by "opening their eyes to the simple problem of plain living and high thinking," and to discard all foreign cloth, foreign eatables, foreign luxuries, liquor, cigarettes, and "all the other vicious ways of life." The "yellow robed fraternity," he hoped, would "burst forth in one voice, 'we are prepared to die for the country'."[143]

Significantly, much as the itinerant maulvis and swamis had done, U Ottama included a message of interreligious unity and solidarity in his discourses that was simultaneously nationalist and universalist. At the very first meeting held at the Shwedagon Pagoda on July 5, 1922 following his release from prison, Ottama spoke in not just Burmese but also Hindustani to an audience of Indians and Burmese.[144] He concluded his lecture with a public show of support to "our Khilafat friends" and an assurance of his sympathy because "theirs is a cause of Europe against Asia, of Christianity against Islam. The same principle applies all over the East and the East is indignant against the West for no other reason than its all-devouring policy. So long as such a policy continues there is an inherent danger to the whole of Asia and no part of Asia can be so stupid as not to sympathize with you."[145] He repeated this message in Mandalay, where he addressed an audience of more than 8,000, sharing the stage with members of the Burma Provincial Indian Congress, the Khilafat Committee, and the Young Moslem Union. Again speaking in Burmese and Hindustani, he assured the Burmans present that he was not a "kala Hpongyi [sic]," that is, an Indian monk, but was "a Burman, born in Burma" who wanted to foster unity among "Indians, Burmans, Muslims, Hindus, and Buddhists." Buddhists, U Ottama reminded his supporters, "had no enemies. To us, all creatures and people of the earth are brethren. We will hail their advent into our country."[146]

Conclusion

Writing in early 1940, in the aftermath of anti-immigrant, anti-Muslim Burmese Buddhist nationalist violence in the Irrawaddy Delta, especially in Rangoon, J.S. Furnivall referred to Burma as a "plural society," in which communities that he identified as simultaneously racially and geographically distinct—that is, "European, Chinese, Indian and Native"—lived together but "separately" with interactions limited to a "market place."[147] Nile Green has similarly traced the divisive discourses of mid-twentieth century Islam and Buddhism, the unraveling of which the contemporary Rohingya crisis brings to the fore, that had roots in the late nineteenth century.[148] Following the shadowy archival presence of revolutionaries, maulvis, pongyis, and swamis, whose politics was embedded in and inseparable from the religiously defined communities and concerns, this essay argues that, far from being a marketplace, Burma's postwar political ecumene was shaped by both local geographies of coexistence and oceanic networks of exchange. These oceanic crossings and riverine ripples were effectively deployed by maulvis, swamis, and pongyis to mobilize Muslims, Hindus, and Buddhists to express their shared and collective temporal sovereignty against colonial rule. It is only by peeling back the many layers of Burma's Khilafat moment that we can locate the historical conjucture at which it was possible for a Burmese Buddhist monk to imagine his nation as one in which migrants and Muslims had an unconditional right to belong.

Between 1921 and 1939, when he died, U Ottama mobilized Buddhist monks and women into political agitation, framing his concerns as simultaneously spiritual and national. His imprisonment in 1921 was the first of many incarcerations he faced, and by early 1931, he went into self-imposed exile in Calcutta, where he stayed till 1936.

U Ottama is hailed as one of the first anti-colonial nationalists of Burma, commemorated for his role in politicizing pongyis and women, and inspiring students to deliver Burma's freedom. This narrow nationalist framework, however, obscures the scale and scope of U Ottama's religious and political consciousness that was enlivened by his Indian connections, thus allowing him to include non-Buddhists in his anti-colonial nationalist politics.

Sunil Amrith has noted that between 1840 and 1940, close to twenty-eight million people traveled from India across the Bay of Bengal to Ceylon, Malaya, and Burma. Of these, approximately twelve to fifteen million went to Burma.[149] In simple statistical terms, the number of sojourners from India who spent at least two to three years there over the course of a century *outnumbered* the "indigenous" population, which was recorded as just under ten million in the census of 1921. The scale of this encounter, alone, suggests a deeply intimate and entangled shared history of India and Burma that has been a pariah for both South Asianists and scholars of Burma. This essay has offered a first step in the recovery of Burma's South Asian history by uprooting the revolutionaries, maulvis, swamis, and pongyis from their territorially-bounded, national and communitarian histories by joining them on their journeys across the Indian Ocean that brought them together from the Indo-Gangetic plains to the Irrawaddy Delta.

Notes and References

1. *Rangoon Times*, February 9, 1905, 1AO Acc-3656, National Archives of Myanmar (NAM).
2. Yehya En-Nasr Parkinson (ed.), *Inversion of Times by A.S. Rafiqi*, Luzac and Co, London, 1911, p. 7.
3. For details see Thant Myint-U, *The Making of Modern Burma*, Cambridge University Press, Cambridge, 2001.
4. 1901 Census of India, vol. XII Burma, Office of the Superintendent of Government Printing, Rangoon, 1902; 1921 Census of India, vol X Burma, Office of the Superintendent of Government Printing, Rangoon, 1923.
5. Government of Burma to Government of India, July 4, 1921, Home, Political, Proceedings, July 1921, no. 1, National Archives of India (NAI).

6. Fortnightly report, political situation in Burma, July–December 1921. 1 AO Acc-4372, NAM.
7. For details, see Nile Green and James L. Gelvin (eds), *Global Muslims in the Age of Print,* University of California Press, 2013, especially the introduction.
8. See, for example, Francis Robinson, *Separatism among Indian Muslims: The Politics of the United Provinces' Muslims,* Cambridge University Press, Cambridge, 2007; Gail Minault, *The Khilafat Movement: Religious Symbolism and Political Mobilization in India*, Columbia University Press, New York, 1982; Mushirul Hassan, *Nationalism and Communal Politics in India, 1916-1928,* Manohar, New Delhi, 1979; and Ayesha Jalal, *Self and Sovereignty: Individual and Community in South Asia Islam since 1850,* Routledge, London, 2000.
9. Mushirul Hasan and Margrit Pernau (eds), *Regionalizing Pan Islamism: Documents on the Khilafat Movement,* Manohar, New Delhi, 2005; and Alam Abu Yusuf, *Khilafat Movement and the Muslims of Bengal,* Raktakarabee Publishers, Kolkata, 2007.
10. Jonathan Saha, "Is It India? Colonial Burma as a Problem in South Asian History," *South Asian History and Culture*, 7(1), 2016.
11. U Maung Maung, *From Sangha to Laity: Nationalist Movements of Burma 1920-1940,* Manohar, New Delhi 1980; E. Michael Mendelson, *Sangha and State in Burma: A Study of Monastic Sectarianism and Leadership*, Cornell University Press, Ithaca, 1975; Robert Taylor, *The State in Burma,* University of Hawaii Press, Honolulu, 2009, Michael W. Charney, *A History of Modern Burma*, Cambridge University Press, Cambridge, 2009; E. Sarkisyanz, *Buddhist Backgrounds of the Burmese Revolution*, Springer, Dordrecht, 1965; Alicia Turner, *Saving Buddhism: The Impermanence of Religion in Colonial Burma,* University of Hawaii Press, Honolulu, 2014.
12. Green, *Global Muslims*, introduction, pp. 3, 10.
13. B.R. Pearn, *A History of Rangoon,* American Baptist Mission Press, Rangoon, 1939, p.1 and Preface.
14. Ibid., p. 1
15. Ibid., pp. 182–183.
16. *Royal Commission on Agriculture in India, vol XII, Burma*, H.M. Stationery Office, 1928.
17. Arnold Wright (ed.), *Twentieth Century Impressions of Burma: Its History, People, Commerce, Industries, and Resources.* Llyod's Greater Britain Publishing Company Ltd, 1910.

18. Pearn, *History of Rangoon*, p. 188.
19. Ibid.
20. Pearn, *History of Rangoon*, pp. 49-50.
21. 1911 Census of Burma, Office of the Superintendent of Government Printing, Rangoon, 1912.
22. l/PJ/6/354 file 1532, Hindu Muslim Riots, 1893, India Office Records, British Library (IOR).
23. See Thant Myint-U, *The River of Lost Footsteps: A Personal History of Burma*, Faber and Faber, 2007, p. 185
24. Raman Mahadevan, "Pattern of Enterprise of Immigrant Entrepreneurs: A Pattern of Chettiars in Malaya," *Economic and Political Weekly*, 13, 4/5, 1978; Michael Adas, "Immigrant Asians and the Economic Impact of European Imperialism: The role of the South Indian Chettiars in British Burma," *Journal of Asian Studies* 33(3), 1974; Michael Adas, *The Burma Delta: Economic Development and Social Change on an Asian Rice Frontier*, University of Wisconsin Press, 1974.
25. See, for example, Adas, "Immigrant Asians and the Economic Impact; and Usha Mahajani, *The Role of Indian Minorities in Burma and Malaya*, Vora and Co Publishers, Bombay, 1960.
26. 1911 census.
27. Wright (ed.), *Twentieth Century Impressions of Burma.*
28. Ben Bansal, Elliot Fox, and Manuel Oka (eds), *Architectural Guide Yangon*, Dom Publishers, 2015.
29. Pearn, *History of Rangoon*, p. 195.
30. Sant Nihal Singh, "As an Indian Saw Burma," *Modern Review*, 7, 1, 1910, pp. 222–229.
31. A.H. Chanea, "Rangoon Muhammadans," *Muhammadan Observer and Moslem Chronicle*, 20 July 1895.
32. "Bengal Muhammadan Association," ibid., 28 June 1899, and "First Anniversary of the Bengal Muhammadan Association," ibid., 22 April 1900.
33. Correspondence between Jamshed Bakht and lieutenant governor of Burma, February 19, 1910. 1AOAcc-3819. NAM.
34. *Rangoon Times*, August 26, 1907, 1AO Acc-3657, NAM.
35. Government of India to Government of Burma, September 7, 1905; *Rangoon Times*, February 9, 1905, 1AO Acc-3656, NAM; and Criminal Intelligence report, August 10, 1915, GOI, Home, Political, B, Proceedings, August 1915, nos. 552–556, NAI.
36. Nasr, *Inversion of Times*, pp. 12–13.
37. Ibid, p. 10.

38. Government of India to Government of Burma, September 7, 1905; *Rangoon Times*, February 9, 1905, 1AO Acc-3656, NAM; Government of India to Government of Burma, August 1907, 1AOACC-3657, NAM; *Rangoon Times*, August 26, 1907. 1AOAcc-3657, NAM.
39. Government of India to Government of Burma, August 1907, 1AOACC-3657, NAM.
40. Nasr, *Inversion of Times*, p. 9.
41. Ibid. Rafiqi letter to Viceroy of India, January 24, 1908, and Rafiqi letter to Colonel Dunlop Smith, Private Secretary to His Excellency, February 11, 1909, pp. 17–20.
42. *Rangoon Times*, August 26, 1907. 1AOAcc-3657, NAM.
43. Wright (ed.), *Twentieth Century Impressions of Burma.*
44. Abdulla Quillam's Obituary of Yehya Parkinson, "The Philomath," January–March 1918, https://medium.com/@yahyabirt/abdullah-quilliams-obituary-of-yahya-parkinson-1874-1918-697ab7b4df9.
45. See dedication in J. Yehya-en-Nasr Parkinson, *Essays on Islamic Philosophy*, British Burma Press, Rangoon, 1909.
46. Nasr, *Inversion of Times*, p. 15.
47. For details, see Timothy Winter, "Yahya Parkinson (1874-1918): Poet-philosopher of the North," University of Cambridge presentation, September 2016, and http://www.ayrshirehistory.org.uk/postings1/parkinson.htm.
48. Report of English, Anglo-vernacular, and Vernacular press for 1911, Home, Political, Part B proceedings, June, 1912, NAI.
49. Special branch diary of the District Superintendent of Police, Hanthawaddy, for week ending July 27, 1907, AO Acc-3657, NAM.
50. Criminal Intelligence Report, August 10, 1915, GOI, Home, Political, B, Proceedings, August 1915, nos. 552–556, NAI.
51. Government of Burma note, and *Rangoon Times*, 1907, 1 AO Acc-3657 NAM; for details on Rafiqi, see, Tim Harper and Sunil Amrith, *Sites of Asian Interactions: Ideas, Networks and Mobility*, Cambridge University Press, 2014, pp. 31–32.
52. Criminal Intelligence Report, August 10, 1915, GOI, Home, Political, B, Proceedings, August 1915, nos. 552–556, NAI.
53. W.F. Rice to James DuBoulay, August 30, 1917, Home, Political, Proceedings, January 1918, no. 27, NAI; and Weekly Report of Director of Criminal Intelligence for first three weeks of December 1915. Home, Political, Proceedings, December 1915, 709–711, NAI; and Proceedings of Commissioners, Mandalay Conspiracy Case, April–June 1917, Home, Political, A, January 1918, 491–497, NAI.

54. For details, see Mushirul Hasan, *M.A. Ansari*, Ministry of Information and Broadcasting, Government of India, New Delhi, 1995.
55. Quoted in Zafar Ahmad Nizami, *Hakim Ajmal Khan,* Ministry of Information and Broadcasting, Government of India, New Delhi. For details on the mission, see Syed Tanvir Wasti, "The Indian Red Crescent Mission to the Balkan Wars," *Middle Eastern Studies*, 45(3), 2009, pp. 393–406. The list of members of the mission listed in Wasti's article are different from the participants mentioned in the sources consulted in this essay.
56. Weekly Report of Director of Criminal Intelligence, December 1915, Home, Political, December 1915, 709–711, NAI, and Ali Ahmed Siddiqi's statement, May 25, 1925, Home, Political, 1925, 320–325, NAI. For details on the medical mission, see Hassan, *Ansari.*
57. Zain Ali, M.A.S. Jamal, Mahbub-ul-Rahman, and Kesovji evidence and judgment, Proceedings of Commissioners; Mandalay Conspiracy Case, April–June 1917, Home, Political, A, January 1918, 491–497, NAI.
58. Evidence of Mahbub-ul-Rahman, Rafiq-ul-Haq, M.M. Naidu, Sheikh Juman, and Zain Ali. Proceedings of Commissioners, Mandalay Conspiracy Case, April–June 1917, Home, Political, A, January 1918, 491–497, NAI.
59. Hasan, *Ansari*; Weekly Report of Director of Criminal Intelligence, December 1915, Home, Political, December 1915, 709–711, NAI; and Report of the Director of Criminal Intelligence, August 17, 1915, Home, Political, Proceedings, August 1915, NAI; Tassaddaq Hussein and Zain Ali evidence, Proceedings of Commissioners, Mandalay Conspiracy Case, April–June 1917, Home, Political, A, January 1918, 491–497, NAI.
60. Wasti, "Indian Red Crescent Society" confirms this meeting.
61. Zain Ali, Naidu, Maqbub, Rafiq-ul-Haq, and Shekh Juman evidence, Proceedings of Commissioners, Mandalay Conspiracy Case, April–June 1917, Home, Political, A, January 1918, 491–497, NAI.
62. Ibid.
63. For details of the mutiny and revolutionary networks in Singapore, see Tim Harper, "Singapore, 1915, and the Birth of the Asian Underground" in Tim Harper and Sunil Amrith (eds), *Sites of Asian Interaction,* Cambridge University Press, Cambridge, 2014.
64. Hussain Khan evidence and judgment, Proceedings of Commissioners, Mandalay Conspiracy Case, April–June 1917, Home, Political, A, January 1918, 491–497, NAI.
65. Hussein Khan, Mangoo evidence and judgment, ibid.
66. Rafiq-ul-Haq evidence, ibid.
67. Juman Sheikh evidence and judgment, ibid.

68. Weekly Report of the Director of Intelligence, first three weeks of December, 1915, Home, Political, Proceedings, December 1915, 709–711. NAI.
69. Ibid.
70. Naidu evidence, Proceedings of Commissioners, Mandalay Conspiracy Case, April–June 1917, Home, Political, A, January 1918, 491–497, NAI.
71. Ibid; Criminal Intelligence report, 26 January 1915, Home, Political, January 1915, 278–282 NAI and Governor of Burma to Viceroy of India, 10 December 1915, Home, Political, 1916, March, 619–665, NAI.
72. Tassaddaq Hussein evidence, Proceedings of Commissioners, Mandalay Conspiracy Case, April–June 1917, Home, Political, A, January 1918, 491–497, NAI.
73. Naidu evidence, ibid. See also "The Rangoon Chulia Moslems," *The Indian Social Reformer*, 27, 1917, p. 206.
74. Hussein evidence, ibid. Proceedings of Commissioners, Mandalay Conspiracy Case, April–June 1917, Home, Political, A, January 1918, 491–497, NAI.
75. Naidu evidence, ibid.
76. Maung Po Thein evidence, ibid.
77. Government of Burma to Government of India, December 11, 1915, Home, Political, March 1916, 619–665, NAI, and judgment of the Special Commissioner appointed under Defence of India Act 1915 for Trial at Mandalay 1916, Home, Political, Proceedings, September 1916, 403–410, NAI.
78. Statement of people detailed under Defence of India Act 1915, Home, Political, 1921, Part I, 1–51 KW, NAI.
79. For details see Crispin Bates, *Subalterns and the Raj: South Asia since 1600*, Routledge, 2007.
80. Statement of people detailed under Defence of India Act 1915, Home, Political, 1921, Part I, 1–51 KW, NAI.
81. Opening statement and judgment, Proceedings of Commissioners, Mandalay Conspiracy Case, April–June 1917, Home, Political, A, January 1918, 491–497, NAI
82. Judgment, ibid.
83. A. Majid note, April 17, 1924; Diwan Bahadur Rangachariar note, March 24, 1925; Government of India note, 24 March 1925, Home, Political, 1925, 320–25, NAI; Government of Burma note, December 8, 1919 and May 1920, Home, Political, May 1920, 416–479, NAI; and Superintendent Port Blair to GOI, February 17, 1918, Home, Political, Proceedings, January 1919, 207–216, NAI.

84. Malaviya to Rangachariar, March 24, 1925, Home, Political, 1925, 320–324. NAI.
85. Musmat petition to Government of Burma, July 21, 1924, Home, Political, 1925, 320–325. NAI.
86. Rangacharir to Home Member, March 24, 1925, Home, Political, 1925, 320–325, NAI.
87. Siddiqi Statement, May 25, 1925 and release statement, July 1925, ibid.
88. Government of Burma to Government of India, August 30, 1917, Home, Political, Proceedings, January 1918, 27, NAI.
89. Statement of people detained under Defence of India Act 1915, Home, Political, 1921, Part I, 1–51 KW, NAI.
90. For details, see Minault, *Khilafat Movement*, Introduction, and Jalal, *Self and Sovereignty*, Chapter 5.
91. Quoted in Minault, *Khilafat Movement*, p. 62.
92. Jalal, *Self and Sovereighty,*, p. 196 and Minault, *Khilafat Movement*, pp. 68–70.
93. Robinson, *Separatism among Muslims*, p. 299.
94. Minault, *Khilafat Movement*, pp. 76–77.
95. Quoted in, J.T.F. Jordens, *Swami Shraddhananda: His Life and Causes*, Oxford University Press, Delhi, 1981, pp. 110–111.
96. Khilafat Delegation to Viceroy, January 1920, K.K. Aziz (ed.), *The Indian Khilafat Movement 1915-1933: A Documentary Records*, Sang-e-Meel Publications, Lahore, 2006.
97. Government of Burma to Government of India, February 17, 1919, Home, Political, March 1921, 16, NAI; Government of Burma to Government of India, May 16, 1919, Home, Political, July 1921, 48, NAI.
98. "The Rangoon Chulia Moslems and the Viceroy," *Indian Social Reformer*, 27, 1917.
99. l/PJ/6/354 file 1532, Hindu Muslim Riots, 1893 (IOR).
100. Government of Burma to Government of India, August 3, 1920, Home, Political, August 1920, 112, NAI.
101. Tin Maung Maung Than, "Some Aspects of Indians in Rangoon," in K.S. Sandhu and A. Mani (eds), *Indian Communities in Southeast Asia*, p. 618; Government of Burma to Government of India, October 1920, Home, Political, December 1920, 59, NAI and Viceroy to Secretary of State for India, 5 December 1920, Home, Political, January 1921, NAI.
102. *The Weekly Rangoon Times and Overland Summary*, October 30, 1920.
103. Chief Inspector of Police to Secretary, Government of Burma, November 17, 1920, Home, Political, June 1921, 248–282, NAI.
104. Ibid.

105. *Rangoon Times*, November 1920, L/PJ/6/1731, Part I, IOR.
106. GoB to GoI, November 5, 1920, Home, Political, December 1920, 66, NAI.
107. *Rangoon Times*, November 1920, L/PJ/6/1731, Part I, IOR.
108. Government of India memo on Separation (n.d.), Legislative, 147, 1930, NAI.
109. U Ottama set up his kyaung (monastery) in Sittwe, Arakan, named the Shwe Zedi Kyaung, in 1903. Significantly, this was the site of the first pro-democratic rally in Myanmar in 2007, http://content.time.com/time/world/article/0,8599,1917122,00.html.
110. U Ottama's speech at Amoy reproduced in Min Kuo Press, January 20, 1929, Home, Political, 1929, file 145, NAI; U Ottama history sheet, Home, Political, 31/5 KW, 1931, NAI.
111. U Ottama history sheet, ibid.
112. Turner, *Saving Buddhism.*
113. U Ottama history sheet, ibid., Home, Political, 31/5 KW, 1931, NAI.
114. U Ottama speech at Amoy, 20 January 1929, ibid.; U Ottama history sheet, ibid.
115. "Demands of the Strikers, 1920," Myanmar Literature Project, Working Paper, 10:4.1.
116. For details, see Maung Maung, *From Sangha to Laity*, pp. 21–23.
117. U Ottama, history sheet, ibid.
118. S. Chatterjee, *Meeting the Personalities*, Rasika Ranjani Press, 1956, p. 1.
119. Government of Burma to Government of India, December 10, 1920, Home, Political, December 1920, 66, NAI.
120. Government of Burma to Government of India, February 21, 1921, Home Political, 1921, 3, KW, NAI; Government of Burma to Government of India, December 10, 1920 and November 15, 1920, Home, Political, December 1920, 271–276, NAI.
121. U Ottama speeches at Sukalat, Febbruary 4, 1921, Tamatkaw, February 5, 1921, and Dedaye, February 2, 1921, L/PJ/6/1748, file 2735, IOR.
122. Ibid, and U Ottama history sheet, ibid.
123. Viceroy's telegram, March 29, 1921. L/PJ/6/1748 file 2735, IOR.
124. *Rangoon Mail*, March 13, 1921, Home, Political, March 1921, 306, NAI.
125. Viceroy's telegram, March 24, 1921. L/PJ/6/1748, file 2735, IOR; Deputy Commissioner Pyapon to Municipal Secretary, July 10, 1921, 1–15(D) AO-01605, NAM.
126. Fortnightly report, political situation in Burma, July–December 1921, 1 AO Acc-4372, NAM.

127. Fortnightly report, political situation in Burma, July–December 1921, 1 AO Acc-4372, NAM; Government of Burma to Government of India, May 3, 1921, Home, Political, June 1921, 13, NAI; Government of Burma to Government of India, April 18, 1921, Home, Political, June 1921, 51, NAI.
128. For details, see Robert Eric Colvard, "A World Without Drink: Temperance in Modern India, 1880-1940," especially Chapter 4, PhD Dissertation, University of Iowa, 2003; Nandini Bhattacharya, "The Problem of Alcohol in Colonial India (c.1907-1942)," *Studies in History,* 33, 2, 2017, pp. 187–212.
129. Government of Burma to Government of India, April 18, 1921, Home, Political, June 1921, 13, NAI.
130. Government of Burma to Government of India, April 18, 1921, Home, Political, June 1921, 51, NAI.
131. *Rangoon Weekly Times and Overland Summary*, April 10, 1921.
132. Ibid, and Fortnightly report, political situation in Burma, July–December 1921, 1 AO Acc-4372, NAM.
133. *Rangoon Weekly Times and Overland Summary*, April 10, 1921; GoB to GoI, January 23, 1923, Home, Political, January 1923, 25, NAI.
134. Ibid.
135. Government of Burma to Government of India, July 4, 1921, Home, Political, July 1921, 1, NAI; Fortnightly report, political situation in Burma, July–December 1921, 1 AO Acc-4372, NAM.
136. Fortnightly report, political situation in Burma, July–December 1921. 1 AO Acc-4372, NAM.
137. Ibid.
138. Ibid.
139. For details on the Buddhist temperance movement that predated the 1921 boycott, see Alicia Turner, "The Bible, the Bottle and the Knife: Religion as a Mode of Resisting Colonialism for U Dhammaloka," *Contemporary Buddhism,* 14, 1, 2013, pp. 66–77.
140. Fortnightly report, political situation in Burma, July–December 1921, 1 AO Acc-4372. NAM.
141. Ibid.
142. Ibid.
143. Press abstracts, March 24, 1921. L/PJ/6/1748, file 2735, IOR; U. Ottama, *Supplement to New Burma*, July 5, 1922, Speeches, 1922, pamphlet.
144. U Ottama History Sheet, ibid. U Ottama, *Supplement to New Burma*, July 5, 1922, Speeches, 1922, pamphlet.
145. Ibid.

146. Ibid.
147. J.S. Furnivall, *Colonial Policy and Practice: A Comparative Study of Burma and the Netherlands,* Cambridge University Press, 1948.
148. Nile Green, "Buddhism, Islam, and the Religious Economy of Colonial Burma," *Journal of Southeast Asian Studies*, 46(2), 2015, pp. 175–204.
149. Sunil Amrith, *Crossing the Bay of Bengal: The Furies of Nature and Fortunes of Migrants*, Harvard University Press, Cambridge MA, 2013, pp. 28, 104.

6

The Bengali Muslim

Language and Space-Making at the Ocean's Margins

Iftekhar Iqbal

The evolution of Muslim public space followed a similar pattern across pre-colonial South Asia. At the heart of these developments, from Bombay to Bengal, were the Sufis, who sponsored forms of "space-making" at the interface of their transregional itinerary and everyday life around a built environment. Using a "pious network," whether through reclaiming a forest patch or engaging in revenue-generating activities in an urban enclave, the Sufis made themselves an indispensable part of the public space.[1] This practice of space-making assumed a new meaning in Bombay in the colonial economic condition since even deceased Sufis inspired such a process that their tombs continued to be the sites of religious and economic networks. This was an arena where a highly plural and "liberal" religious economy is said to have emerged without the dominance of a rational, reformist Islam.[2]

Colonial Bengal reveals intriguing ruptures. Although Sylhet, Dhaka, and Chittagong (a major port on the Bay of Bengal) had visible Sufi establishments since at least the tenth century, these made little mark on the increasingly globalized economy of colonial Bengal, including in the cosmopolitan city of Calcutta. Esoteric establishments such as Sufi shrines continued to attract a considerable following, but these were more connected to a devotional rather than an economic pathway. This is reflected in the distinctive rise of formal and rational forms of Islamic practices which overshadowed the remnants of once-vibrant Sufi practices, both in its spiritual and institutional appeal.[3] This temporal divergence in colonial public space in the two regions of

Indian Ocean rim raises questions about multiple modalities of space-making among South Asian Muslims.

This chapter suggests that the process of space-making in the nineteenth and twentieth-century Bengal largely took place at the site of language. Without extensive industrialization and urbanization, Bengal saw remarkable mobility of agrarian labor and non-agrarian actors beyond its borders, and the importance of language grew with corresponding pace and scope of popular mobility. Among the four languages—Arabic, Bengali, English, and Urdu—the first two prevailed for historically specific reasons of religiosity and nationalism. But what remains unexplored are the circumstances in which transregional mobility of the Bengalis also led to the increasing attachment of universalist aspirations to those two languages. An exercise in this direction resonates with current debates that consider Bangladesh's public space to be split into two contested linguistic-cultural zones. Arabic is at the center of Islamic pedagogic and pious practices, whereas Bengali, the state language, is at the core of national imagination, secular values, and syncretistic ethnocultural spaces. Arabic is considered an Islamic religious symbol confined to madrassas and mosques; Bangla is perceived as the springboard of Bengali identity. Interrogating the linguistic lens of identity formations, this chapter suggests that language also exists in close conversations with mobility. In the course of the nineteenth and early twentieth centuries, global demands for commodities led to the expansion of agricultural production bases and corresponding labor mobility along the connected littoral regions of the Bay of Bengal where Bengali acquired remarkable national and transregional salience. At another level of spatial crossings across the Middle East and the Malay World, Arabic continued to be the modus operandi and a dominant code of communication for the Bengali Muslims on the move in trade, work, and pilgrimage. This chapter demonstrates the ways the Bengali Muslim mobility along and across the eastern Indian Ocean rim and the connected riverscapes provided for both Bengali and Arabic language as material sites of both space-making and cosmopolitan encounters that reverberated back to the public space of postcolonial Bangladesh, although only to be misrecognized as either a religious or a national signpost.

Mosaic of Mobility in the Ganga-Brahmaputra Delta

The continuity of pre-colonial expansion of agrarian frontiers in the Eastern Bengal delta in the course of the nineteenth century was accompanied by changing ecological circumstances, new commodities, and new approaches to religion. The shifting of rivers toward Eastern Bengal and increasing deforestation in the Himalayan foothills speeded up the geological process of siltation, resulting in the formation of chars or alluvial lands, which eventually became the new sites of production beyond the reclaimed forests of the Sundarbans. In the wake of the decline of the textile industry and the increasingly moribund ecology of western Bengal and parts of Bihar, the productive sites of reclaimed forest and alluvial lands became prime targets for landless and unemployed peasants. Migrant capital and labor played a crucial role in forging closer connections across the Bay of Bengal involving new rice and jute frontiers.[4]

The volume of jute exports jumped forty-fold between the 1830s and 1870s, and during the decade of the 1860s, the value of raw jute exports increased from Rs 4.1 million to Rs. 20.5 million. The demand for jute that was created following the stoppage of Russian hemp trade to Britain during the Crimean war remained uninterrupted until the First World War, barring a few scattered years of slump.[5] In terms of rice, average annual exports in the late nineteenth century were about 1.5 million maunds. The largest share of the supply of rice for Kolkata was furnished by the coastal districts, including the Sundarbans. During the early 1870s, between 7 and 8 million maunds poured in annually through the Kolkata and Eastern canals, which connected the Sundarbans, Barisal, parts of Jessore, and the country around the Meghna river. The amount represented almost 90 percent of the total export of rice from Kolkata. Despite occasional slumps, Eastern Bengal, in the course of the nineteenth century, remained remarkably export-oriented and commercially vibrant.[6]

The coastal buoyancy was replicated further inland. The first jute mill in India was established in the central deltaic area of Sirajganj in the 1860s, but an earthquake prevented the expansion of the industry there, leading way to the banks of the Hugli river. Sirajganj, however, remained a major trading hub, where, in 1872, for instance, the value of total export and import crossed Rs 10 million. The thriving trade and commerce were represented by the fact that between 1872 and 1931 the percentage of non-agricultural population grew by more than 50 percent. The Pabna district, in which Sirajganj was situated, was linked to the adage: "Je ashe Pabna tar nei bhabna" (He who arrives in Pabna worries no more). Like the coastal districts, Sirajganj, situated on the west bank of the Brahmaputra, which connected the Bay of Bengal with Assam and Eastern Bengal, played a key role in agrarian production, trade, and commerce.

With the growth of jute, rice, and tea production in Assam, the Brahmaputra valley beyond Sirajganj became the high street of trade and commerce of eastern India by the late nineteenth century, gradually assuming similar importance as the Ganga. Between 1900 and 1905, the export of tea rose by 300 percent and jute by 50 percent.[7] By the turn of the century, the region of Eastern Bengal and Assam represented a sixth of the total trade of India. The establishment of the new province of Eastern Bengal and Assam marked the growing imperial interest in accessing China and Southeast Asia as well as the Indian Ocean through the Chittagong outlet, in addition to Kolkata.[8] In the seven years of the life of the new province, the "spirit of swadeshi" was spurring industrial activities, implying that the swadeshi movement found a new territory that was now more geo-commercially connected to the Bay of Bengal through the Ganga and Brahmaputra rivers. So, when the new province was revoked in 1911, there was renewed demand for an apex body of chambers of commerce incorporating European, Hindus, Muslims, and Marwaris at the expense of the politicians and lawyers who had not seen the potential of the new province.[9]

It was in this agro-economic buoyancy of the nineteenth century that new forms of public appropriation of Islam began to emerge. Unlike the pre-colonial practice of space-making around Sufi shrines, a clearer, textually inclined version of Islam made its way into the new agrarian frontier. The possibility of linking agrarian production with trade and commerce awakened the peasant society to their rights and entitlement in a remarkable way. For Haji Shariatullah, the founder of the first sustained Muslim agrarian movement in colonial Bengal, known as the Faraizi movement, the idea of *tawheed* (oneness of God) and *adl* (justice) was instrumental in organizing unemployed weavers, emerging in the wake of the decline of textile industry in early colonial Bengal, against the landlords. For Dudu Mian, who succeeded Shariatullah in the late 1830s, it was a suitable moment to blend the idea of God's sovereignty with agrarian enterprises in the new agro-ecological and commercial frontier of Bengal. He pronounced that all land belonged to God and that *langol jar jomi tar* (the land belongs to him who possesses the plow).[10] This was a clear reflection of the growing importance of smaller units of cultivable land under individual ownership in an ecological condition that created new lands through the siltation process and reclamation of forests.

The saintly tombs and Sufi shrines, which had been catalysts to remarkable land reclamation process since the pre-colonial times, were now perceived as rent-seeking institutions that had no active economic role. The nineteenth-century Faraizi reformism that called for closer Quranic regulations of Islam and decrying of grave-reverence cannot be thus understood as merely Wahhabi influence or as mark of distaste for Hindu forms of reverence for the dead. The Faraizis were ardent traders in jute and other commercial products and were keen to secure occupancy rights, using entitlement to land for productive purposes and responding intelligently to critical dynamics of the market in both coastal and river port cities. Through the Acts of 1859 and 1885, individual rights of land reclaimers were made legally binding. The state and the peasant got closer as customary rules were renegotiated in the given ecological conditions outside the jurisdiction of Permanent Settlement of revenue. The persistence of custom in the agrarian economic sphere was a recognition of the fact that global capital could operate in Bengal within the local contexts. Therefore, when the globally tuned agrarian production process facilitated the accrual of certain individual rights in property, these happened to be of local, customary origin.[11] This also provided a context where new forms of agro-religious assertion, which was conducive to the commercialization of the agrarian economy, was tolerated by the colonial administration with calculated indifference. Such conditions enabled the Faraizis to take on colonial capitalist enterprises more directly than via any esoteric establishments, such as a Sufi shrine.

It is in this evolving agro-commercial entanglement that we need to examine Faraizi embeddedness in agrarian politics vis-à-vis the more ideologically driven politics at the regional and pan-Indian level. The Tariqh-i-Muhammadia radical movements, which arrived in Bengal via northern India, didn't go down well with the Faraizi followers, who seemed to be a relatively more active group with a greater stake in the productive agrarian domain. On the other hand, the "modernist" and urban associational culture, what sometimes resembled Alexis de Tocqueville's idea of associationalism, as promoted by figures like Syed Ameer Ali and Khwaja Salimullah, came in close contact with the pre-1857 radicals like Maulana Kermat Ali of the Tariqh-i-Muhammadia group, who in turn contributed to Muslim nationalist politics.

The Faraizis, while they didn't acknowledge the political sovereignty of the British, appropriated the regime's vulnerability to administer the fluid ecological zones and asserted a kind of politics that allowed them to remain indifferent to the War of 1857 as well as to the late nineteenth-century radicalism in northwestern India. This implied Faraizi indifference to ideologies that were not conducive to their own agro-productive milieu. In such circumstances, while contestations among the Bengali Muslims were documented in contemporary vernacular literature, there was a relative lack of communal conflict between Muslims and non-Muslims. For the Faraizis, tensions seemed to be more acute with the non-agrarian forces of Muslim factions than with the non-Muslim communities in agrarian Bengal. The idea of *jatek-gathan* or "nation-formation" as expressed in a *puthi* (vernacular Bengali text) in the 1870s thus offered a more egalitarian sense of the society along lines of class, religion, and market in this maritime zone. But if anything was clearly lacking about the idea of jatek-gathan, it was the spatial configuration of it. For the Bengalis, neither the Sundarbans nor the chars of the deltaic heartland were the last frontier. Up the Brahmaputra Valley in Assam and down the Irrawaddy Delta in Burma and beyond appeared to be the territories where the process of mobility and space-making would continue.

Up the River: Agro-Ecological Expansion along the Brahmaputra Valley

Although the migration of Bengali peasants and traders across Assam dates back to modern times, there were striking trends in this direction by the turn of the twentieth century.[12] By the 1890s a major cultivable portion of the Sundarbans had been reclaimed and the silts that formed productive lands were becoming a liability in many places as riverbeds were raised. While demographic pressure was increasingly felt in the Eastern Bengal plains, the nineteenth-century agrarian and economic growth came to an end with the emergence of a group of non-agrarian social forces, leading to sharecropping and landlessness. During the decade preceding the onslaught of global economic depression, rent receivers increased by 62 percent while the number of vulnerable sharecroppers increased by 49 percent. In the 1940s, the sharecroppers constituted 29 percent of the total agricultural population.[13] It was these broader shifts in ecology and economy in the Eastern Bengal plains that induced the migration of Bengali Muslims along the Brahmaputra valley in Assam.

The migration replicated the earlier agrarian experiences in deltaic Bengal. While in Bengal the cultivation of major agricultural produce including jute and rice was showing signs of decline after decades of growth about the beginning of the First World War, jute cultivation in Assam increased remarkably. Binay Chaudhuri suggests that Assam agriculture was in near stagnation until the first decade of the twentieth century when the Eastern Bengal peasants arrived with appropriate skills. "Nearly all" jute growers were Muslim migrants from the Eastern Bengal districts, who accounted for 56 percent of the increase in Assam's population between 1911 and 1921. The range of productivity corresponded with the scale of migration from Bengal to Assam, as reflected in the fact that between 1901–02 and 1946–47, the net sown area in the plain districts of Assam increased by 97.08 percent.[14]

Although apparently the Bengal Muslim under pressure in the deltaic plains moved upward into Assam, they were in fact not getting any further from the Bay of Bengal as they remained active in the valley of the Brahmaputra, which was, by all means, a formidable arm of the sea.[15] The Indian Ocean continued to inform the Bengali agro-ecological itinerary and commercial dynamics in the wake of dislocations in productive process in deltaic plainland, and in a way which Pearson would describe as ocean's shoreward or amphibious existence on the land.[16] Despite the fact that the Bengali Muslims occasionally engaged themselves in trade and profession, it was mainly the agrarian production that remained their mainstay in Assam.[17]

The transregional mobility can be appreciated from the perspective of Islam as a form of resistance to intermediary rentier extraction along the ecological bases of production that connected the Indian Ocean. A long-term trajectory is useful here because most historical studies have considered agrarian politics, or resistance, in Bengal as scattered and disconnected.[18] Yet little changed over a century since Dudu Mian's employment of agro-political Islam as a form of resistance in deltaic Bengal. At the latter end of this continuum, Maulana Abdul Hamid Khan Bhasani's program in the Brahmaputra valley retained the agro-political quest of the Faraizis. After performing hajj at an early age, like Haji Shariatullah and Dudu Mian, Bhasani returned to Bengal where he was mentored by Syed Nasir Uddin, a spiritual figure who had migrated from Baghdad to Sirajganj and later on in Assam. About that time, Bhasani got in touch with major political leaders of the time, including C.R. Das, Subhas Chandra Bose, and Prafulla Chandra Ray.[19] From 1924 onward until the partition of India, and especially between 1928 and 1938, Bhasani used to move up and down the Brahmaputra valley in order to mobilize Bengali peasants. He was elected to the Assam Legislative Assembly through the 1937 elections.

Bhasani's politics in Assam made three specific contributions. He struggled for securing rights on land on a century-old slogan of "langol jar, jomi tar" in order to put an end to the practice of evicting peasants on whims.[20] He resisted the Line System, which tried to contain Bengali migrants in specific pockets and stifle their free movement along the Brahmaputra valley. Bhasani also resisted the disparity in the system of measurement of the agricultural produce, which left loopholes to the disadvantage of the primary producers. It would seem that a century of resistance by the Bengali Muslim peasants showed a continued attachment to the production bases and networks that the river valleys offered to them.[21] It was in this continuum of human assertion through ecological fluidity and river-based connectivity that Bhasani proved to be a peasant leader. Bhasani's political engagement not only presented an example of continuity of agro-Islamic polities in the long span of a century, it denoted that oceanic history had an itinerary beyond the maritime ports, making deep inroads as far as the upper reaches of the Brahmaputra. In the case of Bengali Muslim peasants in Assam, it was this river through which the Indian Ocean prompted space-making that was both multisited and associated with extensive mobility across an agrarian world without a frontier.

Down the Coast: Moving across Urban Enclaves

If the oceanic dynamics induced the Bengali mobility and space-making inside the agrarian spaces in Assam, it enabled them to leave markedly urban footprints in lower and central Burma. The Bengali Muslim engagement in Burma is perhaps older and more extensive than in the Assam region as it fell on the maritime trail of Muslim merchants from western Asia to Southeast Asia and also because of Bengal's intriguing political relations with lower Burma. Bengali Muslim political connections with Burma started in 1430 when a Bengal Sultan helped King Narameikhla to regain his throne, followed by the settlement of many Bengali soldiers in Arakan. Since then, the relationship between Arakan and Bengal saw extreme ups and downs, ranging from Arakan's loyalty to Bengal Sultans (in 1513)[22] to the enslavement of 80,000 Bengali skilled textile workers (in 1644).[23] In the centuries of vicissitudes and fortunes, many Bengalis rooted themselves in Arakan and other parts of lower Burma where a "highly cosmopolitan" Bengali cultural milieu emerged.[24] It is no coincidence that one of the reasons for the British annexation of lower Burma was that the Burmese king granted trade monopoly of Rangoon port to a "native" Muslim than to the East India Company.[25] A fresh wave of

Bengali migration started with the annexation of lower Burma and continued until the Japanese invasion in 1942.

In the first Anglo-Burmese war, heavy causalities among British soldiers led to the calling of 700 Chittagong lascars, dubbed as "natural watermen," for the Bengal Marine.[26] Bengalis in Burma, scattered across Arakan, Rangoon, Pegu, Hanthawady, Basin, and Mandalay, increased from around 205,000 in 1901 to 301,000 in 1921. According to a local Bengali magazine, the number was more than 500,000 as the lower-class Bengali, who were called *kurungi* by the Burmese, were not included in the census. Of the Bengalis, a majority were from Chittagong, followed by those from Noakhali and Comilla, implying a considerable Muslim population.[27] Those Bengalis who married Burmese women lost their *Bangalitto* [Bengaliness] by one or two generations. While a majority of the Hindus were service holders, many Bengali Muslims were businessmen.[28] A thriving Bengali community was sustained through regular coastal transport. African-American writer Juanita Harrison, who traveled from Chittagong to Rangoon in a packed local steamer in the 1930s, refers to the regular commutation of a huge number of people of different origins and religions between the two places.[29] On the commercial front, numerous Bengalis dealt with milk products and groceries in Burmese towns, but there were also major commercial firms like Abdul Sobhan Khan's Jubilee Stores and Jubilee Press, and Makshud's Burma Swadeshi Stores Limited. Many Chittagonians made fortunes through business in wood, rice, and sawmills. Jamal Brothers, for example, became millionaires.[30]

A process of urban space-making was visible in politics and civil society initiatives. The Rangoon chapter of the Burmah Provincial Khilafat Committee kept the political sphere alive in the 1920s, touching many lives. Didarul Alam of Chittagong had given up studies during the noncooperation movement and came to Rangoon, where he edited, until his death at a young age of 26, two Bengali papers: a monthly magazine, *Juger Alo* (Light of the Era) and a weekly, *Sammilani* (Rendezvous).[31]

Different civil society organizations in Rangoon included Bengal Mohammedan Association (club and library), Khadim ul Islam, and Chittagong Moslem Society. Bangla Sahitya Sammilon was founded by a group of forty Hindu and Muslim literary activists. The literary journal of this organization, *Sammilani*, was edited by Moulvi Muhammad Abdul Monem. Bengali Muslim women came forward through school and college education, Mosammat Ashia Khatun being the first woman to succeed in matriculation from Rangoon University, securing the highest place. She was the daughter of Chittagong's Abdul Majid, an interpreter for the Akyab government. A women's association oversaw some of the developments in the field of women's public engagement and welfare. A night madrassa was established on the Rangoon Botatang Mosque's rooftop. Around this place lived both poor workers as well as wealthy contractors of Fatikshori of Chittagong. Abdul Bari Chowdhury established and managed many charitable *maktab* (Islamic nursery), madrassas, schools, and mosques. The Hindu community in Rangoon equally thrived, and the spirit of philanthropy often crossed the communal boundary. Soshibhushon Niyogi, for example, donated to both Hindu educational institutions and madrassas.[32] With the emergence of an inclusive Bengali civil society in Rangoon, religious identities were able to give way to a broader sense of the Indian community. In such a social space, there was a reflection of the anti-colonial politics in India and also of relatively healthy communal relations among the Indian community. If Bengali Muslim mobility induced the formation of a new social space around the agrarian domain in Assam, in lower Burma, it was a more urban development that was taking shape, although often in tension with the Burmese community in Rangoon.[33]

The urban experience among Bengalis in Burma was reproduced across the Southeast Asian rim of the Indian Ocean. Their mobility across the ocean, especially the regions beyond its immediate coastline, could be understood in larger social domains and broader spatial crossings. When the first Portuguese sailors arrived in Malacca in the fifteenth century, they looked to the Malaccans as "white Bengalis with beards,"[34] denoting the Bengali presence in the region from earlier times. Tomé Pires's *Suma Oriental*, completed in 1515, describes Samudra Passin on the north coast of Sumatra as a cosmopolitan city with an "important Muslim population among whom Bengalis were especially prominent."[35] The idea of Bengali origin of Malayan Islam, as hinted by Fatimi, is recently contested by Hooker on the ground that Bengali Hanafi school didn't match with Malay Shāfi'ī school. Hooker admits that his criticism did not exclude a "Bengali element in the Muslim population of the archipelago."[36]

In the mid-nineteenth century, Punjabis and other Indians were considered by the Malays as Bengalis.[37] At the turn of the twentieth century, many of the qazis, or religious officials conducting marriage and other social ceremonies, were of Bengali origin. The police staff of Penang were mainly drawn from immigrants from Bengal and Madras.[38] By the First World War, many Bengalis joined the anti-colonial forces that participated in the Singapore Sepoy Mutiny in 1915, some of them being possibly executed along with other Indian activists. In the interwar period, the Bengali Muslim community in Malaya played a significant role in the religious and social life of the region, especially under the auspices of the Bengal Muslim Association. At Penang, as the Second World War was raging, Arab, Bengali, Malay, and other Indian Muslims collected funds to donate to the earthquake victims in Turkey.[39] In March 1950, the Bengal Muslim Association of Singapore fed more than 400 people at the Queen Street Mosque in connection with a ceremony to celebrate the Prophet's birthday.[40] They had been organizing such welfare activities from much earlier time.

Medinipur's Din Muhammad, along with some fellow businessmen, was kidnapped in Mandalay in 1858 from a remote area and sold for an ox by some Kachins, and eventually found himself married to a Kachin woman. He was 'rescued' in 1868 by Anderson, an English doctor.[41] By the time the first Ho settlers began arriving in northern Thailand, following the collapse of the Yunnan Muslim rebellion, a community of Bengal Muslims had already been settled in the Chang Khlan area of southern Chiangmai in Thailand.[42] In the early twentieth century, a considerable number of them were in Bangkok, a majority of whose profession was tailoring. Amu Ostagar, the royal tailor and chief technician of a big firm, married a Thai woman, with whom he had children and breathed his last in Calcutta in 1915.[43] It seems that from Eastern Bengal to the Malay world across lower Burma there were forms of urban space-making in which the Bengali Muslim constituted a significant element.

Language and the Shifting Universal

In a widening web of mobility in and beyond Bengal, languages must have been a major element. The question of linking language with transregional mobility has assumed greater significance in the light of recent studies on the quest for the universal in linguistic translations and vernacularization of Arabic-Islamic texts in South and Southeast Asia.[44] As in many other regions of the Muslim world, the Quran was not translated in full into Bengali by a Muslim until the turn of the twentieth century. Many scholars, including Ronit Ricci, have rested the matter of untranslatability of the Quran in South and Southeast Asia to the question of its sanctitude and literary finesse. Scholarly focus has recently been on the semi-sacred sources such as *Kisas Al-Anbiyah*, or the stories of the prophets, in vernacular literature.[45]

Yet the question of the untranslatability of the Quran in Bengali can also be read as a sign of a continued quest for trans-spatial entanglement than a mere theological or lingua-aesthetic barrier. Bengali participation in the Arab-Islamic cosmopolitan corners through mercantile networks across the Indian Ocean gave way to new sets of necessities for Arabic as a mode of communication.[46] The nineteenth-century peasant leaders, including Titu Meer, Haji Shariatullah, and his successors in the Faraizi movement, were not only pilgrims but pupils in educational institutions and networks within Arabia. Arabic, for them, was a language of divinity and spiritual quest, but at the same time it was a mode of communication with the "cosmopolitan zones" where they found themselves moving to.[47] The need to use Arabic as such was felt across the pedagogic domain of the madrassas for centuries in deltaic Bengal, Assam, lower Burma, Malaya, and Western Indonesian islands. In the commercial circuit across South and Southeast Asian maritime spaces, Arabic remained a central language of communication, even if it was through more "untranslated" terms such as madrassa, jamat, or *zikr* (recitation of the

Quran or remembrance of God), as Ricci has shown. The use of the "untranslated" among the array of "translated" rather recognizes the need to keep the central text in its original linguistic form. In other words, there was an urge not to translate the Quran because it was seen as a master sourcebook for communicability across a vast span of the Indian Ocean rim.

Aspects of the communicability rested with the natural environmental setting of the Indian Ocean. The changing role of Islamic prayers and invocation of Islamic ritual practices had a *longue durée* yet adaptive resonance from Java to Zanzibar. For example, "*sadaka*" became a form of self-appropriating "part of a wide variety of communicative forms, intentions and consequently a prayer as social phenomenon." David Parkin suggests that sadaka and *dua* (supplication to God in addition to regular prayer) formed part of a communicative prayer that engaged with divinity through the sea and other spirits, and through these, the fishermen wanted to control their own destinies. The control that the sea spirits exercise over the oceans in which they work is a force to be appeased, lest one of themselves be taken in sacrifice.[48] Such communicative forms of prayers were not uncommon among the seafaring Bengalis. The Indian Ocean was also a site for a connected program of piety and prayers. In all these efforts, Arabic was a lingua franca, even in its more fragmented and vernacular forms.

Another aspect of communication could be explained in relation to the hajj and higher studies, which offered spaces for the exchange of ideas as exemplified in the case of peasant leaders like Haji Shariatullah, Dudu Mian, and Maulana Bhasani. In the postcolonial times, particularly since the 1970s, the need for communication has increased even more. For millions of Bengali expatriates working in the Gulf, Arabic proves to be a sign of the universal as it is during the hajj, commerce, and other forms of activities. To date, a hermeneutic practice of the study of the Quran in the wide range of madrassa institutions continues across Bangladesh, and South and Southeast Asian regions, including in Western Bengal, where, in more recent times, Hindu students have also attended. The debates among the liberal circles in Bangladesh that madrassa education produces radicalism and worthless citizens tend to underestimate the distinct aspirations for trans-spatial crossings and the multifaceted universal that is latent in the Arabic-Islamic pedagogic reproductions.

On the other spectrum of the linguistic question, Bengali emerged as a popular language about the same time that Arabic reached the deltaic shore. The Arabic speaking sultans of Bengal post the fourteenth century patronized Bengali language and attached to it greater public importance. During the apparent royal neglect of Bengali in the Mughal period, it continued to flourish at a popular level and in the court of Arakan. The extensive development of Bengali in early colonial times strengthened it as a language of many avenues. In the agrarian domain, the Faraizis profusely used Bengali in puthi and printed books, from the early nineteenth century, to mobilize political support. In the early twentieth century, Bengali dialects, by now bloomed through the Bengal renaissance, were greatly used in Assam, lower Burma, and other neighboring areas. Bengali became the second language in Rangoon after Burmese, putting behind the Arakanese and the Karenese,[49] whereas in Assam, it was perhaps the first language, putting Assamese in the second position. In the last decades of colonial rule, in the cities of Kolkata and Dhaka, Bengali Muslim literati carved out a remarkable aesthetic space and aspired for transcendence, while Islam remained a fountain of multiple and often competing outreaches to the wider world.[50] In Chittagong, Kazi Nazrul Islam's following suggestion in 1929 could not be more timely:

> Let your Islamabad [Chittagong] be a centre of Oriental culture—Arafat Moidan [the open ground of Arafat that draws all the pilgrims during the Hajj]. Let the pilgrims of home and abroad throng here. Today we are indebted to the newly awakened world—we will not only pay back our debt to it, we will make the world indebted to us ... let this be your ultimate efforts. So far we held our empty palms on the air ... it's time for us to put our palms downwards [to pay back]. If we can't do that, the sea is not very far, let our disgrace end forever in the endless depth of the sea ... I suggest you take up the responsibility of setting up a centre for knowledge and civilization like Santiniketan of Rabindranath.[51]

A cosmopolitan urge now found a greater voice in creative imaginations through Bengali, referring to an intellectual debt to the world alongside a quest for affective identity. Bengali, now equipped with more power and pathways, served the same purpose of communication beyond a fixed point of time and space. By the time Nazrul was writing, Bengali-speaking Muslims had become part of a global diaspora strongly rooted not only in Assam and Burma but far beyond and across the Indian Ocean, including in Britain and the USA.[52] It was not until Samia Khatun's chance encounter in New South Wales with a 500-page Bengali puthi from the 1860s that we know that such Bengali texts were moving along with cameleers in an Australian desert.[53] The ascent of Bengali in the worldview of the Bengali Muslims took a significant boost with the language movement of the 1940s and 1950s, which was not merely a first step toward securing cultural autonomy under the threat of Urdu predominance at the state level, but also a search for transcendence and trans-spatial connectivity. Urdu had a nascent career in Bengal in the elite circle and religious seminaries from the late Mughal period, but as the Bengali mobility increased more along the Indian Ocean rim rather than across mainland India, it lost mass appeal, although many Urdu words and style continued to be featured in Bengali creative literature. The successful language movement of 1952 finally sealed the fate of Urdu in Bengal. When in 1999 the United Nations accepted a proposal from Bangladesh to adopt February 21 as International Mother Language Day, the continued urge for using Bengali as a site of transnational entanglements became apparent. In terms of English, the Bengali Muslims began to engage the language quite late by the late nineteenth century, prompting a curious case of misreading of their reluctance as a sign of religious conservatism and resentment of the lost power that was. In the light of new researches, it may perhaps be suggested that reservations about engaging the English language by the Bengali Muslim community until well into the second half of the colonial period was a reflection of their nervousness of being displaced from trans-spatial passages of communication which both Arabic and Bengali had already offered to them. This hesitation could only be understood from the perspective of shifting linguistic lanes in the high street of global mobility and communication.

Although the historical currency of Arabic and Bengali stems from two different temporal planes, each of the languages emerged as a sign of the universal. Arabic made its mark in transoceanic spaces across both the "translated" and "untranslated" zones in South and Southeast Asia. Bengali served to aid social cohesion and resistance in the zones of agrarian production and urban social space along the Indian Ocean rim of Eastern Bengal, Brahmaputra valley Assam and Lower Burma. The notion that Arabic was exclusively an Islamic preserve while Bengali was a vehicle of secularity thus makes little sense if these communicative synergies linked with spatial crossings are considered. Both the languages thrived in society while negotiating fleeting temporality. Bengal Muslim identity, as it was manifest in the medium of both Arabic and Bengali, is a parallel quest for keeping up with mobility near and far, although the temporal frame through which it is vented gets changed. The use of Arabic and Bengali in the real world found different channels, but the urge to take language beyond the bound of one's ethnospatial confines and to reach the wider world was always there. Does it follow, then, that the language may exist independently of the normative hanger of identity?

Conclusions

The question of Bengali Muslim public space cannot be adequately understood through the competing discourses of religion and secularity alone. This is not merely because the ontological regime of religion and secularity is unmanageably multiple and unstable, as Amartya Sen and Talal Asad have shown, [54] but that such debates often overlook the implications of spatial crossings through which traits of identities are continuously recreated and remapped.[55] The stake of the Bengali Muslims in this context is broader as they have in modern times had an extensive global and transregional sojourn.

In Bengal, aspects of space-making took a different form than what Nile Green observed in Bombay. For the Bengali Muslim, Islam and economic affairs were not centered on a specific seaport alone, carrying its dynamics far inside the landmass through the rivers; it took on both urban and agrarian characteristics given the different spatial contexts and lack of industrialization; it was in its most typical form opposed rather than centered on a saintly tomb. The moral economy had an element of resistance unlike a tomb-centric esoteric organization of the mundane. In other words, spirituality and rituals had a temporal stake in Bengal, where forms of "liberalism" emerged at a site where Islam responded to capitalist changes more directly with compatible rationality.

Communicational urges through linguistic practices eroded, if partially, the political-ideological meanings attached to these languages within national imagination. Bengali took its precedence as a sign of the universal when such a perception of Arabic waned. Bengali remains more visible because it lingers on the linguistic convergence of the nation in Bangladesh. At the same time, it has a greater transnational stake in widening diaspora in Western Europe, North America, parts of Southeast Asia, or the Middle East. Arabic, which couldn't find a national berth, retained the transnational window. Along with commerce, pilgrimage and employment options in the Middle East and the Malay world from the 1970s onward, this transnational communicational necessity has made it even more appealing as it is reflected in the hermeneutic of the madrassas. So, if the question of communication and multiple entanglements in an ever-globalizing world is taken into consideration, it would seem that the anxiety about the ideological properties of language was not merely about Islamic or secular consciousness. It was also linked to the problem of misrecognition of the shift from one sign to the other or, in other words, the unintelligibility of the power of the language to live a life across time and space.

Notes and References

1. Nile Green, *Making Space: Sufis and Settlers in Early Modern India* (New York: Oxford University Press, 2012); Richard Eaton, *The Rise of Islam and the Bengal Frontier, 1204-1760* (Berkeley and London: University of California Press, 1996).
2. Nile Green, *Bombay Islam: The Religious Economy of the West Indian Ocean, 1840-1915* (Cambridge: Cambridge University Press, 2011).

3. For a discussion on the dismemberment of Sufi tradition in the colonial environment, see Iftekhar Iqbal, "A Genealogy of Society: Mapping the Relationship between *Samaj* and Civil Society in Bangladesh," *South Asia: Journal of South Asian Studies*, 40, 1 (2017), 162–174.
4. Sugata Bose, *A Hundred Horizons: The Indian Ocean at the Age of Global Empire* (Cambridge, MA: Harvard University Press, 2006), p. 13.
5. Sugata Bose, *Peasant Labour and Colonial Capital: Rural Bengal since 1770*, The New Cambridge History of India (Cambridge: Cambridge University Press, 1993), p. 53.
6. Iftekhar Iqbal, *The Bengal Delta. Ecology, State and Social Change 1840-1943* (Basingstoke and New York: Palgrave Macmillan, 2010), pp. 18–92.
7. Syed Murtaza Ali, *History of Chittagong* (Dacca: Standard Publishers Limited, 1964), pp. 118–119.
8. Iftekhar Iqbal, "The Space between Nation and Empire: The Making and Unmaking of Eastern Bengal and Assam Province, 1905-1911," *The Journal of Asian Studies*, 74, 1 (2015), pp. 69–84.
9. Peter Swan, *The Declaration of Delhi. How Not to Rule. An Open Letter to the World's Workers of Bengal, Eastern Bengal and Assam* (Calcutta: The Englishman Press, 1912).
10. Iqbal, *The Bengal Delta*, p. 70.
11. For an insightful treatment of the debates about the role of custom in the governance of agrarian Bengal, see Andrew Sartori, "A Liberal Discourse of Custom in Colonial Bengal," *Past and Present*, 212 (August 2011), 163–197. See also Sartori's contribution in this volume.
12. That the Bengalis were a well-known ethnic group in Assam is testified by the fact that early British visitors in the region were called "Boga (white) Bengalis." See Jayeeta Sharma, *Empire's Garden: Assam and the Making of India* (Durham, NC: Duke University Press, 2011), pp. 49, 53.
13. For a political-ecological perspective on this shift, see Iqbal, *The Bengal Delta.*
14. B.B. Chaudhuri, *Peasant History of Late Pre-colonial and Colonial India* (Delhi: Pearson Education in India, 2008), pp. 331, 473.
15. The Brahmaputra was first conceived as an "arm of the sea" by the first surveyor-general of India, James Rennell. See James Rennell, "An Account of the Ganges and Burrampooter Rivers," *Philosophical Transactions of the Royal Society of London*, 71 (1781), p. 112.
16. Michael Pearson, *The Indian Ocean* (London: Routledge, 2003).
17. For example, *Kapurai*, the oil merchants of Assam, were Chittagong Muslims. Golam Haider established a *tanga* (horse-drawn cart) service between Guwahati and Shillong, followed by the opening of a motor

service and oil stores. The company was later sold to his fellow-villager, Jomait Ullah and Sons, which later became a limited company. See Gyanendra Mohon Das, *Banger Bahire Bangali* (The Bengalis Beyond Bengal) (Calcutta: Indian Publishing House, 1931), p. 384.

18. For example, Ranajit Guha, *Elementary Aspects of Peasant Insurgency in Colonial India* (Delhi: Oxford University Press, 1983).
19. During the flood and epidemic in 1922 in Mymensingh, Bhasani's "labour, selfless work for the poor and honesty" made C.R. Das offer him the post of the deputy leader of the relief center. See Abu Noman Khan, "Maulana Bhasanir Jibansrot," in Mohsin Sostropani (ed.), *Majlum Jononeta Maulana Bhasani Smarak-Sonkolon* (Dhaka: Maulana Abdul Hamid Khan Bhasani Porishad, 2002), pp. 259–264.
20. Abdul Hye Sikder, *Jana Ajana Maulana Bhasani* (Dhaka: Farhana Books, 2002, 2005), pp. 155–157.
21. For a long view of peasant resistance in Assam, see Arupjyoti Saikia, *A Century of Protests: Peasant Politics in Assam since 1900* (New Delhi: Routledge, 2013). For a recent contribution on the life and time of Maulana Bhasani, see Layli Uddin, "In the Land of Eternal Eid: Maulana Bhashani and the Political Mobilisation of Peasants and Lower-class Urban Workers in East Pakistan, c. 1930s-1971" (PhD thesis, Royal Holloway, University of London, 2015).
22. Moshe Yegar, *Between Integration and Secession: The Muslim Communities of the Southern Phillipines, Southern Thailand, and Western Burma/ Myanmar* (New York and Oxford: Lexington Books, 2002), p. 23.
23. Stephen van Galen, "Arakan at the Turn of the First Millennium of the Arakanese Era," in Jos Gommans and Jacques Leider (eds), *The Maritime Frontier of Burma: Exploring Political, Cultural and Commercial Interaction in the Indian Ocean World, 1200-1800* (Leiden: KITLV Press), p. 159.
24. Swapna Bhattacharya, "Myth and History of Bengali Identity in Arakan," in Gommans and Jacques Leider (eds), *The Maritime Frontier of Burma*, pp. 199–212.
25. Hiram Cox, *Journal of a Residence in the Burman Empire* (London: John Warren, 1821).
26. Alister McCrae and Alan Prentice, *Irrawaddy Flotilla* (Paisley: James Baton Company, 1978), p. 42.
27. It is estimated that about 40 percent of all Bengalis in Burma Delta was from Chittagong. See Michael Adas, *The Burma Delta: Economic Development and Social Change on an Asian Rice Frontier, 1852-1941* (Madison, WS: The University of Wisconsin Press, 1974), p. 86.
28. Das, *Banger Bahire Bangali*, pp. 403, 403 fn, 420.

29. Where "at one end of the Boat are a Hindoo resturant and a Mohammed one Both very clean I had dinner from the Mohammed. Chicken curry with Rice. The curry doesn't taste nothing like the dried curry powder we get. Here they use the fresh Curry. I ate so much and too fast so with the Sea became seasick and felt wonderful after. When I came on boad they said that European women were not allowed to travell as Deck Passenges. I answered I had my ticket and I couldnt pay any more and if they didnt like it they must pay the differents. everything is going lovely now." Quoted in Pearson, *The Indian Ocean*, 242.
30. Das, *Banger Bahire Bangali*, pp. 471, 476.
31. Ali, *History of Chittagong*, 118–119.
32. Das, *Banger Bahire Bangali*, pp. 431–433.
33. For an exploration of Bengali migrations and diaspora in colonial Burma, see Devleena Ghose, "Burma-Bengal Crossings: Intercolonial Connections in Pre-Independence India", *Asian Studies Review*, 42, 2 (2016), 156–172.
34. D.R. Sardesai, *Southeast Asia* (Dhaka: UPL, 1981), p. 84.
35. M.B. Hooker, "The Translation of Islam into South-East Asia," in M.B. Hooker (ed.), *Islam in South-East Asia* (Leiden: E.J. Brill: 1988), p. 4.
36. Hooker, "The Translation of Islam," p. 6.
37. Thomas R. Metcalf, *Imperial Connections: India in the Indian Ocean Arena, 1860-1920* (Berkeley: University of California Press, 2007).
38. Das, *Banglar Bahire Bangali*, p. 296.
39. "Penang Muslims Aid Turkish Sufferers," *The Straits Times*, February 2, 1940, p. 11.
40. *The Straits Times*, March 10, 1950, p. 80.
41. Das, *Banger Bahire Bangali*, p. 425.
42. Andrew D.W. Forbes (ed.), *The Muslims of Thailand vol. 1* (Gaya: Centre for South East Asian Studies, 1988), p. 102.
43. Das, *Banger Bahire Bangali*, p. 439.
44. Robert Feleppa, *Convention, Translation, and Understanding: Philosophical Problems in the Comparative Study of Culture* (New York: State University of New York Press, 1988); Lydia H. Liu (ed.), *Tokens of Exchange: The Problem of Translation in Global Circulations* (Durham and London: Duke University Press, 1999); Anna Mauranen and Pekka Kujamäki (eds), *Translation Universals: Do They Exist?* (Amsterdam and Philadelphia: John Benjamins Publishing Company, 2004); Naoki Sakai and Jon Solomon, *Translation, Biopolitics, Colonial Difference* (Hong Kong: Hong Kong University Press, 2006).
45. For a study on the literary zones of cosmopolitanism, see Ronit Ricci, *Islam Translated: Literature, Conversion and the Arabic Cosmopolis of*

South and Southeast Asia (Chicago: University of Chicago Press, 2011), pp. 153–154; For a study of similar genre but on a different linguistic and cultural landscape, see Farina Mir, *The Social Space of Language: Vernacular Culture in British Colonial Punjab* (Berkeley: University of California Press, 2010).

46. For premodern Muslim Bengal connections with the Indian Ocean world across North Africa, Arabia, and other regions, where Persian, Arabic, and Turkish speakers joined each other, see Rila Mukherjee, "Conclusion: Time, Space and Region in the Northern Bay of Bengal," in Rila Mukherjee (ed.), *Pelagic Passageways of the Bengali Muslims* (Delhi: Primus Book, 2011), pp. 452–472.
47. For a recent exploration of "cosmopolitan thought zones," see Sugata Bose and Kris Manjapra (eds), *Cosmopolitan Thought Zones. South Asia and the Global Circulations of Ideas* (Basingstoke: Palgrave Macmillan, 2010).
48. David Parkin, "Invocation: Salaa, Dua, Sadaka and the question of self-determination" in David Parkin and Stephen Headley eds., *Islamic Prayer across the Indian Ocean: Inside and Outside the Mosque* (Richmond, Surrey: Curzon 2000), pp. 137, 148.
49. Das, *Banger Bahire Bangali,* p. 403
50. As Bose has argued, a new pattern of cosmopolitanism emerged in late colonial Bengali Muslim literarti that focused beyond vernacularization, implying transfusion of pluralist imaginations. See Neilesh Bose, *Recasting the Region: Language, Culture, and Islam in Colonial Bengal* (New Delhi: Oxford University Press, 2014).
51. Quoted in Abdul Quadir (ed.), *Nazrul Rochanavali, vol. IV* (2nd edn, Dhaka: Bangla Academy, 1993), p. 104. Incidentally, about the time Kazi Nazrul Islam propagated cosmopolitan ethos in the port city of Chittagong, Ramnath Biswas, a Bengali globetrotter from Sylhet district, set out to travel the world. After covering Singapore, Malaya, and Thailand in the early leg of his 51,000 miles of global tour on a bike, Biswas was even more eager to respond to "ojanar aroti" (the yearning for the unknown) and evoked a popular poem by Kazi Nazrul Islam, a shorter version of which reads like this:

    I refuse to be caged in the closed doors, I will travel the world over,
    Will see how people are moving in the whirlpool of turning times,
    How people are running
    From one country to another! …
    I will see how the Chinese soaked in opium are riding the wings
    of pain

For one last do-or-die game at the dawn-break
Oh, how Ireland is going to be free
How Turkey is breaking the shackles so fast
How Greece lost the sun at the noon …
I will see the world now
Will see it in the mountain peaks, in the sky, on the air, stars, oceans and the moon,
I will tear the bondage of my own boundary
And announce myself on a hundred horizons
I will dig deep down the earth and then launch myself across the heavens
I venture to see the universe in the palm of my own hands.

See Ramnath Biswas, *Sarbo-swadhin Shyam* (Calcutta: Bhattacharya Sons Limited, 1949), p. 138. This poem is titled "Songkolpo" (Determination), and this version is translated by Iftekhar Iqbal. Originally published in the 1930s, the poem was reprinted in Kazi Nazrul Islam, *Teele Patka Putuler Biye* (Calcutta: Mahalaya, 1370 Bengali year/1963–1964). I am indebted to Professor Begum Akter Kamal for tracking this reference for me.

52. Bengali Muslim sojourns in the regions other than those covered in this essay are getting attention recently in works including Vivek Bald, *Bengali Harlem and the Lost Histories of South Asian America* (Harvard University Press, 2013); Claire Alexander, Joya Chatterji, and Annu Jalais, *The Bengal Diaspora: Rethinking Muslim Migration* (London: Routledge, 2015); Ashfaque Hossain, "The world of the Sylheti Seamen in the Age of the Empire, from the Late Eighteenth Century to 1947," *Journal of Global History*, 9, 3 (2014), 425–446.
53. Samia Khatun, *Australianama: The South Asian Odyssey in Australia* (Oxford: Oxford University Press, 2019), pp. 1–25.
54. Amartya Sen, *Identity and Violence: Illusion of Destiny* (Allen Lane, 2006); Talal Asad, *Formations of the Secular: Christianity, Islam, Modernity* (Stanford: Stanford University Press, 2003).
55. For two major works on aspects of spatial mobility of Sanskrit and Persian in the premodern world, see Sheldon Pollock, *The Language of the Gods in the World of Men: Sanskrit, Culture, and Power in Premodern India* (Berkeley: University of California Press, 2006) and Richard M. Eaton, *India in the Persianate Age 1000-1765* (Chicago: University of Chicago Press, 2019).

7

The Meaning of Muslim Emancipation in Late-Colonial Agrarian Bengal

Andrew Sartori

When people spoke of "Muslim self-determination" and "Muslim emancipation" in late colonial Bengal, what did they have in mind? The question itself may require a moment of reflection: it takes for granted that forms of politics that were explicitly "Muslim" in twentieth-century Bengal were conceived in terms of a normative aspiration to (some idea of) freedom rather than as an affirmation of traditional authority. Regardless, any appropriately modest answer to such a question would presumably have to be that "Muslim freedom" probably meant different things to different people. In this essay, I want to focus on just one cluster of those possible meanings—but on a cluster of meanings that I think was especially important to the broad-based development of Muslim politics in agrarian Bengal. Specifically, I am less interested here in the important histories of the role played in the development of Muslim politics by demands for colonial representation in education, employment, and governance, struggles for the control of collective spaces, attempts to cultivate institutional self-determination in the field of literature, or even the networks of religious education and religious mobilization that connected the ulama of Bengal to North India, the Arabian peninsula, and elsewhere. Rather, I am interested in what I take to be a more fundamental question: If some idea of "Muslim emancipation" appealed to large numbers of Bengali Muslims in the countryside; if they found the idea meaningful to them; if they could be mobilized under its banner; and if that was possible, despite the diversity of otherwise incommensurable interests that were necessarily called upon to travel under that banner, then of what did that appeal consist? What, in other words, made agrarian Bengal so responsive to the idea of Muslim emancipation?

The core argument of this paper will be threefold. First, I shall argue that the politics of Muslim self-determination emerged in part out of the longer history of the formation of a large Muslim population in the Bengal delta. That longer history is a necessary but not sufficient framing for understanding the more specific normative concerns of emancipation and self-determination that saturated twentieth-century Muslim agrarian political thought. Second, I shall argue that one of the dominant frameworks through which the call for Muslim emancipation was elaborated in the countryside was in terms of the right of the *proja* to a proprietary right in the soil. *Proja*s (also known as "raiyats"—literally, "subjects") were the lowest rung in the land-revenue–paying hierarchy (though not necessarily the lowest rung in the rent-paying hierarchy). The association between proja interests in the soil and Muslimness was initially built on the demographic contingencies of eastern Bengal where most (but by no means all) projas were Muslims, and most (but by no means all) upper-echelon rent and interest receivers were Hindus. But the association became most potent intellectually and politically when the connection between Muslimness and property was rendered *intrinsic* rather than merely an accident of such demography, and this was achieved when Islamic piety was interpreted as an intensifier of proprietary status. Third, then, I shall argue that the power and appeal of the ideal of Muslim emancipation in agrarian Bengal primarily turned on its relationship to the idea of proja property rather than on concerns about the relative political or economic status of Hindu and Muslim constituencies. In the agrarian context, Muslim emancipation did not primarily refer to emancipation from Hindu domination and was not primarily concerned with issues of competition or conflict with Hindus. In fact, the conception of the "Muslim proja" could be elaborated with striking indifference to Hindus, or even, in the Khilafat era, in the context of explicit amity. While the ideal of Muslim emancipation certainly could be readily implicated in anti-Hindu sentiments, it did so in ways that were structured by the logical organization of a conception of Muslimness that fundamentally did not turn on its distinction from or opposition to a Hindu other.

Accessing the meanings of Muslim political discourse in agrarian Bengal is obviously more difficult than examining the more articulate and archivally well-represented voices of the regional political and cultural leadership. But it is too important for it to be subordinated to these other voices, or to be repudiated in the name of archival intractability for at least two reasons. First, when we assimilate the history of agrarian understandings of "Muslim emancipation" directly into larger regional and national histories of Muslim political organization, we skew the history of that idea too quickly toward a focus on the history of communal rivalry and conflict. Second, we simply cannot adequately understand the broad-based popularity of Muslim identitarian politics in the late colonial period from within a framework that highlights mobilization of the agrarian masses by political and social elites without understanding the plausibility and appeal of the language used to mobilize them.

This is a substantial lacuna in the historiography of the largest concentration of Muslims in colonial South Asia. And as a result of that lacuna, the history even of so well-studied a movement as the demand for Pakistan seems strikingly incomplete. The 1935 Government of India Act had extended the franchise much more deeply into the countryside for provincial elections. As a result, when Muhammad Ali Jinnah was negotiating the final settlement for British withdrawal, his standing as "sole spokesman" was vulnerable to the electoral fortunes of the Muslim League in Muslim-majority provincial elections, where the League had not always done well. The League's sweeping victory in Bengal in the 1945–1946 elections—as compared to its distinctly lackluster performance in rural districts in the 1937 elections—was thus a necessary condition for his political credibility at the negotiating table. While it is true that by the mid-1940s, as the final settlement approached, it had become clear to everyone that the political center was becoming more important than the provinces—and so that the fate of Bengal's Muslims was increasingly to be that of a subcontinental minority rather than that of a provincial majority—it remains unclear exactly how those constitutional considerations translated to cultivators in the countryside.[1] Without a better understanding of the appeal of the call of Muslim self-determination in agrarian Bengal, I think we are still far from understanding even these broad political trajectories of the subcontinent in the late colonial period.

I

In an exceptionally fruitful discussion of what he calls the genre of "Muslim Improvement Literature" that began emerging in the 1910s and 1920s, Pradip Kumar Datta notes that the development of a "Muslim" identitarianism in rural Bengal was bound not primarily to conflictual or competitive relationships with Hindus so much as it was centered on the Bengali Muslims' relationship to what was conceived as their own inner Hindu.[2] The pamphlets of this genre focused, Datta points out, not so much on great questions of theology or of the proper protocols of worship (the core theme of an earlier generation of nineteenth-century pamphlets)[3] as on the reform of everyday habits. Such reforms especially targeted forms of perceived extravagance that these pamphlets portrayed as significant obstacles on the path to Muslim prosperity. The desires that led the Muslim into such extravagance (and its practical correlate, debt) were then identified in these texts as Hindu. These desires were Hindu, first, because they involved practices like wedding ceremonies that departed from the relative austerity of Islamic ritual, and second, because in rural eastern Bengal the figure of the Hindu was inextricably bound up with the figure of the moneylender, and it was the moneylender who provided the flow of credit that functioned as the condition of possibility for agrarian Muslims' extravagance as well, correlatively, as the primary mechanism of their corruption. What rendered the Muslim susceptible to the temptation that this (actual) Hindu represented was the Muslim's own extravagant desires, which were figured in this genre as the symptoms of his own internalized Hinduism. This was a corruption fueled historically by pervasive syncretic involvement in Hinduized cultural practices. Therefore, this intimate enemy, this inner Hindu, had to be expelled by means of a systematic ethical purification of everyday life, the principles of which formed the core content of this genre. If the Muslim could be freed of his inner Hindu, he would no longer be dependent on the actual Hindu who lived parasitically off his extravagance. Under such circumstances, the Muslim cultivator's productive activity would generate prosperity. "Wealth becomes so important" in these texts, Datta explains, "that it is made into the most important feature of Islam itself."[4] Where wealth was absent, it marked a decline in religiosity, for it was a symptom of Hindu corruption. Where wealth was present, it was an index of religiosity.

Datta's emphasis on categories of communal identification here is a direct function of his own primary object of study: that is, communal violence. That is certainly legitimate in itself, but it does lead to what from another perspective might be taken as a foreclosure of the concerns that drove these kinds of texts. Consider an influential text that Datta himself uses as a key example, the story of Usman narrated in Abdul Hai Bhawali's *Adarsha Krishak* (The Ideal Cultivator).[5] This pamphlet provides an account of a cultivator in Mymensingh (the eastern district where the pamphlet was first published in 1920) who had survived natural disaster to achieve debtless prosperity through a rigorous and unremitting worldly asceticism. The cultivator, Usman, works all day in the fields, and then when too tired for that spends his off hours tending his garden. He buys as little as possible, using the natural resources available to him, building his own house, digging his own tank, constructing his own furniture, hiring labor only when he cannot perform all the work himself. Through a combination of diligence, austerity, and commercial intelligence, Usman has achieved considerable prosperity despite the simplicity of his way of life. There is little doubt that the foundation on which he was able to build this prosperity is his piety, which forms the cornerstone of his ethical commitment to work.

So far, this does indeed all sound pretty much in accordance with Datta's analysis: Islam is bound to prosperity through its role as an ethical practice for the reform of everyday habits. But we should also recognize that nowhere in this text does Usman link the problem of extravagance or laziness to Hinduness. Indeed, there are good reasons to think that he might have balked at any attempt to interpret his vision of Muslim self-improvement in anti-Hindu terms. In other more or less contemporary pamphlets in whose publication he was actively involved (even if he was not their author), a let-Hindus-be-good-Hindus-and-let-Muslims-be-good-Muslims approach was given clear articulation.[6] I am not suggesting that Datta's analysis is anything but persuasive: it is easy enough to see where anti-Hindu sentiment would fit into Bhawali's story. But Datta's account focuses on a moment in the elaboration of a discourse of Muslimness whose specific capacity to generate or articulate anti-Hindu sentiments only makes sense in the context of some *prior* elaboration of a discourse of Muslimness that was *not* fundamentally oriented toward concerns about the relationship between Muslims and Hindus. The question that remains, then, is to identify the constellation of concerns within which a text like Bhawali's *Adarsha Krishak* made sense.

II

First of all, Usman is a figure that must be read in the context of a powerful and well-established association between cultivation and Islam in Bengal whose origins, Richard Eaton has shown, date back several centuries.[7] Agrarian property was already established as a central motif within the logic of this older association—in ways that at once resonate with and differ from the logic of Bhawali's text.[8]

Starting in the sixteenth century, the Bengali delta began to shift eastwards, carrying with it the engine of the agricultural prosperity for which the region was famous. This set in motion a long process of reclamation and sedentarization in regions previously dominated by shifting agriculturalists and fisherfolk who had existed beyond the margins of either Hindu or Muslim social, political, and religious institutions. Largely backed by Hindu financing, a Muslim religious gentry consisting of Sufi holy men (*pirs*) and religious scholars (ulama) began claiming areas not yet brought under the plow, in order to coordinate their clearance for purposes of settled agriculture and to organize local populations into permanent agriculturalists. They sometimes did this after receiving a land grant—whether purchased or conceded freely with a view to expanding cultivation—from the zamindar within whose estate it lay. More often still, they simply took possession of jungle lands that lay beyond the limits of any zamindar's existing estate. But these latter kinds of claims could still only assume legitimate legal standing after receiving recognition from the Mughal imperial authorities, whose public treasury claimed proprietary rights over all uncultivated lands. The retrospective recognition of these kinds of land claims generally created heritable property rights in the land in return for commitments to maintain a mosque or shrine, bring the land under cultivation, and remain loyal to the sovereign. The claims that these Muslim pioneers brought before the state rested on their efforts to bring jungle under cultivation, but the capacity to transform that claim into property rested on confirmation and recognition from a sovereign who claimed to be the primary source of most legitimate rights over land revenues.

In this context, the emergence of a large Muslim population in the eastern districts of Bengal mapped onto a history of land clearances and agricultural sedentarization. Muslim pioneers established shrines and mosques that functioned as the core institutions on which their authority was centered, constructing the foundations for a cult of veneration centered on their role as pious founders, a heritable charisma that attached to their descendants, and an organizational infrastructure that, together with the prosperity generated by wet rice cultivation, served gradually to integrate local populations into Islam (typically in highly syncretic forms). Under these circumstances, the history of Islam in agrarian Bengal was to a very great extent the history of the ax and plow, so that agrarian civilization could be broadly imagined as an intrinsically Muslim phenomenon. The association between Islam and cultivation, with the veneration of pioneering saints at its core, was thus built at the intersection between the derivation of legitimate rights to the soil from the sovereign and the derivation of claims to the soil from the clearance of uncultivated land. In that sense, it was closely connected with hierarchical connections that reached from the sovereign down to the founder's lineage, and from the founder's lineage down to those who in turn derived rights to the soil from the pioneer or his descendants. It was through these forms of vertical integration that Islam came to be imagined as a religion of agrarian civilization.

The centrality of pir veneration and the pioneer-lineage to Bengali agrarian Islam was no doubt specific to the contingencies of regional history, but it nonetheless expressed themes that were articulated much more broadly in early-modern Muslim legal thought across South Asia and the Ottoman Empire, where Hanafism was the dominant school of Sunni jurisprudence. Only recognition by sovereign authority was able to transform Muslim pioneers' claims based on the clearing of land for agriculture into a specifically *proprietary* claim over the soil. The significance of this fact only becomes clear when seen in the light of these broader developments in juristic thinking about agrarian property.

Land revenues were regularly assigned to individuals as a reward for service to the Mughal state. Akbar's treasure seems to have understood the ongoing alienation of these revenues as contingent on the sufferance of the sovereign—and as such did not consider them to possess the character of a heritable property in the strict sense even when rights were transferred across generations.[9] Claims about the primacy of Mughal rights over land revenues would achieve sharp articulation in the writings of the eighteenth-century jurist, Qazi Muhammad A'la Thanwi, who argued that the ability of the Mughal treasury to demand very high rates of land tax implied that those demands were unlimited by sharia constraints on the rate of taxability on legitimate property in agricultural land. In other words, those who held revenue grants from the sovereign could claim proprietary rights neither over those revenues nor over the lands to which they were attached.[10]

But Thanwi's argument was built in part on premises that had been developed to defend the contrary position: that revenue grants legitimately derived from the public treasury constituted strong proprietary rights, including rights of alienation and inheritance. The sixteenth-century Sufi scholar, Jalaluddin Thanesari, argued that the Muslim conquerors of India had never affirmed the proprietary rights of the conquered—and that in any case, the process of conquest had effectively displaced the original occupants of the soil, thus destroying any primordial proprietary claims. Insofar as the proprietorship of soil thus devolved to the public treasury, subsequent revenue grants took on the character of property precisely insofar as they had been duly acquired from the sovereign. In other words, the affirmation of the primacy of the sovereign in the determination of revenue estates served as a means to ground the fully proprietary character of such grants, as much by unburdening them of rival claims from below as by insisting on the limitations on the powers of the sovereign to resume rights over the revenues of the estate.[11]

Thanesari's argument was far from singular. It echoed arguments that had emerged over the course of the preceding century in Mamluk and Ottoman territories that had fundamentally transformed the premises of Hanafi juristic thought in relation to property in land. Classical Hanafi jurists had affirmed the status of private property in land on a dual basis: first, a right to possession based on clearance and cultivation; and second, the concession of the ongoing standing of that right by the conquering Muslim imam both among the conquered and among those Muslims allocated new holdings out of abandoned and uncultivated lands. Possession established presumptive ownership, and the combination of ongoing cultivation and the payment of taxes (*kharaj*) to the treasury served as confirmation of proprietorship.[12] But starting in the fifteenth and sixteenth centuries, these classical assumptions were increasingly displaced by a new approach. Over the centuries since Muslim conquest, they argued, few lands could have remained in the hands of the descendants of their original owners. In the wake of such failures of succession, the legitimate ownership of land passed into the hands of the public treasury. In that case, any individual rights of property could no longer be derived from primordial claims of clearance and cultivation, but rather would have to be derived out of the proprietary claims of the state. The key issue in defending such rights was therefore to establish the process through which property in land had been legitimately acquired *from the sovereign*. Property in agrarian land thus came to be primarily identified with grants of rights over revenue estates derived out of the state's claims on the product of the soil. Smallholders on such estates did not pay kharaj, but rather *rent*—whether directly to the sovereign, to revenue estate holders, or to religious and charitable trusts (*awqaf*). Such payments established no presumptive proprietary rights on the part of the payer. The possessory rights that arose from such payments could be understood in terms of the leasing of usufructuary rights, or of the delegation of some portion of the obligations of the revenue holder in a form of trust not unlike public office. Such usufructuary rights were unlimited by the sharia injunctions on kharaj obligations, and, to the extent that succession from father to sons was the de facto standard, the sharia rules governing inheritance were similarly inapplicable. That was why Thanwi could consider high rates of land tax to be indicative of an absence of property rights.[13]

Postclassical Hanafi jurists did nonetheless retain a conception of individual property distinct from state ownership, especially in its treatment of building, tools, livestock, and trees. Even though the primacy of the sovereign as the source of rights over agricultural land remained undisputed, this conception of private property (*milk*) established the grounds for a parallel set of claims developed around the investment of money and labor in the soil. Land planted with orchards, groves or vineyards, for example, entailed significant effort and expense, but was slow to yield rewards; and as a result, justice required that the cultivator's claims on the soil be respected. Rights derived out of the state's revenue claims could thus come to be paralleled by rights derived out of productive activity, especially in relation to commercial cultivation. This represented in one sense a return to the classical theory, but this second form of right could only assume a specifically proprietary form when it mapped onto the holder of the first form of right. In other words, the proprietor of agrarian *milk* was generally also a revenue-estate grantee.[14]

In eastern Bengal, the point of intersection between these two forms of claim was the pir-lineage—not the zamindar, who stood at too great a distance from the productive use of the land, nor the cultivator, who stood at too great a distance from sovereign authority. Seen in the light of this history, the identification of Islam as a religion of agrarian civilization in Bengal—and by extension, the identification of Islam as an ingredient in the formation of agrarian property—did not necessarily imply any correlative identification of Islam with *smallholding cultivators*, Muslim or otherwise. If Bhawali's vision of Muslim freedom centers on Usman, it certainly proceeds from the deep regional associations between Islam and the ax and plow. But for Usman to be the figural vehicle of Muslim agrarian civilization, the nature of that association had to be dramatically rethought. And it was only through the process of this rethinking that some conception of freedom could come to be identified as a central normative impulse of agrarian Islam.

We can perhaps glimpse the beginnings of this process of refiguration in the emergence of the Faraizi (literally: rigorist) movement across the eastern delta in the first half of the nineteenth century. The Faraizis were a Hanafi reformist movement whose founder, Haji Shariatullah, formulated his conception of Islamic principles on the basis of almost two decades of residence and religious instruction in Mecca. The connection with the Arabian Peninsula seems to have served as a means to bypass established regional hierarchies of religious authority. Shariatullah emphasized strict observance and the maintenance of rigorous monotheism in ways that set his followers apart from most other rural Muslims, whose religious practice included not only broad participation in syncretic practices but also various forms of shrine- and grave-centered pir-veneration, which Faraizis condemned equally as compromises with polytheism (*shirk*). But this assault on regional deviation (*bidat*) from a more austere religious norm entailed a correlative assault on the very foundations of the older association between Islam and agrarian civilization that pir-veneration articulated. And from this perspective, it is especially striking that by the 1840s, under the leadership of Shariatullah's son, Faraizism came to identify its cause with that of Muslim cultivators under the slogan, *langol jar, jomi tar* (the land belongs to the one who plows it). This implied that the basis of agrarian property could be found in a history of productive activity substantially divorced from the primacy of sovereign claims to the soil. These were claims that in any case had fallen into crisis with the advent of a British rule that Faraizis condemned as un-Islamic. The land-to-the-tiller principle thus displaced the revenue-grantee rural gentry from its central role in organizing the relationship between Islam and agriculture.[15] Similar (if fuzzier) impulses were arguably visible in the contemporary Waliullahite Tariqah-i-Muhammadiya reformist movement, which in the iconic figure of Titu Meer combined an insistence on Muslim religious austerity and a repudiation of the legitimacy of British sovereignty with an alliance with the interest of cultivators: "[W]hen the [English] government is turned out, no more rent is to be paid, and the Musalmans are to have the *jote* [that is, the land holdings]."[16]

III

The Faraizis appeared to have intensified the connection between Islam and cultivation by attacking the historical foundations on which that association had historically been built. Unfortunately, they did not themselves leave us any writings of a kind that would help us to understand better how they themselves construed the connection between the agrarian interests they were articulating and their theological preoccupations. Still, through what we know of them, we seem to be getting closer to the world of Bhawali. In saying this, I don't mean to imply that it was the Faraizis' sectarian preoccupations that are relevant to the interpretation of the discourse of Muslim improvement. After all, Faraizis, even at their height, represented only a small section of Bengali Muslims. But their sectarian concerns appeared to have assumed broader social significance in the eastern Bengal countryside as Islam came to be identified with the interests of the cultivator, not merely with cultivation. But that still leaves us with a crucial question: How were the interests of the cultivator construed such that they could be connected with Islam? The category through which that connection came to be most powerfully forged was the question of property.

In the second half of the nineteenth century, the question of property would explode in both colonial law and agrarian politics generally.[17] In 1859–1860, projas of the central and western districts of Bengal refused to grow indigo, a plant from which blue dye was produced. In doing so, they were continuing in the footsteps of earlier Faraizi cultivators who had battled zamindars and European indigo planters for control of shifting alluvial lands of the deltaic frontier, over which property rights (whether in terms of their spatial reference or in terms of the relative standing of rival claims) were at best vaguely defined.[18] Indigo cultivation in Bengal was organized by European planters, who rarely organized its farming directly on their own holdings, but rather bought into leases and property and then advanced money to cultivators in the local area—both their own tenants and others—who were thereby obliged to grow the plant. This organization was advantageous to indigo planters for three main reasons: first, planters could avoid the headaches of organizing their own farms in a context where hired labor was scarce and credit was unreliable; second, they could minimize the cost of production by exploiting the unpaid labor of peasant families; and third, they could transfer the substantial risk involved in any agricultural venture in a monsoonal climate onto the cultivator.[19]

This last element was central to the Indigo Disturbances. On the one hand, planters demanded the right to enforce contracts and supervise the cultivation of the plant once advances had been given. They also claimed such entitlements when debt had accrued to projas for having failed to fully pay off their advances, and this debt was sometimes treated as heritable. In these cases, the planter–proja relationship was being conceptualized as a capital–labor relationship. On the other hand, the fact that the planter was actually functioning as a creditor and a purchaser, coupled with the fact that it was the projas who bore the burden of the risk of crop failures, seemed to imply that the relationship between planter and proja was a contract between independent producers—both in their own way "capitalists." The core demand of the indigo raiyats seemed to be that they should be treated as independent producers entitled to grow whatever it was in their best interest to grow, at a time when the prices of rice and other commercial crops was steadily rising against stagnant and depressed indigo prices. Furthermore, they mounted their claim to the status of free producers on the basis of an independent possessory interest in the soil that confounded any attempt to reduce them to the status of laborers under the planter. In the end, albeit not without some predictable equivocation, the colonial state backed the projas' claims, effectively beginning the process by which over the subsequent two decades indigo cultivation was largely displaced from Bengal to neighboring Bihar.

In response to their political defeat, indigo planters sought either to renew their leverage over projas or to recoup the losses they had sustained by enhancing the rents of tenants who refused to grow for them. But they thereby set in motion a whole new set of conflicts.

In 1859, the colonial legislature had passed an act primarily intended to reform procedure around recovery of arrears of rent and transfer such cases from the hands of the local tax official to the civil courts. In the process, however, the legislators had sought to codify what they understood to be existing law, and in so doing had, first, designated a class of projas as possessing occupancy rights over the soil (meaning they could not be evicted except for nonpayment of rent); second, included restrictions on the circumstances under which landlords could raise such tenants' rents; and, third, had further stipulated that such rent enhancements as were allowed nonetheless also had to be consonant with fair and equitable rates prevailing in the locality. Unfortunately, it gave little guidance on just how to determine what such fair and equitable rates might be. If, in keeping with liberal commitments to the rationality of laissez-faire, the market was deemed to have a capacity to generate multilaterally beneficial outcomes, surely there could be no reason to assume that fair and equitable rates would differ from rates determined by the market? Yet there was considerable doubt as to whether the assumptions upon which the classical political economists had demonstrated the tendency of the market to bring about such fair and equitable outcomes applied in the context of agrarian India. In 1865, the full bench of the High Court determined that the fair and equitable rate was one which should be determined proportionately: that is, if the cause for the enhancement was, say, a 25 percent increase in the gross value of the land's annual product, then the rent could be enhanced by 25 percent. The justification for this principle was that it would preserve the proja's interest in the soil. This was an interest, the lead opinion argued, that derived neither from the landlord (in the way that a tenant's right to the land derives from his or her contract with the landlord) nor from the state (understood as a universal proprietor in parts of colonial India settled on the ryotwari system). Rather, the proja's was a distinct, separate, and primordial interest in the soil, a form of co-proprietorship enshrined in custom and common law. The principle of proportion was thus intended to preserve that interest as a property in the land that extended beyond a mere right of continued possession, to a hereditary stake in whatever surplus the land was generally capable of producing (through its natural fertility) beyond what was necessary to cover the costs of producing the crop (labor and capital).

Some sections of liberal opinion, led by Sir George Campbell, added a further step in the argument when they explicated that the proja's primordial and customary interest in the soil was ultimately derived from the original labor of reclaiming the soil from jungle and rendering it cultivable. This would become a centerpiece of liberal arguments in favor of the reform of agrarian tenancy laws in the subsequent years—arguments that stood in sharp contrast to rival forms of liberal argument endorsing the inviolability of the zamindari form of proprietorship constituted by the colonial state in the late eighteenth century. These developments in liberal colonial thought thus were worked out in the context of, and indeed echoed, the core claim of the indigo-growing projas, that they were independent producers with a stake in the soil rather than laborers contracted by planter capitalists. They powerfully vindicated the slogan of the Faraizis, that "the land belongs to the tiller." The land belongs to the tiller because he makes the land his own by working it and improving it. These new liberal claims about proja property redounded in turn in the demands that would proliferate in the eastern Bengal countryside in the 1870s when projas resisted attempts by zamindars to restore through coercion (for all intents and purposes) their claims to absolute proprietorship over the soil. The core impulse of this peasant politics in the second half of the nineteenth century was thus to insist on the right of property as a foundation upon which to participate in commercial life as an independent producer. At the nexus of peasant politics and colonial tenancy reform was thus the concept of property as the foundation for a vision of independence.

IV

Seen in this light, it is very important that the center of gravity for the normative claims that organized the narrative of *Adarsha Krishak* was not really prosperity as such, as Datta emphasizes. Rather, it was independence and self-determination. Bhawali laid great emphasis on the fact that the elements of Usman's homestead really belonged to him: "One must keep in mind that this is Usman's reservoir, and it really is his reservoir." On the rare occasions when Usman did sit down, it was "after invoking the name of Allah after much labor, on a stool he made with his own hands, by the bank of a reservoir dug with his own hands."[20] Usman's property was a property created by labor. That "rough stool" on which he rested was in reality "more worthy than the jewel- and pearl-encrusted, gilded, noble throne of a world-conquering, independent ruler."[21] This simple self-made stool was his throne and represented a conception of self-determination and independence inseparable from a kind of claim over nature that was grounded in the capacity of labor to create a proprietary interest. If, as Datta rightly notes, wealth was so highly valued in Muslim improvement literature, it was not because it provided the core normative structure that organized that literature. It was rather because wealth functioned simultaneously to sustain the connection between the proja and his property, to represent its material consequence, and to underwrite an institutional infrastructure for Muslim collective life.

It is above all in this context that Islam became crucially important in Bhawali's narrative. Usman's piety functioned primarily in this text as a means to intensify the connection between the proja and his property. For, under circumstances where indebtedness threatened the unity of labor and property in the eastern Bengal of the moment of this pamphlet's composition, Bhawali offered Muslim piety as a resource from which a set of ethical coordinates could be drawn as a means to sustain that connection. Islamic piety, Bhawali argued, was the foundation for a practice of worldly asceticism that rendered debt avoidable and small property economically viable. Usman's lauded prosperity was primarily praised for this reason: that it symbolized just how successful his aspiration to self-determination had been, despite difficult circumstances. In this sense, Usman was not a figure who primarily represented prosperity; he was a figure who primarily represented *freedom*. In fact, it was that very word, freedom, that headed a chapter in the second edition that outlined specific prescriptions for the elimination of vice and the development of a self-sufficient household economy.[22] *Adarsha Krishak* was thus a vision of freedom that turned on the rooting of self-determination in labor and its property-creating capacities, and it was one that identified Islamic piety as the necessary practical infrastructure for a life dedicated to such property-creating labor. What Bhawali's narrative suggested, then, was that in the eastern Bengal countryside, "Muslim emancipation" represented a vision of independent self-determination closely connected to a claim about the property-creating capacity of labor.

At this level, *Adarsha Krishak* was entirely indifferent to Hindus and Hinduism: one can well imagine Bhawali claiming Islam's supremacy as an ethical system, but one could also potentially imagine him acknowledging some form of Hinduism as an alternative (if less potent) foundation for worldly asceticism too. It is not hard to see that Datta is quite right to argue that this (essentially non-communal) discourse of Muslimness could structure a virulently anti-Hindu conception of religious difference—that is, from the moment that the extravagances and unruly desires that a pious life serves to eliminate have been identified as "Hindu." The point though is that this further step would represent the communalization of a discourse of piety whose deeper coordinates were fundamentally indifferent to relationships between Hindus and Muslims. The capacity for any such communalization would of course ultimately turn on the demographic contingencies of eastern Bengal, with its preponderance of Muslim rent and interest payers and Hindu rent and credit receivers. But in Bhawali's discourse of the Muslim cultivator, the identification of the Bengal proja as quintessentially Muslim did not turn on such demographic generalizations, and nor was it in any substantial sense destabilized by the presence of either low-caste Hindu cultivator communities or in some cases very prominent families of Muslim landlords. Rather, stereotypical Muslimness turned on the notion that it was the Muslim proja who was oriented toward the most intense and stable connection with his property. On such grounds, Bhawali could actually suggest that the Muslim cultivator was not only the quintessential Bengali cultivator but also that the Muslim cultivator was the quintessential Bengali.[23]

When a real crisis did occur in Hindu–Muslim relations—whether in the form of the communal violence in Bengal's towns in the 1920s or the collapse in the 1930s of credit relations, which, in eastern Bengal, were also by extension predominantly Hindu–Muslim relations[24]—the experience of those crises in the countryside was necessarily refracted through a conception of Muslimness that was already highly elaborated outside of and prior to that context. Furthermore, the conception of Muslimness at work in Bhawali's narrative was one that already fused religion to "economic" considerations, so that the translation between the Muslim of property and the Muslim who was not a Hindu was relatively straightforward, and called for no radical dilemma on the part of rural Bengali Muslims between privileging religion or class as the most important set of considerations for determining their identities or their interests. This blurred the line separating the so-called secular politics of cultivators and tenants from the so-called communal politics of the Muslim League. (None of this is to suggest that Muslim piety itself derived its power in eastern Bengal from such "economic" considerations. My claim is merely that the way in which Muslim piety entered the domain of Muslim politics in the countryside was through this connection.)

The fact that this conception of Muslimness was initially worked out outside of the historically specific context of struggles over colonial representation (such as the organization of census categories, educational policy, questions of communal representation in state employment and government bodies) should not be taken to mean that it was anything other than historically specific in the way it conceptualized Islam as the privileged religion of agrarian emancipation. The idea of Muslim emancipation cannot be reduced to some timeless conception of peasant religiosity or of peasant community without ignoring the normative force of the concepts of self-determination, independence, and freedom that were so central to this agrarian politics.

V

I do not mean to suggest that this discourse of the Muslim cultivator was the only conception of Muslim emancipation in circulation, even in agrarian Bengal. With the introduction of a degree of local self-governance in the form of local and district boards, questions of communal representation no doubt reached deeply into agrarian society, even if the actual constituencies eligible to vote in such electoral contests (eligibility based on a property qualification) was tiny. Nor do I mean to suggest that the processes by which this discourse came to be hitched to the idea of Pakistan as a vision of Muslim emancipation were straightforward. That story would have to involve a more detailed—and a more contingency-laden—account of the drift of left-leaning proja activists into the Muslim League in the late 1930s and early 1940s.[25] And it would certainly also have to attend to important distinctions *within* the Muslim League left. For example, Abdul Hamid Bhashani, the preeminent leader of the Bengali Muslim immigrants who colonized the Brahmaputra Valley of Assam in large numbers in the first half of the twentieth century, and who would go on to be the preeminent leader of the Pakistani left in the post-Independence era, grounded his political commitments in the claim that labor created property, and that this, in turn, should serve as the foundation of Muslim freedom. Rentier zamindars would, he argued in 1938, "have to give the proja complete independence. The proja has improved the soil through back-breaking labor. It is the proja who is the real owner and he should have full rights over the soil."[26] It was primarily in the face of the threat of eviction, and of claims to the land on behalf of the Assamese "Sons of the Soil," that Bhashani appealed to an ideal of Muslim independence.[27] In contrast, Abul Hashim, the western Bengali leader of the Muslim League left, had his intellectual roots in quite different traditions of Islamic radicalism. He was at best stumbling in his articulation of the discourse of the Muslim cultivator, although he worked hard to incorporate that vision into his political program.[28]

What I do want to suggest here, however, is that it is impossible to understand the widespread enthusiasm for the ideal of Muslim emancipation—including the Pakistan demand of the 1940s as perhaps its single most significant expression—without recognizing that the energy that drove it in the Bengal countryside was to a very large extent generated at the level of claims about peasant property, rather than at the more immediate level of inter-communal competition or hostility.

That energy could flow in many different directions, and it certainly did not point teleologically toward the Pakistan demand of the 1940s. But the success of the Muslim League in winning over a rural electorate that had been less than enthusiastic about it in the late 1930s cannot be understood without recognizing the provincial League's success in harnessing agrarian ideas of Muslim emancipation to its cause.

Notes and References

1. Ayesha Jalal, *The Sole Spokesman: Jinnah, the Muslim League and the Demand for Pakistan* (Cambridge: Cambridge University Press, 1994), Chapter 4; Humaira Momen, *Muslim Politics in Bengal: A Study of the Krishak Praja Party and the Elections of 1937* (Dacca: Sunny House, 1972); Andrew Sartori, "Abul Mansur Ahmad and the Cultural Politics of Bengali Pakistanism," in Dipesh Chakrabarty, Rochona Majumdar and Andrew Sartori (eds), *From the Colonial to the Postcolonial: India and Pakistan in Transition* (New Delhi: Oxford University Press, 2007), pp. 119–136.
2. Pradip Kumar Datta, *Carving Blocs: Communal Ideology in Early Twentieth-Century Bengal* (New Delhi: Oxford University Press), Chapter 2.
3. Rafiuddin Ahmed, *The Bengal Muslims: A Quest for Identity, 1871–1906* (New Delhi: Oxford University Press, 1981).
4. Datta, *Carving Blocs*, p. 71.
5. A.F.M. Abdul Hai Bhawali, *Usman, Adarsha Krishak* (Mymensingh, 1920), p. 1. A second expanded edition was issued as *Adarsha Krishak* (Dhaka, b.s. 1328 [1921/1922]).
6. See, for example, Shah Abdul Hamid, *Krishak-bilap* (Mymensingh, 1922), p. 40.
7. The following two paragraphs draw broadly on Richard M. Eaton, *The Rise of Islam and the Bengal Frontier, 1204–1760* (Berkeley: University of California Press, 1993), Chapters 8–10.
8. For a more detailed discussion of the issues discussed in this section, see Andrew Sartori, "Property and Political Norms: Hanafi Juristic Discourse in Agrarian Bengal," *Modern Intellectual History* (2018), 1–15. doi:10.1017/S1479244318000215.
9. B.R. Grover, "The Nature of Land-Rights in Mughal India," *Indian Economic and Social History Review* 1/2 (1963), 1–23.

10. Irfan Habib, *The Agrarian System of Mughal India, 1556–1707* (2nd edition, New Delhi: Oxford University Press, 1999), pp. 123–24; Zafarul Islam, *Socio-Economic Dimensions of Fiqh Literature in Medieval India* (Lahore: Research Cell, Dyal Singh Trust Library, 1990), Chapter 6.
11. Islam, *Socio-Economic Dimensions of Fiqh*, Chapter 5; Abdul Azim Islahi, "Kharaj and Land Proprietory Right in the Sixteenth Century: An Example of Law and Economics," *Journal of Objective Studies*, vol. 19, nos. 1–2 (2008), 29–44.
12. Baber Johansen, *The Islamic Law on Land Tax and Rent: The Peasant's Loss of Property Rights as Interpreted in the Hanafite Legal Literature of the Mamluk and Ottoman Period* (London: Croom Helm, 1988), Chapter 1; Kenneth Cuno, "Was the Land of Ottoman Syria Miri or Milk? An Examination of Juridical Differences within the Hanafi School," *Studia Islamica*, no. 81 (1995), 121–152.
13. Martha Mundy and Richard Saumarez Smith, *Governing Property, Making the Modern State: Law, Administration and Production in Ottoman Syria* (London and New York: I.B. Tauris, 2007), Chapter 2; Johansen, *Islamic Law on Land Tax and Rent*; Cuno, "Was the Land of Ottoman Syria Miri or Milk?"
14. Mundy and Smith, *Governing Property*, Chapter 3; Cuno, "Was the Land of Ottoman Syria Miri or Milk?"; Sabrina Joseph, "An Analysis of Khayr al-Din al-Ramli's Fatawa on Peasant Land Tenure in Seventeenth-Century Palestine," *Arab Studies Journal*, vol. 6–7, nos. 2/1 (1998–99), 112–127.
15. Muin-ud-din Ahmad Khan, *History of the Fara'idi Movement in Bengal (1818–1906)* (Karachi: Pakistan Historical Society, 1965); Rafiuddin Ahmed, *The Bengal Muslims, 1871–1906: A Quest for Identity* (Delhi: Oxford University Press, 1981).
16. Cited from Ahmed, *Bengal Muslims*, p. 44.
17. I draw broadly in this section on Andrew Sartori, *Liberalism in Empire: An Alternative History* (Oakland: University of California Press, 2014).
18. Iftekhar Iqbal, *The Bengal Delta: Ecology, State and Social Change, 1840–1943* (Basingstoke: Palgrave Macmillan, 2010), Chapter 4.
19. On indigo cultivation in Bengal generally, see Sugata Bose, *Peasant Labour and Colonial Capital: Rural Bengal since 1770* (Cambridge: Cambridge University Press, 1993), pp. 45–52; Benoy Chowdhury, *Growth of Commercial Agriculture in Bengal, 1757–1900* (Calcutta: Indian Studies Past and Present, 1964), vol. I, 73–203; Blair B. Kling, *The Blue Mutiny: The Indigo Disturbances in Bengal, 1859–1862* (Philadelphia: University of Pennsylvania Press, 1966); Chittabrata Palit, *Tensions in Bengal Rural*

Society: Landlords, Planters and Colonial Rule, 1830–1860 (Calcutta: Progressive, 1975), Chapters 4–5; and Tirthankar Roy, "Indigo and Law in Colonial India," *Economic History Review*, vol. 64, Supplement 1 (2011), 60–75.

20. Bhawali, *Usman*, pp. 16–17.
21. Bhawali, *Usman*, p. 17.
22. "*Mukti*" (Freedom), included in the second edition: Bhawali, *Adarsha Krishak*, pp. 203–224.
23. See the foreword to the first edition of Bhawali, *Usman*.
24. The former is emphasized in Datta, *Carving Blocs*, and Partha Chatterjee, *Bengal 1920–1947: The Land Question* (Calcutta: K.P. Bagchi, 1984); the latter in Sugata Bose, *Agrarian Bengal: Economy, Social Structure and Politics, 1919–1947* (Cambridge: Cambridge University Press, 1986).
25. For a detailed discussion of the political shifts of this period, see Joya Chatterji, *Bengal Divided: Hindu Communalism and Partition, 1932–1947* (Cambridge: Cambridge University Press, 1994), Chapter 3; Jalal, *Sole Spokesman*, Chapter 3; Harun-or-Rashid, *The Foreshadowing of Bangladesh: Bengal Muslim League and Muslim Politics, 1906–1947* (Dhaka: The University Press, 2003), Chapters 3–4; and Shila Sen, *Muslim Politics in Bengal, 1937–1947* (New Delhi: Impex, 1976). See also Andrew Sartori, "Abul Mansur Ahmad and the Cultural Politics of Bengali Pakistanism."
26. *Assam Legislative Assembly Debates*, 1938, vol. 2 (IOL V/9/1413), p. 299.
27. On Bhashani in Assam, see Anindita Dasgupta, *The Emergence of a Community: Muslims of East Bengal Origin in Assam in the Colonial and Postcolonial Period* (unpublished dissertation, Guwahati University, 2001), Chapter 6; Saiyad Abul Maksud, *Maulana Abdul Hamid Khan Bhashani* (in Bangla, Dhaka: Bangla Academy, 1994), pp. 1–33; and Layli Uddin, "Pir, Politician and Peasant Leader: The Making of Maulana Bhashani in Colonial Assam, c. 1930–1947" (unpublished M.Phil. thesis, Oriental Institute, Oxford University, 2011).
28. See, for example, his embarrassing comments in the course of debates in 1937 over further reforms to the Bengal tenancy law: *Bengal Legislative Assembly Proceedings*, vol. 51, no. 4 (1937), pp. 1954, 2199–2200. For his commitments to agrarian reform, see his draft manifesto, "Free Pakistan in Free India," *Star of India*, March 23, 1945, 3. For a more detailed discussion of the unfolding of Muslim agrarian politics in this period, see Sartori, *Liberalism in Empire*, Chapter 5.

8

South Asian Islam and the Politics of German Orientalism

Kris Manjapra

The trace of the German philological and historical science shows up just under the surface of works by many major Indian Muslim intellectuals of the twentieth century. For example, Muhammad Iqbal's dissertation of 1908, *The Development of Metaphysics in Persia,* was written at the Ludwig Maximilian University of Munich. In this early work, Iqbal seeks "to prepare a groundwork for a future history of Persian Metaphysics." He makes the cultural history of Persian thought stand out across a vast tableau of temporal change. In this study of origins and historical development, Iqbal locates the roots of Indo-Persian philosophy in the pre-Islamic philosophies of Zoroaster and Mazdak, and then traces their transformation through the influence of "Greek dualism" and "Islamic rationalism," culminating in Sufi thought. The dissertation was an assertion of Indo-Persian and Islamic identity born of what Iqbal asserts to be a great and ancient cosmopolitan legacy. Iqbal's study, written in Heidelberg and Munich, shares its concern with historical origins and distinctive cultural legacies with the work of many other South Asian nationalists who studied in German-speaking universities during this time. Muhammad Shahidullah completed his dissertation on the ancient Buddhist roots of Bengali culture at the Sorbonne and at Leipzig University in 1926. Meanwhile, in the same year, Ali Akhtar Ansari, sponsored by the Nizam of Hyderabad, finished his study of architectural distinction of the Taj Mahal and the art history of Mughal India at Josef Strzygowski's Art History Institute at the University of Vienna. The works of Iqbal, Shahidulla, and Ansari were all important expressions of Indian anti-colonial nationalism and carry the mark of German modes of philological, cultural, or art historical investigation. They each used comparativist and culturalist historical methodologies in a rebellion against the liberal assimilationist historiography of the British Empire. The trace of German methods under the surface of these texts might be interpreted as the imprint of the "devil's handwriting," to use Steinmetz's suggestive phrase. But these traces might also signify something entirely different: the ways that Muslim Indian thinkers used and exploited the splits and conflicts within European epistemology to their own anti-colonial and epistemological ends. The German trace could be recruited in efforts to strike the Anglo-Saxon prose of counterinsurgency.[1]

The widely circulating tropes of Islam as a "religion of the desert" and as a "religion of the sword" opposed to the West and to Christianity are of ancient vintage, going as far back as the time of the Crusades.[2] But throughout the nineteenth and twentieth centuries, political and intellectual entanglements continually transgressed the discursive tableau of the East versus the West. A careful look at the historical record shows that South Asian Muslim intellectuals, as they described and reflected on their own traditions, had a prolonged and intensifying relationship with German speakers and Germanic practices of scholarship from the mid-nineteenth to the mid-twentieth centuries. Studying this interaction is significant not because it adds more documentary evidence to the story of cultural encounter and "understanding" between Asians and Europeans, and between East and West, but rather because it helps us better define the mechanisms of intellectual and political power and their modes of entanglement within a global frame. The British Empire, with its claims of liberal universalism and its metonymic privilege as the chief nineteenth-century metaphor for Europeanness, Westernness, and Progress, can be better historicized if we understand how the *Germanic* West and *South Asian* Islam, with their own historical potentials, disrupted the universalizing discourses of British power in order to assert their own place in the world.

The study of interactions between the Germanic West and South Asian Islam helps us focus the spotlight of history on the inability of British universalism to attain the world hegemony it desired during that century of universalist intoxication in Britain, beginning with Queen Victoria and Gladstone and ending with Churchill, c. 1850–1950.

In fact, the century from the 1850s to the 1950s was one of resistance to Anglo-Saxonism by various groups worldwide. To insist that opposition to Anglo-Saxonism was really resistance to the abstract universal of the West or was mere anti-modern or anti-liberal resistance to Progress is to uncritically accept the British imperial metonymy. Meanwhile, historians who criticize "Western" hegemony by focusing on the David-versus-Goliath duals between local non-Western peoples and dominant global Western forces perhaps unwittingly overlook the political and societal variation within Europe itself that continually disturbed the Goliath-like norm of "Europe." Political efforts to construct zones of cosmopolitanism beyond the British world empire involved colonial and European actors alike.

Representatives of Germanic practices of Orientalism had a particularly intensive relationship with Indian Muslim intellectuals during the century of global entanglement, 1850–1950. Germanic practices for the study of Islam both contributed to British colonial designs but also disrupted them. Orientalism was a double-edged and multipurposed thing, especially as colonial nationalist politics and inter-imperial competition came to the fore by the turn of the century.

The different strands of Germanic Oriental practice that I discuss here emerged somewhat sequentially in the century spanning the 1850s to 1950s but also wove into each other during that period. These Germanic practices were the philological approach, the cultural-historical approach, the existentialist approach, and the geopolitical approach. These practices were patently universalist in scope and conception—seeking to understand Islam as a world whole, not as a regional part. Through these approaches, South Asian Islam attained special significance for German scholars as South Asia was placed at the center of various kinds of worlds: linguistic, cultural, existential, and political. Islam, specifically South Asian Islam, played a role in the Germanic search for intellectual clout in the world. In the age of German *weltpolitik* and Indian anti-colonial internationalism, Germans and Indians conspired in projects to establish alternative universes in opposition to the Anglo-Saxonist world standard.

The Germanic *Weltbürger*, the Urdu *Insan-i-Kamil*, and the Bengali *Mahamanab* were just some of the idealizations of cosmopolitan selfhood that opposed the norms and standardizing institutions of British world power. In the 1850–1950 period, rising social groups continually presented themselves as members of worldwide wholes, not culturalist parts. The Anglo-Saxonist striving for hegemony stimulated counteractions that were also universalist in scope.

British Universalism and the Search for Particulars

The 1850s, the consolidation of the Victorian era, constituted a special moment in the life of Anglo-Saxon universalism. The British assault on Burma in 1852, the battle to secure total dominion over India in 1857, and the establishment of informal British authority over the Ottoman lands in the aftermath of the Crimean War put into place the martial safeguards for an upcoming decades-long project to transform the Indian Ocean into a British lake and the world into a Britain-centered condominium. It was in this context of aggressive Anglo-Saxonism that Islam gained a set of new connotations for Britain's policymakers and for its populace. Anglo-Saxon universalism was informed by normative strategies of portraying all forms of resistance as localized and illiberal threats to the global and liberal Pax Britannica.

British Studies of Islam from these early decades of the aspirational Anglo-Saxonist century were the work of amateur Orientalists, generally colonial officials or Christian missionaries.[3] In 1841, Mountstuart Elphinstone, a high-level administrator in India and once the governor of Bombay, set the post-Mughal pitch of British Islamology when he placed Muslims on the margins of a longer Indic history that stretched back to Hindu and Sanskritic origins. In the ensuing time of the birth of British Anthropology as a discipline, British Islamologists studied Muslims by ethnic group, often with attention to family lines and tribal affiliations but without great interest in living Islamic political or religious worlds.[4]

The 1860s and 1870s saw the rise of the "Wahhabi threat" in the colonial mind. In the period after the 1857 conflagration, the British sought to consolidate their total rule of the subcontinent. Beginning in the 1860s, the British Indian military carried out a series of expeditions, or raids, on centers of resistance in the Punjab and the Swat Valley.[5] In 1871, W.W. Hunter published his treatise, *Indian Musalmans*, a text celebrated by intellectuals and popular writers alike.[6] Hunter's work took the temperature of Victorian society's feverish fantasies about the "treason depots" that infected the expanding overseas empire.[7] As a member of the Bengal Civil Service who prided himself on the amount of time he had spent in the Bengali mufassil, W.W. Hunter wrote in the mode of an amateur ethnographer and perhaps an even more amateur religious scholar.

Hunter envisioned South Asian Muslims as belonging to a network of fanatical tribes stretching from Afghanistan to Bengal—an extended chain of sedition. "The bleak mountains which rise beyond the Punjab are united by a chain of treason depots with the tropical swamps through which the Ganges merges into the sea."[8] This belt of sedition threatened British surveillance since "the coalition dissolves like a mountain mist."[9] Anglo-Saxon universalism associated itself with the Roman Empire, and it is with this simile that Hunter ended his treatise. The ancient Romans, during their age of glory, had successfully thwarted Asian conspiracies. So too would the British by putting down the Wahhabi threat.

The Wahhabi Trials were strung out over the course of two decades after 1857 and served as a grand legal performance of geopolitical reconstruction.[10] The five main trials, including the Ambala Trial of 1864, the Patna Trial of 1865, the Maldah and Rajmahal Trials of 1870, and the Great Trial of 1871, occasioned the interview of hundreds of witnesses, the detainment of many suspects under the special provisions of Regulation III of 1818, a "large body" of imprisoned convicts and at least three death sentences.[11] In the same period, a different strand of British Islamology began to focus increasingly on rediscovering the history of the Mughal state in India and cataloging the modes of rule and governance in terms of the military, the judiciary, the exchequer, and the organization of political economy and education.[12] By the late nineteenth century, just as the Indo-Saracenic architectural style began to stud imperial capital cities, historians such as V.A. Smith and Alfred Lyall presented the Mughal state as a prefiguration of the perfected

Asiatic Monarchy of the British Raj.[13] If British Islamology presented Muslims as small and tribal in the 1860s and 1870s, the tone shifted in the coming decades as the Anglo-Saxonist discourse sought to defuse and incorporate the history of Indian Muslims into a universal history of the British empire.[14]

Germanic Practices and the Search for Universals

Germanic scholars were hired by the British to work in India in large numbers during the period of mid-nineteenth century Anglo-Saxon universalism. The transition from Company to Crown Raj required the creation of a new colonial knowledge fund for the subcontinent, and British officials tapped Central European universities to obtain the experts needed in order to run colleges, organize scientific surveys of India's natural endowment and economic product, and to collect and categorize the troves of subcontinental cultural objects and records, especially ancient manuscripts, acquired for British imperial museums and libraries. German-speaking scholars helped to direct institutions such as the Geological Survey, the Forestry Survey, the Archaeological Survey, and the Manuscript Divisions of libraries in Calcutta, Bombay, Madras, and Lahore.

While the British, in this era of Anglo-Saxonism, tended to see particulars when they studied the subcontinent, the imported Germanic disciplinary practices saw something quite opposite: they saw universals. Especially in terms of the study of Islam, the early German scholars in India focused on the philological traditions and the linguistic worlds through which Islam was transmitted. If British Islamology was chiefly defined by its fascination with ethnicity and tribe, German Islamology in the 1860s and 1870s was most concerned with the genealogies of language groups and textual transmissions. Germanic Orientalist practices contributed to the British project of building up the Raj by establishing authoritative descriptions of the linguistic universes of the subcontinent. This Germanic focus on universals would eventually exercise a disruptive influence on the British Raj beginning in the late nineteenth century.

Just as much as Germanic approaches were beginning to work themselves out within the framework of the British empire, the British empire was affecting Germanic Orientalist practices. Before the 1850s, it was de rigueur for German-speaking scholars to study Islam in the context of either the Ottoman lands or the Semitic lands. Joseph von Hammer Purgstall, in Vienna, institutionalized the Germanic study of Ottoman Islam. Meanwhile, some of his contemporaries, especially Abraham Geiger and Geiger's students, Heinrich Graetz and Ignaz Goldziher, focused on the Arab lands and set Islam within the broader context of Semitic and Judaic cultural and religious inheritances. Some of the most sensitive and penetrating students of Islam in the German context were Jewish and came to their "Philoislamic" studies via Jewish Studies (*Wissenschaft des Judentums*).[15] The Hebrew scriptures and ancient Semitic languages, such as Aramaic, were said to lie at the historical heart of Islam.

But another strand of early German scholarship on Islam, represented by Friedrich Rückert, Heinrich Ewald, and Theodor Nöldeke, tended to place Islam in closer association to Persian and Indian languages and pre-Islamic texts. From the 1850s onwards, in the context of scholarly demands of the British Raj as well as the new kinds of knowledge institutions it created, German Orientalists working in India increasingly studied Islam in the Indo-Persian mode. The place of German scholars wedged within British Indian institutions, and the business of building up a new knowledge regime for the British Raj encouraged the Germanic focus on the universal dimensions of "Indo-Persian Islam." The rise of Indo-Persian Islamic Studies in Central Europe alongside the studies of both Ottoman and Semitic Islam can thus only be understood in the context of the rising institutions of British world power. The Indo-Persian focus of German philologists influenced nationalist universities in India. The inaugural edition of the journal of Rabindranath Tagore's new university, the *Visva Bharati Quarterly*, featured an article by visiting professor Moritz Winterntiz on "The Ethics of Zoroastrianism From a Comparative Point of View." Meanwhile, Julius Germanus's article on "Modern Movements in Islam" appeared in the journal in 1930, just at the time when Tagore was preparing for his journey of cultural diplomacy to Persia and Iraq, which eventually took place in 1932.[16]

German scholars of Indo-Persian Islam, as opposed to either Ottoman or Semitic Islam, sought Islamic textual origins and linguistic genealogies not in Aramaic language and Hebrew Scriptures but rather in ancient Persian and Sanskrit languages and manuscripts, as well as in South Asian vernaculars. The state of Germanic study of Urdu literature far surpassed the level in British-run colleges, both in the subcontinent as in the metropole.[17] And in opposition to the Arabicist trend among many South Asian Muslims at this very time, German Orientalists in the late nineteenth century burrowed into regional vernaculars, such as Sindhi, Kashmiri, Balochi, Brahui, and Pashto, and highlighted the philological continuities linking the North Indian Islamic universe to earlier Zoroastrian, Brahmanical, and Buddhist worlds.[18] The philological study of Islam as a palimpsest of historical textual and linguistic universes contrasted not only with the British Islamological fixation on Muslim tribes but also with the Deoband School's rising Arabicist originalism. The British Empire transported the weight of German philological interest eastward, from the Semitic Orient to the Asian Orient, but ironically, it also transported the focus of many Indian Muslim intellectuals westward from the Mughal and Persian capitals to the Arab lands.

Philology

William Muir wrote the first major modern English-language biography of Muhammad in 1858. But the four-volume work overtly modeled itself on the multivolume *Life of Muhammad* by Austrian Orientalist, Aloys Sprenger. Sprenger's 1852 biography of the Prophet served as the touchstone for Muir's work even as Muir took issue with the positivism of Sprenger's Orientalist practice. Sprenger viewed Muhammad as merely a historical man caught up in extraordinary circumstances.[19] Muir, on the other hand, insisted that Muhammad, as a prophet, must be first understood as a marvelous and extraordinary man. Muir asserted this disagreement with Germanic practices of scriptural criticism, while all the while using Sprenger's work as his authoritative anchor.

The authoritativeness of professionalized German philology served amateur British colonial scholars throughout the coming decades. For example, Thomas Arnold's famous English-language exegesis, *The Preaching of Islam* of 1898, was not at all exceptional in its copious use of Germanic philological and historical sources. British authors relied on German texts in order to make claims about textual and historical origins, even as English sources were more often used to justify political and ethnographic assertions.[20] In the mid-nineteenth century, in the context of Victorian universalism, British Islamologists often found themselves relying on the authority of Central European scholarly authority.

Orientalists such as Aloys Sprenger, Heinrich Blochmann, Rudolf Hoernle, and Aurel Stein in Calcutta, and G.W. Leitner, principal of Government College in Lahore (a position Sprenger had also held) were the leading Indo-Islamic philologists and paleographers of British India as well as the leading interpreters of Muslim texts for the British administrators.[21] The directorship of the Calcutta Madrassa had been in the hands of German scholars from the time of Aloys Sprenger in the 1850s all the way up to the 1900s. Sprenger, a scholar of Arabic, Persian, and Urdu literature, came from Vienna to India as a medical doctor in 1843. He was named the principal of the Calcutta's prestigious Aliya Madrassa in 1850 after serving as principal of Delhi College.[22] Sprenger left his position as principal of the madrassa in 1858, the year the British established direct rule over India. Another Persianist and Urdu scholar, Heinrich Blochmann, from Leipzig, traveled to Calcutta as a soldier of the East India Company in the *annus mirabilis* of 1858. But philological interests constituted Blochmann's main reason for his Indic sojourn. He completed studies at Calcutta University and joined the Aliya Madrassa as a professor of Persian and Islamic texts in 1865.[23] Meanwhile, Rudolf Hoernle took up the principalship of the Calcutta Madrassa after Sprenger's retirement. Hoernle was an Indian-born Persianist and son of German missionaries.[24] He studied and cataloged ancient Prakrits from Central Asia and North India, such as Khotanese, Kuchean, and Sogdian, the ancient languages of North

Indian Buddhism. When Hoernle retired from his post in 1899, Aurel Stein took over. This Anglicized Austro-Hungarian paleographer and archaeologist soon gained international renown for his excavations of ancient Buddhist and Greek artifacts in Chinese Turkistan and his translation of the Kashmiri *Rajatarangini*.[25]

Cultural-Historical Method

Antagonism between the British and German states rose to unprecedented heights in the 1880s. The Berlin Conference of 1884–1885 under Bismarck and the *Weltpolitik* envisioned by Kaiser Wilhelm II in the 1890s inaugurated an era in which Germans no longer saw themselves as surrogates for the British Empire but as worthy opponents to Anglo-Saxon universalism and defenders of German power in the world.[26] German speakers from across the Central European lands sought to define themselves as world citizens, *Weltbürger*, who had their own universalistic aims to pursue. It was no accident that German efforts to write Universal Histories, *Universalgeschichte,* belonged to this very time.[27] To be universal meant to see the historical record universally in terms of "state, religion, and culture" and in terms of the whole human condition.[28] Germans purported to achieve in the scholarly domain what the British claimed to achieve in the realm of the economy—to see it from the god's eye view.

By the 1870s and 1880s, the philological study of ancient languages and textual transmissions was no longer satisfactory for German Orientalists. Propelled by the amassing of new *Realien* (cultural artifacts) thanks to proliferating archaeological digs and projects in colonial collecting, a new approach began to gain traction. "Cultural-historical methods" focused on interpreting cultural artifacts, including pieces of fine art and minor art, textiles, and handicrafts, as well as other objects of cultural life.[29] Because of these cultural-historical practices, Islam was increasingly studied in terms of continuities arising out of pre-Islamic contexts and in terms of interregional comparisons. Out of this era of cultural-historical study came Oswald Spengler's notion of a "Magian civilization" that encompassed Islam and all its earlier cultural predecessors from the time of the ancient Babylonians and

Egyptians to the rise of the Arabs.[30] Similarly, Josef Strzygowski coined the term "Northern civilization" to describe the continuities between Arabia, Persia, Central Asia, and China, and he juxtaposed this cultural world to a "Southern civilization" that comprehended Greece, Italy, and the Southern European lands.[31] The Bengali scholar, Hasan Shahid Suhrawardy, who taught Art History at Calcutta University in the 1920s and worked with one of Strzygowski's students, introduced his conception of "Nomadic Art" to describe the cultural continuities from Spain to North Africa to the Arab Lands and on to Central Asia and Inner China, and between Islamic art and Central Asian art.[32]

By the early twentieth century, German students of South Asian Islam sought to reveal cultural worlds by considering Indo-Islamic forms of music, statecraft, philosophy, and poetry.[33] They considered Islamic social mores and topics such as the cultural roles of women as wives and as mothers in family institutions.[34] According to this new scholarship, German Orientalists came to view the Safavid and Mughal Empires as the blossoming of Islamic high culture.[35] From Josef Horowitz to C.H. Becker to Alexander Gleichen-Russwurm to Annemarie Schimmel, South Asian Islam represented the intersectional peak of the Arabic, Platonic, Zoroastrian, Brahmanical, and Buddhist cultures.

German Orientalist practices, not English ones, anchored the professional study of South Asian Islamic art history in the subcontinent. Particularly through the work of figures such as Joseph Horowitz on Sanskritic transmissions into Islamic texts, and the work of Ernst Kühnel, Ernst Dietz, and Ernst Graztl on Sultanate and Mughal art history, Indo-Islamic art study obtained its own standing amidst Western scholarship.[36] There is little wonder that German institutions of scholarship became such a magnet for Indian Muslim thinkers in this period of cultural-historical research. The disciplinary pull was strong enough to bring Muhammad Iqbal to Germany in the early twentieth century.

Iqbal studied under Fritz Hommel, an Arabicist in Munich, and received his PhD in 1907. This foreshadowed a rising trend of Indian Muslim advanced study in Central Europe in the coming decades. Such study and travel were political and witnessed the Indian preference for

Germanic (but also Russian and French) Orientalist practices instead of British ones. Muhammad Shahidullah, leading scholar of the Bangla language movement, completed advanced studies in Freiburg. Zakir Husain and Sattar Kheiri, both of whom went on to play leading roles at Aligarh University, are other well-known exemplars of Germanic entanglements among Indian Muslim thinkers.

In 1905, Josef Horowitz, an Arabic and Urdu specialist, began teaching at Aligarh University. He remained in India until the beginning of the First World War. After returning to Frankfurt in 1915, Horovitz wrote his anti-British and pro-Indian tract, *India under British Rule.*[37] Fritz Krenkow was another German-born scholar to join Aligarh, teaching there from 1929–1930. From 1923 onwards, Krenkow curated and published Arabic texts for the Jamia Nizamia, the Muslim university in Hyderabad. Krenkow also helped found that university's *Islamic Culture* journal. A convert to Islam, he wrote in the inaugural edition of *Islamic Culture,* "[L]et us therefore strive, whether Shi'a, Sunni or Khariji, to prove by our conduct, our unity of purpose and an unswerving faith that we have one Imam which is accepted by all alike … and that is the Kor'an!"[38] At Aligarh, Otto Spies also taught Urdu literature from 1932–1936.[39] Meanwhile, Johann Fück joined Dacca university (1930–1935) as director of Arabic and Islamic Studies. Fück had studied under Joseph Horovitz in Frankfurt and showed great fascination for Muhammad Iqbal's work. Germanic practices and practitioners were now contributing to Indian nationalist institutions and not to British imperial ones, as had once been the case in the mid-nineteenth century.

In the 1930s in India, Herman Goetz made important contributions to the disciplinary field of Indo-Islamic Art history, beginning as a student of Indian miniatures.[40] In an article about images of Muslims in Hindu art, Goetz discussed historical and aesthetic aspects of Vijayanagara temple reliefs showing Tughlaq Muslim rulers.[41] In another article, his Germanic cultural-historical practice led him to explore depictions of Persian costumes in sixteenth and seventeenth-century Dutch paintings.[42]

German scholars of South Asian Islam emphasized the universal, not the particular. And this played directly into the scholarly objectives of Indian nationalism. From 1947 to 1953, Goetz served as director of the Baroda Museum and Picture Gallery. He was also a founding assistant director of the National Gallery of Modern Art, remaining in India until 1961 before he moved to Heidelberg.[43] Goetz's example fits into a pattern that includes other Germanic Orientalist practitioners, including Muhammad Asad in Lahore, Stella Kramrisch in Calcutta, and Walther Kaufmann in Bombay, who helped organize and build up the knowledgeable and cultural institutions of Indian nationalists during long sojourns in the interwar and postwar years. However, the majority of these Germanic practitioners were of Jewish ethnicity, and their work for Indian institutions after 1933 was more a necessity than choice.

In the 1930s, the longstanding and intensifying association between Germanic Orientalists and Indian Muslim nationalists became increasingly obvious to colonial administrators, and they grew increasingly alarmed. During that decade, four leading professors of Aligarh University had all obtained PhDs at German institutions and three had German wives.[44] British officials felt that Aligarh had become a hotbed of conspiracy.[45] If in the 1850s to 1870s it was the particularism of Muslim tribes and the "fanaticism" of religious allegiance that threated the British, in the 1930s it was rather the illicit transnationalism of Muslim intellectuals and their connections with the European arch enemy that raised alarms.

Existentialism

So far, we have considered two modes of Germanic Orientalist practice: philology and the cultural-historical approach. Both of these modes contributed to a third Orientalist practice in the context of the cultural and political catastrophe of the Great War. Germans and Austrians experienced the Great War as the end of the world as they knew it. The war cost millions of lives and witnessed the demise of two Central European empires, the Hohenzollern and the Hapsburg. The war brought about the dismantling of German colonies and the final deathblow to the nineteenth-century patrician hegemony over German society. This was no Wilsonian Moment for German-speakers, but the Disgrace of Versailles.

The devastation led to a process of self-Orientalization among Germans, and Islam became one of the pathways for Germans to reject the West and to shuttle themselves into an alternative universe of meaning. Muhammad Asad (a.k.a. Leopold Weiss), a young Ukrainian journalist in Berlin who converted to Islam in 1926, wrote that Europe "stood in the sign of a spiritual vacuum. All the ethical valuations to which Europe had been accustomed for so many centuries had become amorphous under the terrible impact of what had happened between 1914 and 1918."[46]

When Muhammad Asad arrived in British India in 1934, he was taken under the wing of Muhammad Iqbal and became one of his closest intellectual collaborators. Their common terms for interaction rested on the disciplines both men shared: philology and cultural-historical analysis but also existentialism.

Asad formed an existential bond with Islam, as is easily seen from his early autobiographical account, *The Unromantic Orient,* as well as from his late reflections.[47] In Central Europe, the 1920s and 1930s were a period in which Islam, and particularly South Asian Islam, grabbed the attention of German-speaking youth as a new source of personal meaning. This may have been especially due to the native emphasis on mediation and mysticism in South Asian Islam, and its traditions of devotion and asceticism that cut deep into Persian and South Asian contexts. The supposed distance of South Asian Islam from rationalized, Protestant monotheism, not the proximity with it, attracted existentialist German converts in the Weimar years. The existentialist study of Islam in the Weimar period detached Islam from conventional notions of Semitic faith and associated it more with Orientalist views about South and East Asian spiritual intension.[48]

The fact that Muhammad Asad should travel to British India in order to find his spiritual home after converting to Islam fits into a larger trend. In the 1920s, Fritz Krenkow, considered above, converted to Islam and took up work as an Arabic translator in Hyderabad and later as a professor at Aligarh University, before returning to Germany to work at the University of Bonn. And Leo Nussimbaum, a German-speaking popular intellectual of Russian descent, converted to Islam and took the name Bey Essad in Berlin.[49] These conversions do not just belong to the personal history of specific individuals. Weimar Muslim converts to Islam–many of whom were Jews and from the outer regions of Central European states—arose from the specifically Germanic existentialist practices of constructing worlds of meaning for Western audiences using Asian cultural resources.

The existentialist turn of German-speakers to Islam can be understood in relation to the spate of German conversions to Buddhism, Hinduism, Zoroastrianism, and Taoism that also took place in these years. We know that Muhammad Asad came to Islam after studying Taoism, for example.[50] Interest in Taoism rose sharply after the war, especially after the republication of Richard Wilhelm's translations of Laozi.[51] As much as the East Asian texts became new Bibles for the German youth, so too did Sufi poetry. The *Rubaiyat* became one of the most popular and most translated "Oriental" texts in Germany in the 1920s.[52] Koranic Studies also experienced a rise in these years.[53] Similarly, Sufi practices of breath and body control attracted scholars such as Annemarie Schimmel to the study of South Asian and Persian Islam.[54] Informing this Asianate study of Islam was a critique of the dualistic worldview of Christian monotheism, in which the realm of the body is assumed to be sequestered from the realm of the mind and the realm of God from the realm of the profane. Orientalists pitted the apparently integrative and non-dualistic teachings of Asian philosophy and scripture against a Christian conventionalism that they wished to reject.

Geopolitics

Especially from the start of the Great War onwards, South Asian Islam came to be studied in yet another mode: the geopolitical. During the First World War and afterward, for Orientalists hired by the German state, Islam came to be seen as encompassing a political geography that contained the greatest storehouse of anti-British sentiment on earth. Muslim lands also correlated to the locales of some of the world's greatest natural wealth in terms of oil from Arabia and coal and agricultural product from India. The Muslims of the Arab World and Turkey were a major fascination of German political planners in the years leading up to the First World War. But the politics of Indian Muslims became a fixation during the course of the war and afterward, especially with the rise of the Khilafat movement.[55] As early as 1915, just as T.E. Lawrence and Wilhelm Wassmuss were competing to win allies amongst the Arabs, political thinkers such as Max von Oppenheim maintained that the true potential for dismantling the British Empire would come from the "revolutionized" Muslims of India.[56] It was this vision of South Asian Muslim revolt that informed early Soviet foreign policy in the 1920s as well.[57] Both German and Russian planners, thinking in terms of sheer numbers, observed that Indian Muslims represented the largest reserve of potential mercenaries for a world war against British global power.

The publication of the journals *Welt des Islam* in 1910 and *Der Islam* in 1912 demonstrate the rise of a patently colonial view among German state planners about the Muslim lands.[58] C.H. Becker, a leading scholar of Islam from Hamburg and a member of the Prussian Ministry of Culture, uttered the famous words: "[T]he future of Islam can only involve its integration into European civilization, otherwise its days are numbered."[59] Becker's form of Orientalism recalled the British Islamology of the nineteenth century. He, like Martin Hartmann and Eugen Mittwoch, and the Dutchman Snouk Hurgronje, all studied ethnic and tribal characteristics in order to better understand and potentially control Muslim populations.[60]

Hans Rohde in *Der Kampf Um Asien* (1924) argued that the Indian war of 1857, the opening of the Suez Canal in 1869, the Russo-Turkish war of 1877, and Britain's acquisition of Egypt in 1882, all had the effect of securing the two main poles of British political domination of Asia—one in the Arab lands and the other in India.[61] With the hydrocarbon revolution of these decades and the pouring of black gold out of Arabia, as well as the continued extraction of precious agricultural commodities from the subcontinent, Arabia and India served as the foundations for British world power—the two treasure chests used to underwrite British expansion.[62]

Rohde maintained that British efforts to control the ninety million Muslims of India would make it the "greatest Mohammedan power of the world," thus satisfying the "inveterate English struggle to give its world power a secure foundation." Without a pacified Muslim population, Rohde wrote, British world power could not persist. This thesis informed German geopolitical planning from the 1910s to the 1940s.

The German state after 1933 sought to use the political energies of Muslims along the Indian Ocean Rim to fulfill the perverse aims of Nazi universalist striving. Nazi state planners wanted to woo Muslims along the "revolutionary belt." Nazis warped the Germanic Orientalist tradition of studying universal dimensions of Islam to fit their aims. The Nazi study of geopolitics focused on the regions of Afghanistan, North India, and Chinese Turkistan as a major focal point of future geopolitical tension. The peoples of Uyghur Khaganate, Barkul, Turfan, and Kashgar, whose linguistic inheritances had long been of interest to German philologists, now became interesting as martial subjects in the eyes of German geopoliticians. There was a growing interest in the geopolitical position of Islam in China, especially given the resistance movements among the Muslim Chinese Hui peoples in the late nineteenth century.[63] Paul Schmitz saw the national movements across the Muslim world in the 1920s and 1930s as evidence of the political unity of Islam, which contrasted with the exacerbated political "disorder" (*Zerrissenheit*) of Europe.[64]

In the context of a dismembered and disordered Europe after the Great War, Nazi geopolitical thinkers spuriously proposed that Islam was a twin of German fascism. "Islam and National Socialism share many parallels and analogies," one commentator wrote.[65] The Nazi struggle to create "Middle Europe" (*Mitteleuropa*) was equated with the so-called "Pan-Islamic" pursuits of Muslims against the West.[66] In a complete perversion of both the actuality of Islam and of the philological, cultural-historical, and existential interpretive practices of German Orientalism, Nazi interpreters projected their violent will-to-power onto the Muslim world. At a time when Nazis thought they would replace failed "European solidarity" with a racist Germanic one, German state planners saw in universal Islam their own Nazi ideal of militant, annihilationist political unity. [67] In addition to cultivating close ties with the Grand Mufti of Jerusalem in a project to coopt

Arab politics for Nazi ends, Heinrich Himmler was of the opinion that "Mohammedanism is a practical and sympathetic religion for soldiers." He purportedly proclaimed himself a "Mohammedan," willfully perverting any meaning such a proclamation could possibly have.

During the Second World War, Indian Muslims who had returned home to India from Central Europe engaged in radical politics, speaking out against the British and in favor of the Axis powers. Indian Muslim thinkers wove together their own political analysis with Germanic geopolitical practice, proposing that India might spring out of the British imperial lock thanks to leverage from Germany, Italy, and Japan.[68] In 1940, Obeidullah, who had spent long years in Central Europe in the interwar period, spoke in Delhi after Juma prayers saying that Germans might soon invade India through Iran, thereby ending British rule.[69] Sattar Kheiri and his German society at Aligarh University organized pro-German meetings and sought to obtain funding for university programs at Aligarh from the German consulate.[70]

Conclusion

This paper has considered different Germanic Orientalist practices for the study of South Asian Islam—the philological, the cultural-historical, the existential, and the geopolitical. These Germanic practices, with their universalist scope, served to anchor an emerging German identity in the world, on the one hand, but these practices also helped Indian nationalists to resist the particularizing strategies of aggressive Anglo-Saxonism on the other.

Today, German national discourse seems increasingly concerned to assert and defend its "Westernness" and to strengthen its own faith in a new European universalism with Germany at the center. Indeed, the Germanic fascination with Western universalism, deeply rooted in Phil-Hellenism, has a robust and long legacy. But an equally long-standing and powerful impulse of German national discourse has asserted the proximity of the Germanic West to the Orient and has envisioned the universalisms of Asia in ways that disrupted the exclusive universalist pretensions of Northwestern European power. Germanic Orientalist practices contributing to Anglo-Saxonism in the decades after 1857 soon reversed their charge and began to interfere with the British Empire's efforts to normalize itself as the global standard.

Studying the ways in which Germanic practices and the colporteurs of those approaches informed and infused Indian Muslim nationalist projects does not amount to a story of Western imposition on the East or Eastern enslavement to Western discourse. What is important here is not the phenomenon of borrowing or emulation per se but rather the modalities of Orientalist practice, on the one hand, and the changing politics and positions of these practices on the other. Islam can be antagonistically juxtaposed to the West in the recurring "Clash of Civilizations" refrain only if we agree with the modern Empire's perspective that place and position do not matter and that some parts actually do legitimately stand in for wholes.

Notes and References

1. Muhammad Iqbal, *Metaphysics in Persia* (London: Luzac, 1908); Muhammad Shahidullah, *Les chants mystiques de Kanha et de Saraha* (Paris: Adrien Maisonneuve,1928); Ali Akhtar Ansari, "Tadsch Mahal und seine Bedeutung für die Geschichte der indische Baukunst," (Vienna: PhD Dissertation, Fachbibliothek Kunstgeschichte, Vienna University, 1926); George Steinmetz, *The Devil's Handwriting: Precoloniality and the German Colonial State in Qingdao, Samoa, and Southwest Africa* (Chicago: University of Chicago Press, 2007).
2. Talal Asad, *Formations of the Secular* (Stanford: Stanford University Press, 2003).
3. David Arnold, *Science, Technology and Medicine in Colonial India* (Cambridge: Cambridge University Press, 2009).
4. Mountstuart Elphinstone, *The History of India* (London: J. Murray, 1841); Brian Hodgson, *Miscellaneous Essays Relating to Indian Subject* (London: Trübner, 1880).
5. *Frontier and Overseas Expeditions from India,* 3 vols., (Calcutta; Superintendent Government Printing, 1910).
6. W.W. Hunter, *The Indian Musalmans* (London: Trübner, 1871).
7. Alfred Lyall, *Asiatic Studies* (London: J. Murray, 1882), 229.

8. Hunter, *Indian Musalmans,* 1.
9. Ibid., 23.
10. The Great Wahabi Case of 1870, 1899.
11. Hunter, *Indian Musalmans,* 60.
12. Ibid., 71.
13. V.A. Smith, *The Early History of India* (Oxford: Clarendon Press, 1904).
14. This shift is discussed by Karuna Mantena, *Alibis of Empire* (Princeton: Princeton University Press), 2010.
15. Abraham Geiger, *Was hat Mohammed aus dem Judenthume aufgenommen* (Bonn: F. Baaden, 1833); Dirk Hartwig et al., eds., *"Im vollen Licht der Geschichte": die Wissenschaft des Judentums und die Anfänge der kritischen Koranforschung* (Würzburg: Ergon, 2008); Susannah Heschel, "Abraham Geiger and the Emergence of Jewish Philoislamism", in: *ibid.*, 65–86; also see Robertson Smith, *Kinship and Marriage in early Arabia* (London: A. and C. Black, 1885); Susannah Heschel, "Revolt of the Colonized," *New German Critique,* 77, 1999, 63; John Efron, "From Mitteleuropa to the Middle East," *The Jewish Quarterly Review,* 94:3, 2004, 490–520.
16. M. Winternitz, "The Ethics of Zoroastrianism from a Comparative Point of View," *Visva Bharati Quarterly,* vol. 1, no. 1, 1923, 33–53; J. Germanus, "Modern Movements in Islam," *Visva Bharati Quarterly*, vol. 8, nos. 1–2, 1930, 74–98.
17. Major scholars of Urdu were Joseph von Hammer-Purgstall, Aloys Sprenger, F. Krenkow, J. Horovitz, and Friedrich Rosen.
18. See Ernest Trumpp on Sindhi, Wilhelm Geiger on Balochi, and G. Raverty on Pashto.
19. "De-mystifying" prophets by arguing they were just men caught up in extraordinary circumstances was a standard form of German "high criticism" of religious texts. Theodor Noeldeke, *Das Leben Mohammeds,* (Hanover: Rümpler,1863)*;* Krehl, *Das Lebem Muhammad* (Leipzig: Otto Schulze, 1884); Hans Haas, "Das Bild Mohammads im Wandel der Zeiten," in*: Zeitschrift für Missionskunde un* Religionswissenschaft 31, 1916, 161; Frants Buhl, *Das Leben Muhammeds* (Leipzig: Quelle & Meyer, 1930); Tor Andrae, Die Person Muhammeds in Lehre und Glauben seiner Gemeinde (Stockholm: Norstedt & Söner, 1917); Hubert Grimme, *Muhammed* (Münster: Milnster, 1892); H.R. Reckendorf, *Mohammed und die Seinen* (Leipzig: Quelle & Meyer, 1907); Aloys Sprenger, *Das Leben und die Lehre des Mohammed* (Berlin: Nicolai, 1869); Gustav Weil, *Mohammed, der Prophet* (Stuttgart: Metzler'schen, 1843).
20. Arnold's book used 192 sources in total, of which 61 were German, 52 English, 39 French, 24 Dutch, and 16 others (mostly Italian and Spanish).

21. Jalal, *Partisans of Allah: Jihad in South Asia* (Cambridge: Harvard, 2008), 160; Aurel Stein, *Serinida,* five vols. (Oxford: Clarendon Press, 1921).
22. Ikram Chaghtatai, ed., *Austrian Scholarship in Pakistan* (Islamabad: PanGraphics, 1997); Nina Berman, *German Literature of the Middle East* (Ann Arbor: University of Michigan Press, 2011).
23. "Heinrich Ferdinand Blochmann," *Encyclopaedia Iranica* (New York: Bibliotheca Persica Press, 1999), http://www.iranicaonline.org/articles/blochmann-heinrich-henry.
24. "A.F. Rudolf Hoernle," *The English Historical Review*, 26: 104, 1911, 795–796.
25. He was born in Sikandra, near Agra. G.A. Grierson, "Augustus Frederic Rudolf Hoernle," *Journal of the Royal Asiatic Society of Great Britain and Ireland* (1919), 119.
26. Pau Rohrbach, *Der Deutsche Gedanken in der Welt* (Königstein: Langewiesche, 1912).
27. Sabine Mangold, *Eine "weltbürgerliche Wissenschaft: die deutsche Orientalistik im 19. Jahrhundert* (Stuttgart: F. Steiner, 2004).
28. Burckhardt, *Weltgeschichtliche Betrachtungen* (Berlin: W. Spemann, 1905).
29. Otto Höver, *Kultbauten des Islam* (Leipzig: W. Goldmann, 1922); See C.H. Becker and R. Strothmann, *Der Islam* "Bibliographie", 1929, for works on carpets, textiles, paintings, etc.
30. Spengler, *Der Untergang des Abendlandes* (Leipzig: Wilhelm Braumüller,1918), 785.
31. Josef Strzygowski, *Die Stellung des Islam zum Geistigen Aufbau Europas* (Wien: Abo Akademi,1922), 26.
32. Suhrawardy collaborated with Stella Kramrisch; Ernst Diez, *Die Kunst der islamischen Voelker* (Berlin: Akademische Verlagsgesellschaft Athenaion, 1922).
33. Alexander von Gleichen-Russwurm, *Die Kulturwelt des Orients* (Hamburg: Hoffmann und Campe, 1900), 247.
34. Sara Kohn, *Die Eheschliessung im Koran* (London: S. Austin & Sons, 1936).
35. Ibid.
36. Ernst Kühnel, *Kunst des Orients* (Potsdam: Akademische Verlagsgesellschaft Athenaion, 1923).
37. Horovitz, *Indien unter britischer Herrschaft* (Berlin: B.G. Teubner, 1915).
38. Fritz Krenkow, "The Unity of Islam," *Islamic Culture,* 1, 1927, 27.
39. Annemarie Schimmel, *German Contributions to the Study of Indo-Pakistani Linguistics* (Hamburg: German-Pakistan Forum, 1981), 26.

40. Goetz, "The Early Muraqqa's of the Mughal Emperor Jahangir," *East and West,* 8:2, 1957, 157–185.
41. Goetz, "Fruehe Darstellung von Moslems in der Hindu-Kunst," *Oriens,* Vol. 18/19, 1965, 193–199.
42. Hermann Goetz, "Persian and Persian Costumes in Dutch Painting of the Seventeenth Century," *The Art Bulletin,* 20: 3, 1938, 280–290.
43. Karl Jettmar, "Hermann Goetz," *East and West,* 26: 3, 1976, 540.
44. "Reports son Activities of Germans, Italians and Japanese," September 9, 1938, OIOC, L/PJ/12/506.
45. OIOC, L/PJ/12/659.
46. Muhammad Asad, *Road to Mecca* (London: M. Reinhardt, 1954), 62.
47. Ibid.
48. The Rosenzweig and Martin Buber translation of the Hebrew Bible is example of the eastward push in Jewish Studies.
49. Bey Essad, *Blood and Oil in the Orient* (New York: Simon and Schuster, 1932).
50. Asad, *Road to Mecca.*
51. Richard Wilhelm's translation of Laozi's *Tao te King* (Jena: Diederichs, 1911).
52. Friedrich Rosen's translation of Omar Khayyam's *Rubaiyat* (Berlin: Deutsche Verlagsanstalt) appeared in 1921.
53. Horovitz, *Koranische Untersuchungen* (Berlin: de Gruyter, 1926).
54. Schimmel, "Studien zum Begriff der mystischen Liebe in der frühislamischen Mystik" (Marburg: PhD Dissertation, 1954); *The Ornament of the Saints* in: *Studies of Isfahan,* 1974; *Pain and Grace* (Leiden: Brill, 1976).
55. Mirza Djevad Khan Kasi, "Das Kalifat nach Islamischem Staatsrecht," in *Die Welt des Islams,* 5, 1918, 189.
56. Oppenheim, *Denkschrift,* 1915 (Berlin: Verlag Das Kulturelle Gedächtnis, 2018); Oskar von Neidermayer, *Im Weltkrieg vor Indiens Toren* (Hamburg: Hanseatische Verlagsanstalt, 1936.
57. Manjapra, *M.N. Roy,* 2010.
58. Becker, *Islamstudien* (Hildesheim: G. Olms, 1967), 31
59. Becker, "Die Religion in Geschichte und Gegenwart."
60. Becker, "Materialien zur Kenntnis des Islam in Deutsch-Ostafrica," 1911, 10.
61. Hans Rohde, *Der Kampf um Asien,* 15.
62. Ibid.
63. Martin Hartmann, *Zur Geschichte des Islam in China,* Leipzig, 1921; Wilhelm Filchner, *Hui-Hui: Asiens Islamkämpfe,* 1928.

64. Schmitz, *All-Islam! Weltmacht von Morgen?*, 245.
65. Lindemann, *Der Islam,* 3.
66. Zaki Ali, "Grossdeutschland und der Islam," in Reichardt, *Der Islam vor den TOren,* 1939.
67. Lindemann, 5; also see Othmar Krainz, *Das Schwert des Islam,* Deutscher Hort Verlag, 1938; Thomas Reichardt, *Der Islam vor den Toren,* Leipzig, 1939.
68. L/PJ/12/506.
69. L/PJ/12/506.
70. "DIB's Reports on Activities of Germans, Italians and Japanese," L/PJ/12/506.

Index

R

T

Notes on Editors and Contributors

Sugata Bose is the Gardiner Professor of Oceanic History and Affairs at Harvard University. His books include *A Hundred Horizons: The Indian Ocean in the Age of Global Empire* (2006), *His Majesty's Opponent: Subhas Chandra Bose and India's Struggle against Empire* (2011), *The Nation as Mother and Other Visions of Nationhood* (2017), and, with Ayesha Jalal, *Modern South Asia: History, Culture, Political Economy* (4th edition, 2017).

Ayesha Jalal is the Mary Richardson Professor of History at Tufts University. Her books include *Self and Sovereignty: Individual and Community in South Asian Islam* (2000), *Partisans of Allah: Jihad in South Asia* (2008), *The Pity of Partition: Manto's Life, Times and Work across the India-Pakistan Divide* (2013), and, with Sugata Bose, *Modern South Asia: History, Culture, Political Economy* (4th edition, 2017).

Sunil Amrith is the Mehra Family Professor of South Asian Studies at Harvard University. His books include *Crossing the Bay of Bengal: The Furies of Nature and the Fortunes of Migrants* (2013), and *Unruly Waters: How Rains, Rivers, Coasts and Seas Have Shaped Asia's History* (2018).

Eric Tagliacozzo is the John Stambaugh Professor of History at Cornell University. His books include *Secret Trades, Porous Borders: Smuggling and States along a Southeast Asian Frontier* (2005), and *The Longest Journey: Southeast Asians and the Pilgrimage to Mecca* (2013).

Seema Alavi is Professor of History at the University of Delhi. Her books include *Islam and Healing: Loss and Recovery of an Indo-Muslim Medical Tradition* (2008) and *Muslim Cosmopolitanism in the Age of Empire* (2015).

Sana Aiyar is Associate Professor of History at the Massachusetts Institute of Technology. She is the author of *Indians in Kenya: The Politics of Diaspora* (2015).

Iftekhar Iqbal is Associate Professor of History at the Universiti Brunei Darussalam. He is the author of *The Bengal Delta: Ecology, State and Social Change* (2010).

Andrew Sartori is Professor of History at New York University. His books include *Bengal in Global Concept History: Culturalism in the Age of Capital* (2008) and *Liberalism in Empire: An Alternate History* (2014).

Kris Manjapra is Associate Professor of History at Tufts University. His books include *M.N. Roy: Marxism and Colonial Cosmopolitanism* (2010) and *Age of Entanglement: German and Indian Intellectual Encounters across Empire* (2014).